ROPOLITAN UN

L'

r

24 126
25,

21,

D0538853

0115126 X

CIOB Handbook of Facilities Management

The CHARTERED
INSTITUTE OF
BUILDING

CIOB Handbook of Facilities Management

Edited by Alan Spedding

Longman
Scientific &
Technical

Longman Scientific & Technical
Longman Group Limited
Longman House, Burnt Mill, Harlow
Essex CM20 2JE, England
and Associated Companies throughout the world

© Longman Group Limited 1994

All rights reserved; no part of this publication may be reproduced, stored in any
retrieval system, or transmitted in any form or by any means, electronic, mechanical,
photocopying, recording, or otherwise without either the prior written permission of the
Publishers or a licence permitting restricted copying in the United Kingdom issued by
the Copyright Licensing Agency Ltd, 90 Tottenham Court Road, London W1P 9HE.

First published 1994

British Cataloguing in Publication Data
A catalogue entry for this title is available from the British Library

ISBN 0-582-25742-5

LEEDS METROPOLITAN
UNIVERSITY LIBRARY
170115126x
B23EL
227639   10 5.95
24. 5. 95.
658.2 CHA

Set by 8 in 10/12 Plantin
Printed and bound in Great Britain
at Bookcraft (Bath) Ltd

Contents

Foreword   vii

Editor's note   ix

The authors and acknowledgements   xi

1 Facilities management   1
   Alan Spedding & Roy Holmes

2 Strategic property management   9
   Derek Worthing

3 Property development, valuation and management   25
   Stephen Hargitay

4 The legal environment   43
   Mark Tyler, Nick Hadley & Tony Kitson

5 Design in practice – planning and managing space   74
   John Worthington

6 Life cycle appraisal   94
   Roger Flanagan & Laurence Marsh

7 Construction procurement   115
   Alan Park

8 Built asset management practice   137
   Roy Holmes

9 Documentation and cost-effective management of property   155
   Alan Spedding

10 The indoor environment: strategies and tactics for managers   181
   Adrian Leaman & David Tong

11 Facilities management and the organisation   196
   Alan Jordan

Glossary   216

Index   220

Foreword

For far too long the management and maintenance of the built environment has been the poor relation of the new build sector of the construction industry. Now, facilities management has begun to be recognised as a key element of an organisation's strategic plan, with responsibility for its effective pursuance firmly located within the boardroom.

It is surprising, in view of the importance of the subject in contributing to the lowering of overheads and the general improvement of efficiency and quality, that its acceptance as a management function has been so long delayed.

Research indicates that poor facilities management performance exists within both the public and the private sectors and, as a consequence, vast under-utilised resources are tied up which could otherwise be released for more productive activity.

For some time there has been a need for a basic handbook to cover the management of facilities. To meet this need the Chartered Institute of Building commissioned this work as a guide to facility owners and practising facilities managers alike. It is also intended that this book will prove helpful to students sitting the facilities management option of the final examinations of the Chartered Institute of Building and to other students engaged on the increasing number of courses being offered both in the UK and overseas.

I warmly recommend this volume to all managers as a valuable primer in the subject of facilities management and as a first step to a better understanding of its relevance to their business.

Victor E Michel FCIOB
Chairman
The Management of Facilities Committee
Chartered Institute of Building

Editor's note

Any student or practitioner in the field of facilities management will know that there are numerous definitions of the scope of this relatively new professional area. One may be entitled to ask if it is really new, but the increasing interest in facilities management, as evidenced by the appearance of newspaper articles and journals devoted to the topic, suggests that a chord has been struck with potential clients and providers of this service. The definition which has been quoted in the first chapter of this book is potentially comprehensive, and therefore it has to be recognised that any handbook of this length cannot cover the field in its totality.

It is only relatively recently that the words facilities management have been seen in the technical press in the United Kingdom. Apart from the efforts of one or two notable pioneers, there appeared to be little general interest in the topic within the property field during the boom days. The Editor had his curiosity aroused on learning of the existence of courses for FM executives at MIT Boston, and attended a course there as well as attending the first International Congress of the International Facilities Management Association in Washington DC in 1989. The fact that delegations attended not only from North America but also from a number of European and Far Eastern countries indicated that the facilities management movement had been growing steadily throughout the world.

The last three or four years have seen an acceleration in the use of the term facilities management or facility management, together with an increase in the number of textbooks which address the needs of practitioners and students. Many of these textbooks, however, deal with relatively narrow aspects of facilities management because of the background of their authors; alternatively, they attempt to deal with the whole field in a relatively superficial way. This handbook does not attempt to cover the whole field but to fill in some of the gaps for the busy practitioner and also the student.

The Editor is grateful to the Chartered Institute of Building for sponsoring this publication and also to the authors who have given their time and expertise in making their contributions to the handbook. We have been careful not to try to define the nature of facilities management in terms of any traditional professional grouping, but to portray some of the complexities and richness of this very interesting and challenging field.

There is a distinction to be drawn in most cases between the core business of a firm or organisation and those activities which are support or non-core activities; facilities management is frequently associated with the latter. It is an intention of this handbook to indicate some of the inter-relationships which have to be considered in order to make sure that the coordinated operation of property and services help to support the efficient management of a firm's business.

A careful reading of this handbook, and some of the additional reading recommended, will, we hope, indicate some of the directions in practice and research which have the greatest potential for the future of all those who build, maintain, and operate buildings.

Bristol 1994   Alan Spedding

The authors and acknowledgements

The Chartered Institute of Building wishes to thank the authors for their contribution, and wishes to point out that, although the overall scope of the book has been produced under the guidance of the CIOB, the opinions and information contained in each chapter are those of the individual authors and do not necessarily represent the considered viewpoint of the CIOB.

Roger Flanagan

Roger Flanagan is Professor of Construction Management and Head of Department at the Department of Construction Management and Engineering at the University of Reading. He has been involved in a number of books in the area of life cycle appraisal and has undertaken research projects for the Engineering and Physical Sciences Research Council, the Royal Institution of Chartered Surveyors, the Royal Institute of British Architects and CIRIA.

Nick Hadley

Nick Hadley is a partner in the Property Group of McKenna & Co. Before becoming a solicitor he obtained a PhD in law at Birmingham University. He specialises in property development and investment transactions and has wide experience of acting for institutions, landlords, tenants and developers. In addition to being a speaker at seminars on property law he is in charge of the Property Group's precedents and editor of the Group's principal property bulletins.

Stephen Hargitay

Stephen Hargitay is the Professor of Property Investment and the Director of Studies of the School of Valuation and Estate Management at the University of the West of England. He is a Visiting Professor at the National University of

Singapore and at the University of Reading and a tutor/examiner in property investment at the College of Estate Management. He is the author of a number of books and papers on property investment and the application of computers in the property profession.

Roy Holmes

Professor Roy Holmes, a Fellow of the Chartered Institute of Building, spent many years in construction management before entering the academic world. He is a Reader in the Faculty of the Built Environment, University of the West of England and Director of the Facilities Management Research Unit. He also has joint responsibility for leading the MSc course in facilities management and lectures on his specialism, built asset management, on a number of MSc and MA programmes at Bristol and other universities. His work on maintenance management is well known both nationally and internationally and his research has resulted in a national framework for coding maintenance. Currently he is involved in a research project in China, and he has presented papers at a number of international conferences. His main interest is optimal system support for maintenance management and the cost-effectiveness of systems.

Alan Jordan

Alan Jordan is a chartered mechanical engineer and had a career spanning 15 years in project and operational engineering management in the UK and overseas before becoming a facilities manager at Allied Dunbar in 1986. Since then he has been involved with most aspects of premises management, property strategy and construction programmes.

As a divisional manager Alan developed a subsidiary company, FM², with the objective of seeking external facilities management work for Allied Dunbar's property department. Following a management buy-out in January 1994 he is a senior manager with FM², now an independent private limited company specialising in site facilities management, relocation and facilities consultancy.

Alan is co-author of *Are you managing facilities?* published in conjunction with the Industrial Society.

Tony Kitson

Tony Kitson is a partner in the Planning Group of McKenna & Co. Prior to joining the firm in 1988 he had 15 years' experience as a solicitor in local government. He now specialises in the planning and environmental law aspects of commercial, industrial, residential and infrastructure developments. He has spoken at seminars on planning and environmental law, local authority law and administration and rating reform. He is a contributor to the *Solicitors' Journal*, the *Law Society Gazette*, the *Journal of Planning and Environmental Law* and McKenna & Co publications on planning, highways, compulsory purchase and rating.

Adrian Leaman

Adrian Leaman is Director of Research at the Institute of Advanced Architectural Studies at the University of York. He is Managing Director of Building Use Studies of London, a firm which specialises in research into the operation of buildings to help designers improve building performance.

Laurence Marsh

Laurence Marsh is a Research Fellow at the Department of Construction Management and Engineering at the University of Reading. He has been active in the area of life cycle appraisal and is currently undertaking research into auto-ID systems in the construction industry

Alan Park

Alan Park is a Chartered Quantity Surveyor and a Chartered Builder whose experience in facilities management started on site in the petrochemical industry in the early 1970s followed by work in Saudi Arabia and Kuwait. Work in the Glasgow Underground modernisation project management group was followed by a partnership in quantity surveying, and then a directorship of Architects Stride Treglown, managing director of Stride Project Management and the QA manager for both companies. He currently practises in facilities and project management consultancy, and his interests include membership of the CIOB Facilities Management Committee.

Alan Spedding

Alan Spedding is Professor of Construction Economics and Acting Dean of the Faculty of the Built Environment at the University of the West of England, Bristol. He is a Chartered Structural Engineer, a Chartered Quantity Surveyor, and is also an Affiliate of the British Institute of Facilities Management. He spent his early career with a building and civil engineering contractor, and after National Service in the Royal Engineers joined a consultant quantity surveying practice in Liverpool, and subsequently began to teach.

His professional involvement includes Vice-Presidency (Europe) of the Commonwealth Association of Surveying and Land Economy and membership of the International Committee of the Royal Institution of Chartered Surveyors. He is currently researching on a number of projects which include SERC supported work on priority indexing in maintenance management, and a British High Commission/British Council, ODA funded project on building maintenance management in India.

David Tong

David Tong is a senior consultant with DEGW Strategic Consulting Limited where he is responsible for user-related research studies. He is a psychologist but has always worked with architecture and design professionals. David's career began in housing management, working for the leading housing association CCHA, and later in the Psychology Department at the University of Surrey, where he managed research into human behaviour in emergencies. In 1984 he joined Building Use Studies Limited where he undertook a range of research and consultancy assignments for major private and public sector clients. He is a member of the Market Research Society and the Ergonomics Society.

Mark Tyler

Mark Tyler is a partner in the Healthcare Group of McKenna & Co. His practice comprises advisory work and litigation in the areas of health and safety product liability. As well as presenting seminars on safety-related issues he is a frequent contributor to journals such as *Property Management, Facilities* and *Property Journal*. His published work includes contributions to *Buildings and health*; *The Rosehaugh guide to the design, construction, use and management of buildings* (RIBA Publications) and *New balance: buildings and the environment – a guide for property owners and developers* (produced jointly with Jones Lang Wootton and Gardener & Theobald). He is a member of the CBI Health and Safety Consultative Committee.

Derek Worthing

Derek Worthing is the Director of Studies for the School of Building Surveying and Facilities Management at the University of the West of England. Formerly he worked in both the public and private sectors where he practised as a Chartered Building Surveyor. His research and consultancy interests include strategic property management and the application of the facilities management approach to historic buildings.

John Worthington

John Worthington is Professor of Architecture at the University of York, and is also Director of the Institute of Advanced Architectural Studies, and Deputy Chairman of DEGW Limited, a well-known architectural and facilities management practice in London.

He has lectured widely in the UK and overseas and has published extensively. His wide range of consultancy activities includes work on user requirements, space planning and fitting out of buildings and regeneration of urban areas.

Chapter 1

Facilities management

Alan Spedding & Roy Holmes

Introduction

This handbook presents a view of the rapidly developing professional field of facilities management. It introduces and refers to a variety of topics relating to buildings and their surroundings and to activities within buildings. The potential scope and depth of the field means that the handbook does not contain a definitive treatment of the subject, therefore throughout the text the reader is directed to other publications and sources of information that will lead to a wider and deeper knowledge of the subject-matter.

The publication is aimed at members of professions related to the built environment in the expectation that many fields such as building design and technology and related engineering technology will be familiar to many readers. However, the authors are aware of the growing interest in facilities management from other professions and expect the handbook to appeal to other managers and students. It is assumed that, in this case, specialist professional advice on building is readily available, and the wide literature on building technology is readily accessible. In order, however, to put the field into context, the handbook includes discussions which should enable the reader to understand the relationships between design and planning of space in buildings, the efficient operation of buildings, and the legal, financial and strategic issues involved.

A range of experts have been involved in the writing of the handbook and the work has been coordinated and edited by Professor Alan Spedding of the University of the West of England, Bristol. The idea of the publication was developed by a Steering Group at the Chartered Institute of Building (CIOB) under the joint chairmanship of Stuart Bradburn and Roy Holmes, and the original brief was to revise the existing CIOB handbook on maintenance management which was a guide to good practice. For that purpose the Steering

1

Group produced a matrix of subjects to be considered for the revision of that document. It soon became clear that there was considerable overlap between the views taken of maintenance and facilities management and as a result the brief was subsequently enlarged to embrace facilities management related to the built environment.

During the course of preparing the document the approach has been discussed with a number of interested groups. In particular, we became aware that the Chartered Institute of Building Services Engineers was in the process of revising their 1990 publication on building services maintenance management (Technical Memorandum 17). The revision will be published in mid-1994 and the reader is recommended to give close attention to this important field.

The CIOB has taken a particular view of facilities management which is reflected in Figure 1.1. Figure 1.1 highlights the areas of built asset management, strategic property management, organisation – people and processes, valuations and contract procedures. This model has been used as the basis for the facilities management syllabus in the new educational framework of the CIOB. These five main groupings of activity take place within the practice environment of facilities management, which also relates to the organisation's business environment, and encompasses all of the particular processes of facilities management many of which are made more efficient by the use of information technology (IT).

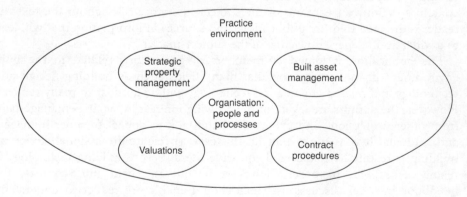

Figure 1.1 Facilities management

Figure 1.1 has not been used as a model for this handbook although each chapter can be ascribed to a grouping of activity as indicated above and as discussed in a little more detail later in this introduction.

Clearly the business environment will be particular to any organisation and the alternatives cannot be covered in this handbook. However, reference is made to those legal and procedural factors which affect the development and management of buildings.

Our intention is to make clear that the nature of facilities management is such that all of the topics in this handbook are interrelated and the CIOB has recognised the potential for overlap between material in different chapters. Consequently, although each of the chapters is an essay on a particular topic within the scope of facilities management, the editor has drawn attention to links between chapters where considered appropriate.

A comprehensive view of facilities management in the rapidly changing business and information technology environment has been taken by the CIOB, and therefore it is recognised that there is considerable scope for additional material to be published by CIOB in the field. However, it is felt that this handbook will complement much of the material already available, and will provide a basis upon which further CIOB papers may be published.

Definition

Several groups have attempted to define the scope of facilities management, or facility management, and some of these relate to particular views from the more traditional professional fields. Although there are some notable figures who have been pioneers in the UK facilities management profession it is probably true to say that the concept was first given its identity in the USA, and this book has been written using the American Library of Congress definition:

> The practice of co-ordinating the physical work place with people and work of the organisation integrates the principles of business administration, architecture and the behavioral and engineering sciences.

This definition is very broad, and it encompasses the functional professions of many people who are engaged in facilities management.

In some countries, such as in the UK, there are clearly recognised property management professional bodies which do not exist to the same extent elsewhere. Therefore, many people in the UK have perceived facilities management in terms of conventional property management functions. What has not tended to be acknowledged by many is the potentially comprehensive view of facilities management, and therefore some definitions give much more prominence to the management of the buildings and their functioning rather than the management of buildings for business and people. In this respect Dr Frank Duffy of DEGW Architects of London has commented to us that the growth of facilities management has been spurred on by demand-side thinking relating to the deficiencies observed by building users, and that a supply-side property-orientated viewpoint is not necessarily the major interest for facilities managers.

However, whichever definition of facilities management is favoured by the reader, it is the intention of this handbook to make it clear that facilities management is an umbrella term under which a wide range of property- and user-related functions may be brought together for the benefit of the organisation and its employees as a whole.

Why facilities management?

The suitability of buildings for their purpose is becoming more important to employers as the interaction between buildings, people and processes becomes more recognised and as the nature of much business activity changes particularly in countries like the UK where there has been a shift out of heavy industry. The total costs of large highly serviced, even intelligent buildings operated in expensive locations, in many cases by multinational corporations, have focused interest on their efficient operation. Costs of energy and security, repairs and maintenance are inevitably becoming more significant in the overall running costs of buildings, even if in some cases repairs and maintenance in many properties are being reduced to such a level which may be storing up trouble for the future. Departments or sections of organisations are often charged by management for space which they occupy and therefore, they are becoming more aware of the costs of space, and are demanding more effective quality and performance in their accommodation.

Due to factors of supply and demand in the market for buildings, and the changes in economic activity in many developed countries, the rush to build speculative offices and commercial premises has, at least for some time, abated. The ease with which investment property could be disposed of on the property market has given way to a more cautious attitude on the part of institutional investors and potential owners and tenants. Thus the escalation in property values which could mask the operating cost penalties of many properties no longer applies, and the flexibility and suitability of many buildings, including some relatively modern highly serviced ones, are under scrutiny.

Similarly the growth of technology in business operations has focused attention on the building as a resource which should be adaptable to the changing needs of business. Indeed, the concept of the one person, one workstation is being challenged in today's IT-rich environment, and many organisations are using computing as the means by which space may be shared between people in a more effective manner. Thus property increasingly demands more active management, depending of course on its function.

Benefits of facilities management

Although facilities managers may offer to operate individual contracted-out services on behalf of the organisation, the function should be that of managing the property in the best interests of the core business. Thus a long-term view, coupled with techniques such as life cycle costing, may indicate to the facilities manager that more money should be spent selectively on the building in order to maximise returns rather than the more conventional view of cutting building costs without carefully considering the effects on the users or the occupants.

It will be appreciated that, in organisations where salary costs are high, the potential contribution of property to overall efficiency of the organisation may be hidden, but nevertheless may be much greater than at first expected. Layout of the building, and adequacy and servicing of space, clearly have production and efficiency implications for manufacturing industry, and it has been increasingly realised that similar considerations apply to office and other types of work space. The effect of interaction of space and its planning, provision of furniture and equipment, together with staff amenities, is difficult to evaluate. Nevertheless the relationships between the workplace and its environment and the people who use the buildings are becoming somewhat clearer as a result of research in the field. Therefore, the aim of facilities management should be not just to optimise running costs of buildings, but to raise the efficiency of the management of space and related assets for people and processes, in order that the mission and goals of the firm may be achieved at the best combination of efficiency and cost.

Growth of facilities management

Studies into the efficiency of workplace organisation have been undertaken quite extensively in this century. Similarly, concepts of value in building and the concepts of construction economics have been progressively refined in the second half of this century. The growth of large national and international companies, together with improved communications, mobility of people, and IT, means that attention has now begun to focus more on the connections between buildings and people.

The formation of the International Facility Management Association (IFMA) in the USA was a significant point in development of the profession. When the first International Facilities Management Symposium in Washington DC was organised by IFMA in 1989, delegates attended from many countries of the world, not only the USA and Canada, but also from the UK, Australia, Japan, Netherlands, Switzerland and Germany, and facilities management organisations exist in each of these countries. It is interesting that in Japan in particular, the facilities management function has been promoted through government agencies, whereas elsewhere the onus has tended to be on individual, independent professional associations to develop facilities management, and the viewpoint of facilities management has tended to be coloured in many countries by the existence or otherwise of strong professional bodies in the property management and architectural fields.

The scope of facilities management

In addition to those matters which relate to people in buildings, a comprehensive view of facilities management will involve all of those elements which practitioners in the UK might see as coming under the heading of strategic property management. It also requires the understanding of the detail of the operation and conservation of property which is often referred to as built asset management. Of course, many of these factors relate to the design and layout of buildings which also affect the way in which the organisation and the management of people and processes impinge on the effectiveness of the organisation. This means that concepts of facilities management should be in the minds of the design and construction team from the initial feasibility studies of proposed developments or refurbishments, and should be carried through into 'as built' documentation and the operation of property.

As referred to in the introductory paragraph, the CIOB has expressed these concepts in Figure 1.1 where they have identified their view of the major areas in facilities management for professionals in the built environment. The role of each of these major areas is now examined in rather more detail, in relation to the topics in this handbook.

Strategic property management and valuations

In the handbook we have included not only strategic property management as a topic but also the principles of life cycle costing, and complementary topics of property development, and therefore the text deals with two different and sometimes opposing aspects of property; firstly, to provide and sustain suitable space at an economic cost and, secondly, to provide an acceptable return over time for the cost of investment. Both aspects influence decisions to develop, acquire or to dispose of property either from the investor's or owner's viewpoint or from the user's viewpoint.

The first aspect focuses on matters such as existing property related to need, location, property appraisal, and consideration of the options for providing space. Within this area a series of evaluations is normally undertaken, and are referred to. The second aspect will relate to investment and returns on that investment compared with alternatives, and the evaluation of quality, amounts and standards of space provided. In both these areas of strategic property management a number of issues should interact, such as life of building components, value for money, environmental standards and special needs of the user.

Contract procedures and built asset management

Because of the relationships between building design processes, the construction of buildings and their eventual maintenance and operation, the CIOB has highlighted the areas of Contract Procedures and built asset management.

The matters discussed under the heading of construction procurement in this handbook also have some relevance to later material on contracting-out of services in the operation of buildings. Clearly, the procurement of building

6

work also relates to built asset management which is concerned with conserving the physical assets when built. In practice these topics embrace maintenance, renewal and improvement work to buildings and their surroundings and to the services relating to those buildings. The handbook also includes consideration of the documentation needed to manage property effectively and some of the aspects of asset management which involve service charges and comparative benchmarking.

A primary task of built asset management is organisation and controlling response maintenance, planned maintenance, renewal and improvements. Data from response maintenance, which is sometimes referred to as emergency or day-to-day maintenance, is valuable for indicating trends in failure and the likely periods for inspections to be undertaken. Planned maintenance consists of condition-dependent work which involves inspections of buildings and services to assess the need and the priority of the work, and non-condition-dependent work which consists of cyclical and other work that has to be carried out irrespective of the condition of the elements such as under health and safety at work and other statutory regulations.

The essential corollary of maintenance is the control of overall cost-in-use, and the staffing and energy costs involved and these aspects are also outlined.

Organisations: people and processes

This aspect of facilities management is concerned with people and their interaction with the building. Facilities management activities may be focused on the workforce in an organisation, in respect of the provision of satisfactory space and internal environments. They can also be focused on the processes undertaken in the organisation, which includes the provision of specialist services and monitoring the carrying out of tasks.

The main thrust of these aspects of facilities management is to optimise the design of space and its procurement, its utilisation, as well as the internal environment. It follows that much of the work involved concerns the management of use of space, and the provision of an environment that will support the processes involved.

Organisation will also embrace the management of support services, which are part of the facilities management brief, as well as services which are more related to core business activities and which are outside the scope of this publication.

Practice environment

Practice environment is the 'glue between the parts'. In other words, in addition to specific facilities management techniques and processes it also contains those aspects which, in themselves, have no unique connection with

7

facilities management. However, because facilities management relates to an overall function it involves a range of enabling processes which include the financial management, legal and professional environment within which facilities management takes place. It is this aspect of facilities management which should inform the corporate image and quality of service. It does so by professional ambience and by the confidence created among employees and customers when the service is competently and effectively delivered.

Because it is the 'glue' in facilities management, the thread that is woven between the many parts, it is difficult to attribute a specific chapter to it, but within the publication it will be found in various contexts, seeking to remind the reader of the expectations and responsibility placed on all professionals involved in this work.

Concluding note

Finally, an underlying theme in this particular publication will be the fact that data and management systems cost money to operate, and the organisation should be clear about which levels of control of various processes it is willing to pay for. An important factor to be borne in mind is that data throughout the facilities management system must be coordinated and consistent in their collection and use. Facilities management may operate at various levels and although this handbook has tended to keep to strategic and managerial levels, operational levels have been considered where appropriate.

It is suggested that no single, conventional, profession is likely to encompass the necessary level of expertise in all aspects of facilities management in its initial educational stage, so this handbook is intended to help people who wish to improve their expertise in the field to develop further. In the end, however, effective facilities management depends not just on knowledge and systems, but on the professionalism and management abilities of the people who work in the field.

Chapter 2

Strategic property management

Derek Worthing

Introduction

The essence of strategic property management is the realisation that the built estate is a valuable resource which, along with other resources, such as manpower and finance, can help to deliver the corporate goals of an organisation. It follows that, for an organisation with a large property portfolio, the built estate needs to be managed appropriately in order to play its part in achieving the corporate goals of that organisation. Property-related decisions must be made in a context where there is a clear understanding of the corporate goals of an organisation and of the social, political and economic forces which affect those goals. Strategic property management is a process where the value of the built estate as a resource is recognised, and its salient features understood and measured. This information is fed into the corporate plan, in order to help ensure that property furthers an organisation's strategic objectives.

All too often organisations with large property holdings ignore the built estate, and merely produce an uncoordinated shopping list of projects which emerge from planning decisions lacking a property insight. Indeed, many organisations lack a systematic understanding of their own holdings, and do not pursue an explicit property management strategy. In a number of cases property values will not appear on the 'balance sheet'. Yet the significance of property as a resource should be obvious. As Valente points out:[1]

> According to Central Government statistics, commercial property assets in this country have a total value of approximately £500 billion (current replacement cost). Of this, it is estimated that around £225 billion of commercial property assets is held by the corporate sector, which is substantially higher than the £50–60 million which is estimated to be held by institutional investors in this country. Only the public sector holds more property than the corporate sector.

He goes on to observe:

> The Hanson Trust holds more property assets than MEPC, whilst the Forte Group and the National Westminster Bank can be considered to be the fourth and fifth largest 'property companies' in this country in terms of value of assets held on their respective balance sheets. Another way of looking at the importance of property to the corporate balance sheet is from the point of view of property as a cost overhead. The 100 companies interviewed paid as much in rent as they did in interest payments, which is not an insignificant amount given the level of corporate debt over the last 2–3 years.

A lack of information on property holdings is perhaps only an indication of a more serious deficiency which fails to recognise the potential value of property in helping effective service delivery. Often this is because neither those responsible for strategic plans, nor those running the estate, recognise the potential of that estate in helping to deliver long-term goals. The problem is compounded by the fact that those that run the estate often do not have a place at board level (or its public sector equivalent), and at a lower level, organisational problems which act against strategic property management may also include:

1. The separation of property operations along professional lines, e.g. architects concerned with new buildings separated from building surveyors concerned with refurbishment and maintenance.
2. Separate resource allocations for capital and revenue including the effect of decisions on future estate investment. For example, cut backs on maintenance which both reduce capital value and require greater capital expenditure in the future.
3. Conflict between central property departments and client departments' perspectives and priorities, particularly as this affects long-term plans for the whole estate.

Problems with conventional property management

It might be said that 'conventional' property management tends not to see property in strategic terms, lacking a sense that property is a resource that can be pro-actively manipulated in order to optimise its potential in the long term. Property may be seen rather in negative terms only as a cost burden with a depreciating physical expression, and its management may tend therefore to be organised reactively merely to keep things 'ticking over', rather than seeing property as a catalyst which can both effect change and increase the effectiveness and value of the core business. Another characteristic of conventional property management is the tendency to concern itself almost entirely with the physical elements of the built estate, and ignore other salient features such as location, function, space, value. Where property is viewed from all levels of an organisation in this reactive manner with no clear property policy objective, it is perhaps unsurprising that property often becomes a burden on future developments rather than an asset for unlocking the organisation's potential.

Objectives

The concern of strategic property management is to ensure that a coherent view of property is fed into the overall strategy of the institution. From the organisation's strategy there should emerge a subsequent estate strategy which ensures that the organisation's built estate enhances its primary processes, and that the organisation has the right type of property, in the right location, in the right condition and at the right time. It is also important to ensure that the organisation has the optimum amount of property necessary to support its strategic goals and that there is, as far as possible and within the context of changing requirements, no underused nor surplus property. Avis et al.[2] gave the following example of well-defined property objectives from an organisation in the public sector:

1. Provide economically and efficiently for the present and future needs of clients, either by arranging for the reallocation of space within the existing estate, or by building, purchasing or leasing additional property as necessary.
2. Keep outgoings on the leased estate such as rental payments and service charges to the minimum achievable through efficient negotiation of rent reviews and lease renewals with landlords.
3. Hold an estate sufficient to meet objectives (1) and to dispose of any surplus accommodation quickly and effectively.
4. Reduce the amount of vacant space to the minimum possible.
5. Maintain the operational fitness and value of the estate by timely and adequate maintenance.

Given that the estate is a resource that exists to support the function of an organisation and its corporate goals it is important to realise that the facilities do not operate in isolation. No doubt the built estate can be run efficiently in isolation, but it cannot be run effectively unless property-related decisions are made interactively with decisions regarding the manpower and financial resources at an organisation's disposal and in the light of a coherent strategic planning culture with clear corporate goals. The facilities manager must understand the corporate goals of an organisation and the interaction and relative importance of the social, political and economic forces which affect those goals. Obvious examples of the consequences of this lack of understanding include expenditure on the maintenance of buildings that are to be rendered obsolete in the strategic plan.

One of the common problems with our concept of buildings is that they are often seen as an end in themselves rather than a corporate resource so that in the private sector they are seen mainly in terms of a financial investment, and all too often in the public sector (and probably in much of the private corporate sector as well) as a 'free good'. This assumes that there are no explicit penalties if more buildings and land are held than is necessary or if those assets are poorly managed or inefficiently used. For a facilities manager, in either sector, the task must be to optimise the built estate in relation to its primary role of supporting the primary process of the organisation. In relation to the strategic goals of the organisation this may mean that the costs of occupancy must be taken into account but a return on investment from the building itself may be a lesser consideration.

A framework for decision

Both public and private organisations with large property holdings need to introduce a rational framework for strategic decision making. What seems clear though is that there are two hurdles for both private and public sector organisations:

1. Acknowledgement of the importance of real estate in corporate activity.
2. Translating that acknowledgement into coherent strategic plans for the estate.

One particular organisation that has developed such a framework is the National Health Service. The impetus for a coherent estate strategy was the publication, in 1983, of a report entitled *Under-used and surplus property in the NHS*.[3] This report set in motion a process which led to the creation of a systematic approach to the strategic planning of NHS property culminating in a system which consisted of seven interrelated stages as follows:

1. *An estate data base.* To include estate terriers, open market, existing use and replacement values; property overheads.
2. *Performance analysis.* To include questions relating to remaining life, whether too much or too little property is being held (and whether it is in the right geographical position) and an appraisal of each building and site condition and functional suitability.
3. *Rationalisation.* In which the strategic plan for the organisation is developed by the appropriate multidisciplinary team with reference to the key resources of finance, manpower and the estate.
4. *The evaluation of alternative strategies.* The strategic options of the estate which evolve from stage 3 are subjected to option appraisal.
5. *An estate investment programme.* A financial profile showing the capital and revenue implications of decisions made.

6. *Estate control plan.* The encapsulation, for each individual site, of all decisions that have been reached, the cost implications and a programme of implementation.
7. *Estate operational plan.* The extension of the process of rationalisation to all assets including the maintenance of the built estate.

The coherence of this process and the general lessons learnt by the NHS are pertinent to other organisations with a large property portfolio whether public or private sector. As Davies observes, in reference to the NHS estate[4]

> An efficient organisation will take all facilities, their acquisition, valuation, performance, maintenance, disposal and location into account in its resource and strategic planning. It will not be able to afford more property than the function requires, so it regulates its holdings including plant and equipment regularly to match the demands for its services and ensures that all space is effectively utilised. The effective organisation maintains its property in good condition recognising that both its internal and external appearance presents to the public in general, and the patient in particular, an image of the whole organisation and is also closely related to staff morale. The crucial importance of the functional aspects of a plan need not, indeed will not be allowed to, conflict with the quality of the environment and the level of amenity for both patient and staff. The relationship between a good building and its external environment and a caring efficient service is a close one ... It will have ensured that the revenue consequences of new property can be met, that physical standards are maintained at an appropriate level and that the resource implications of this are identified and planned for over time. Such an organisation will ensure that the actual costs of operating property can be readily identified and related to indicators of performance, trends and alternative ways of providing a service.

Appropriate estate information

The lack of recognition of the estate's potential as a resource is often compounded by a lack of status afforded to those who provide estate services, aggravated by a cultural divide between those occupying the buildings and those who are managing them. From a strategic planning point of view therefore it is important that those who provide estate services understand and take part in the organisation's strategic planning process, allowing the estate to play a creative role in the delivery of that plan. For this to happen data must be available on the estate at an appropriate level for strategic planning purposes. The necessary information will include:

1. What is owned, and how much it costs to run.
2. Value and enhanced value of the stock.
3. An appraisal of the performance of the buildings.

In appraising buildings it is important to ensure that qualitative judgements are made along with quantitive ones. The work on building appraisals carried out in the fields of post-occupancy evaluation (POEs) is a useful reference point, particularly the emphasis on the importance of user involvement.

Preiser *et al.*[5] suggest that POE should cover:

- *Technical elements*, such as fire safety, structural integrity, sanitation, durability, acoustics and lighting.
- *Functional elements*, such as operational efficiency, productivity, work flow and organisation.
- *Behavioural elements*, such as privacy, symbolism, social interaction, density and territoriality.

The performance of a building might be appraised by considering the following:

- physical condition
- functional suitability
- space utilisation
- health and safety and statutory compliance
- energy

Physical condition

This should produce broad indications of the physical condition of the building and its services, and show the cost of repairs to bring the estate up to a specified minimum level of condition. Physical condition is often homed in on by technical professionals as the key criterion. In practice, however, important factors such as space or functional suitability may be more crucial in either preventing or allowing the exploitation of the estate's potential.

As with all surveys, determining the appropriate level of information is important. For strategic purposes broad categories are sufficient to provide a starting point for more detailed maintenance or minor works programmes. In practice, issues such as a rating for inherently unsatisfactory buildings in good condition, or alteration of the physical criteria rating because of the function can cause problems.

Functional suitability

This is an important issue because there may be buildings which are inherently unsuitable for their purpose no matter how much money is spent on them, but they might accommodate another function more effectively than their present one. The appraisal should cover the suitability of the whole site as well as individual buildings, because buildings may be individually suitable but the site may not be. For example, a university campus or a hospital should be considered in relation to its location with reference to centres of population, transport, amenities, relationship with other sites, as well as the site's characteristics, and access. There is also a need to consider overall effectiveness such as the under- or overprovision of a particular functional unit.

For individual buildings, assessment may include, for example:

1. Space – including critical dimensions for its function and a consideration of the relationship between spaces.
2. Services.
3. Amenity – this will obviously vary with the type of organisation in question, but may range across assessments of the impression created for clients, visitors, the public, the working and social conditions for staff and the mix of public/private areas.
4. Location – this may include factors such as access and relationship to (related) departments.
5. Environmental conditions.

Space utilisation

For both the public and private sector, space allocation and utilisation have become a major issue. In many parts of the public sector there has been, and continues to be, enormous pressure to account for the efficient use of space and sell off that which can be identified as surplus. While there are obvious difficulties, particularly when the organisation is going through a period of uncertainty, a property space evaluation can potentially deliver significant savings. In the private sector the saving on rent can often be significant and will be the obvious driving factor. However, even in the private sector (where the companies concerned are themselves owners of large property portfolios) the amount of unused or inefficiently used space is significant despite the assumption of greater efficiency, driven by factors such as rent. For example, Valente[1] refers to a survey which considered 175 million sq. ft of industrial floorspace occupied by 100 companies. Of this 5 per cent or 9-10 million sq. ft was unoccupied (and this figure would probably have increased). As Valente observes:

> . . . whilst such a vacancy level is largely a function of the current economic climate, it may also reflect the fact that the majority of companies have no incentives or indeed penalties to ensure the most efficient use for floorspace. Only one-third of the companies interviewed charged internal rents for example and only around 20% had a corporate policy on space standards.

In both the public and private sector there is, it seems, sometimes a problem in convincing people that buildings and the space within them are not a 'free good'. Attempts to tackle this include sticks, such as real or notional charging systems, or carrots, such as performance-related space. However, it is likely that the best way forward is to demonstrate how the realisation of space saving can improve service delivery or profits by reducing revenue costs.

There are many problems with space utilisation surveys from adopting appropriate methodologies through to the 'politics' of space. Measurement is also difficult because of the dynamic nature of space. Space utilisation is concerned with the use of space over time, the frequency of use and occupancy rates while in use. In reality 100 per cent usage of space is certainly transitory, probably unachievable and almost certainly undesirable.

It is particularly important with space to relate decisions to the organisation's strategic plan. There have been cases where buildings or sites have been sold off because of short-term contingencies only to find that similar space was the key to delivering future plans.

To the practical difficulties of measurement can be added the problem of the cultural divide, referred to earlier, between the space occupier and the property manager. If the property manager cannot grapple with the way space is actually used (rather than how the designer envisaged its use), how links between spaces work and the way patterns in the social interaction of the users occur, then space appraisal will be meaningless. As Shove[6] observes in reference to space utilisation in higher education:

> . . . what constitutes good space utilisation in terms of property management may be quite unlike that which constitutes good space utilisation defined in terms of the effective integration of activity, accommodation and time.

This same clash is often seen when commercial letting agents fail to understand, or acknowledge, that their net rentable space is not the same as the net effectively usable/suitable space, and that the net usable space can change over time and between clients. There is often the need to address the cultural divide and this must include involving the user in space, and function, appraisals.

In practice other problems arise in making judgements; for instance, there may be impressions of overcrowding, when the problem is due to poor management. Indeed the opposite may be true and undermanning might be confused with underutilisation. Another serious problem is that staff often find the process of appraisal threatening. There is a perceived or implied criticism of any (space) appraisal, and the link between space and status adds to the potential problem. There may be a tendency to bias opinions to imply that a space is usually more widely used than it appears to be. There may also be a tendency with staff who have grown up with a space problem, to be efficient in dealing with it, but not to recognise the problem of effectiveness.

Health and safety and statutory compliance

It is important that an assessment is made of the building for compliance with statutory obligations, and its performance in terms of protecting the health and safety of its users. This may take on a particular perspective for certain organisations. For example in the National Health Service, fire safety assessment is a prominent consideration.

Energy

Energy usage is an obviously important factor in the performance of a building, and needs to be monitored, and improved where possible.

Coordinating appraisal information

For these surveys only broad-brush indicators are necessary because in practice 'accuracy' is less important than consistency, and what is required is a comparative evaluation. It is obviously important to provide an estimate of costs associated with the buildings, whether the strategic plan indicates retention, alteration or disposal. The cost information required at this stage will include costs to retain serviceability and to carry out improvements to an acceptable level of condition.

It is important that double accounting is avoided in respect of overlapping improvement in two or more categories, such as an improvement in thermal performance which may accrue from improvements in physical condition. It is also very important to try to assess whether or not problems can be overcome in reality. In relation to space this can be difficult because of the organisational issues involved, but with function, and condition, a practical assessment of potential improvements should not be difficult to assess.

To be of any value the surveys have to be seen as interactive, and it may be necessary or desirable to devise a weighting system to give comparable data. For example, what overall rating should be given to a building which is in good condition, has low energy costs and where space is used well, but where its functional suitability is poor?

However, it must always be remembered that appraisals are intended to provide appropriate information for the organisation's strategic plan and that individual details may not be the most pertinent in determining the future use of the resource. It is important for the 'property professional' to understand the distinction between, and dynamics of, a building's physical decay and its obsolescence (i.e. its socio-economic life).

The estate appraisal should enable all the issues and problems pertaining to the estate to be brought together and fed into the strategic process. It is important that objective assessments of 'where are we now' are brought to the table in order that they can be measured against a 'where do we want to be' scenario. This is necessary so that both difficulties and opportunities can be assessed in option appraisals without the restrictions to creativity that prejudgements, or specialist concerns, might bring. For instance, a maintenance surveyor might see physical condition as being the primary factor in a building's performance to the virtual exclusion of other factors. The strategic plan may indicate a need to retain the building but improve its performance, but if improvements are difficult to achieve and the building or site has a relatively high market value, then its performance assessment may lead to a decision to sell.

Performance indicators

Performance indicators (PIs) are a useful management tool for measuring the current position of the built estate and in comparing progress towards the organisation's objectives. They are particularly useful where a large organisation is broken down into smaller geographically diverse units all serving the same purpose, such as in hospitals, housing or retail outlets, where managers can consider the performance of their unit against another similar one.

Perhaps the most important point about PIs is that they should be used, not in a competitive sense, but as a management tool which allows comparative performance to be measured. If there is a difference between say the cost per unit of area to maintain a school in central London and one in rural Cumbria, there are almost certainly explanations other than inefficiency. The purpose of a PI in this case would be to highlight the difference and register it as worthy of further investigation. PIs may also be useful in pinpointing the source of a particular problem. For instance, cause and effect may be indicated if the PIs for a particular estate show energy use higher than the norm plus a low maintenance expenditure per unit area, a high building area per functional unit, and poor condition. An explanation may be that the poor condition results from a surplus of inefficiently used buildings which stretches the maintenance budget.

The use of performance indicators implies:

- having legitimate comparisons
- two variables
- target(s)

To be of value PIs must obviously be based on comparable, consistent and reliable data, they should be complementary and holistic, they should be part of an integrated system but, above all, they should be relevant. Obviously to be relevant the PIs must relate to the goals of the particular organisation. The PIs shown below have been used by the NHS, but illustrate the type of indicators that can be used for all types of property organisations.

- hectares of land related to population
- disposal of land against percentage of land held
- building area related to available beds
- building area related to resident population
- plot ratio
- cost to bring estate up to condition 'B'
- annual maintenance expenditure per unit area
- energy usage per unit volume
- maintenance staff related to building area

Identifying surplus land or buildings

Space audits will help to identify underutilisation and to show how space can be used more effectively, possibly identifying areas of land or buildings which can be shown to be surplus to immediate requirements. This will include a consideration of how the operational delivery of the service might be adjusted in order to use space more effectively and the lessons learnt should, as with POE, inform the design of new buildings.

Identification of surplus land and buildings can only be achieved by considering current and future plans. Any changes necessary to the estate, in order to allow it to play an active part in the delivery of the strategic plan, need to be subjected to option appraisals. These option appraisals will identify how much of the existing estate may be retained, as well as opportunities for reordering the present estate to improve throughput. They will also identify requirements to demolish, rehabilitate or build new (perhaps on additional land) over the strategic period. It is only after this stage that one can start to identify surplus land with some confidence, and perhaps just as importantly, when that surplus land might be available. However, in both the public and private sectors there is a danger that scaling down today, in the case of estates by lack of care and injudicious sales, will restrict the exploitation of opportunities in the future.

Forecasting change in demand

Clearly in order to make strategic plans for property there must be a strategic plan for the organisation. Often the strategic plan for a private sector organisation will have a relatively easily identifiable objective such as to make a profit or to increase a share of the market. In the public sector the objective may be simply stated but more complex to achieve, for example to improve the health of the population.

A strategic planning process needs to be put in place which includes a policy framework, the consequence of that policy, a comprehensive information base, and procedures to produce and implement the plans. Of course, over time, the strategy of the organisation may not be fixed, and therefore the plan must allow for review and adjustment. While the longer the planning period the more uncertainty is introduced, particularly in relation to factors outside the control of the organisation, it is clear that short planning periods can cause problems because the lead time for effecting property decisions may be greater than for other factors. Additionally, the objectives of organisations will differ and therefore so will the scope and complexity of the subsequent strategic plan.

A simplified example of some of the strategic issues which face the estate of a university is given in the appendix to this chapter.

Planning for estate change

The absence of a strategic plan may result in property failing to play a vital part in realising an organisation's objective. This might arise because part of a property holding is sold in order to realise capital, which prevents expansion or indeed an eventual enhancement of its value. An option appraisal process will be necessary to identify and evaluate the range of solutions which could fulfil the estate strategy, and a key challenge at this stage is the creativity needed to identify options to be appraised. The strategic plan should highlight the implications for sites, and buildings in order that a clear programme of new build, rehabilitation, maintenance and repair, demolition, sale (in part or whole) and purchase is put in place related to forecasts of future operational requirements.

Clearly, the implications of the strategy need to be related to the current and projected financial resources available, and need to be seen in the context of enabling improvements in the performance of the built estate and therefore service delivery. As well as understanding, for instance, the long-term problems of underfunding maintenance of property, the projected expenditure on the estate needs to be balanced against:

1. Capital accrued from disposals.
2. Revenue savings from disposals and more efficient utilisation of the property resource.
3. Improved service delivery resulting from more efficient and effective buildings.

Estate control plans

The NHS[7] views the production of the estate control plan as being a key document which encapsulates all the key decisions emanating from the strategic plan, and which will form the link between rationalisation proposals and the future management of the rationalised estate. The document states that:

> This stage therefore provides the final formal opportunity in the system of critically examining the future use of all buildings, land and associated plant with the aim of providing the most effective physical environment for the provision and delivery of services. It will normally need to be supported by feasibility studies which will explore possibilities and examine the key available options.

As the NHS approach is so coherent it is worth considering their approach more closely. Estatecode points out that the estate control plan stage (see 'A framework for decision' stages 1–7, p. 12) cannot be satisfactorily completed until a series of questions have been answered. These questions relate to external space, internal space, functional suitability, physical condition, location, shape and layout related to safety standards and cost of compliance and, lastly, energy performance and pay-back periods of improvements. All of these issues are pertinent to strategic property management and the reader will find the estatecode documentation a useful source of further information.

Appendix

This example illustrates some of the factors which influence the type of strategic property decisions which are required for a higher education institution, in particular:

- changes in student numbers
- changes in delivery of courses
- changes in the type of courses

Factors affecting these elements include the fact that higher education numbers have expanded dramatically over the previous decade in large part due to government policy, but government has now put a ceiling on recruitment of full-time students. It is likely that growth in the numbers of part-time students will still be encouraged. Part-time attendance (e.g. one day a week) produces a more intensive demand on rooms and services due to the traditionally longer day, but this may produce efficiency gains. There is also a move towards a more intensive use of space by increasing the 'working day' for full-time students as well as part-timers. There are also calls for greater use of weekend teaching to accommodate the wishes of, for instance, postgraduate part-time students for whom pressure of work does not allow weekday attendance. Changes in the way that courses are delivered to provide a more student-centred approach will affect the space requirements, such as type and size of rooms, and will generate a greater need for library accommodation and private study facilities. Changes in type of courses might include, for instance, a move from humanities-type courses to engineering-based courses with a subsequent requirement for laboratories and other specialist rooms.

For the university in this example a long-term objective is to concentrate all of its activity on its main site A with its location near rail and motorway links and room for physical growth (see Figure 2.1). At present the university is located on a number of sites which causes problems including:

- Students and staff at the outlying sites do not identify with the institution.
- There is a duplication or at least extra cost to essential services, e.g. portering, cleaning, library and catering.
- Staff, and in some cases students, have to move between sites.
- Equitable provision of university-owned accommodation and other resources is difficult and its siting favours those on the main campus.

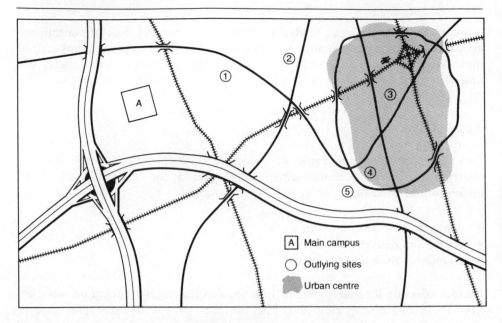

Figure 2.1 Multi-site university property

- Timetabling constraints and the uneven nature of room occupation throughout the day is a problem in all universities. With split sites the efficient use of space is likely to be a greater problem than would be the case if the same volume of buildings were on site.

Therefore the strategic plan envisages that the services provided at sites 1–5 will be transferred to site A in the next 15 years. The plan envisages that three departments which are currently separate and located on sites 1–3 should be combined and relocated as soon as possible at site A as a Faculty of Combined Studies.

For the main site it will be necessary to ensure that a control plan is put in place to ensure that the activities of sites 1–5 are moved to the main site at agreed times over the next 15 years. This may necessitate:

1. The reordering of the existing accommodation, if space utilisation surveys show that by more efficient use of space, some of the activities can take place in the existing accommodation. Also, existing accommodation may be more functionally suitable for the users now operating at sites 1, 2, 3, 4 or 5.
2. Rehabilitation or extension of existing premises.
3. New build.

It will undoubtedly also require:

1. Extra library accommodation

22

2. Extra car parking (or better public transport!).
3. Extra catering services, toilets and support services.

The requirements of the faculties which are to move and their physical and teaching relationship to other faculties should be considered.

It is worth noting the effect of car parking on the effective management of the estate for this university. Public transport to the university is a problem, because the main site is on the edge of the city. The bus company has improved its service, but also peaks and troughs of the teaching day mean that the provision of effective public transport is difficult because the students do not all arrive at 9 a.m. and leave at 5 p.m. Apart from environmental considerations, the amount of valuable space required for cars is considerable and might distort rational estate decisions. A change in timing of the teaching day/week could therefore have quite wide-ranging implications for the estate, possibly bringing more efficient use of buildings and land.

It is important that short-term decisions such as selling currently 'surplus' land to raise capital do not lead to the main site lacking room for expansion even though capital sales may be valuable.

In the short term it may well be sensible for the Faculty of Combined Studies to come together on one of the peripheral sites, in order to begin to address some of the split site problems mentioned previously including the more efficient and effective use of space. It may be possible, for instance, with some reordering of space and function plus minor extensions to existing buildings, to locate the activities of sites 2 and 3 at site 1 thus freeing up two sites for sale. This could be more cost-effective than the present situation and, despite the need for investment to bring some buildings up to an acceptable condition plus extensions, it may well be more cost-effective and more viable than the sale of three sites and the relocation of their activities in mainly new accommodation on site A. Factors affecting this decision might include a comparison of each site on the basis of:

- Functional and space suitability of all of the existing departmental locations both as current and assessing flexibility for new uses.
- Communications links with main site.
- Ease of access, and car parking space.
- Proximity to student accommodation.
- Physical condition, energy usage, health and safety condition, including how much it will cost to bring the buildings to an acceptable condition and to achieve economical running costs.
- Which site has the highest realistic capital value.

Clearly there are several potential strategies which might be pursued by the university and only a detailed examination of the alternatives will give a reasonable chance of choosing the best solution.

References

1. Valente J 1993 *Role of property managing cost and releasing value.* Paper given at RICS 'Cutting Edge' Conference
2. Avis M, Gibson V, Watts J 1989 *Managing operational property assets* Department of Land Management and Development, University of Reading Graduates to Industry
3. Davies C (Chairman) 1983 *Underused and surplus property in the National Health Service* Enquiry Report, HMSO
4. Davies C 1988 *Facilities management in the health service.* Paper presented at RICS Building Surveyors National Briefing, March
5. Preiser W F E, Rabinowitz Z, White E 1988 *Post-occupancy evaluation* Van Nostrand Reinhold
6. Shove E 1993 *The black holes of space economics* Buildings and Society Research Unit, University of Sunderland, January
7. Department of Health 1989 *Guidance on the estate control plan (part of estatecode)* Advisory Group on Estate Management, Estate and Property Management Directorate, February

Chapter 3

Property development, valuation and management

Stephen Hargitay

Introduction

This chapter is intended to introduce some principles of estate management which the facilities manager should understand when dealing with the decision to develop and to investigate the budgetary, taxation and related issues concerned with long-term property management. It will also take into consideration the various factors in forecasting the life of the buildings from the investment point of view.

The facilities manager can provide an active input into the traditional work sphere of both the property manager and the developer, and can also provide an interface between the various property specialists where the design and functioning of the workplace is concerned. When working with various property specialists and professionals the facilities manager must understand and appreciate the procedures and implications of the design, construction and economic viability of buildings in order to provide effective management of the buildings throughout their lifetime.

Assets are created through the processes of property development and these assets need to be managed primarily to maintain their value and to optimise their operating performance. Facilities management is part of this management process and is particularly concerned with the provision for anticipating and dealing with change relating to property.

The facilities manager, in the context of property management, is one of the principal providers of strategic information. Traditional property management does not provide the information that senior executives need and the traditional approach is usually reactive. Property management is mainly concerned with the routine administration of individual properties, tenancies and rent collections. Traditional property management is particularly inadequate for the management of property investment portfolios and cannot provide appropriate strategic management. The facilities management approach, on the other hand, should be able to deal strategically with operational and investment assets. The Facilities Manager should be able to make positive inputs into decision making concerning the design, development, acquisition, disposal, refurbishment and efficient management of operational and investment assets. The facilities manager's task is to interpret and translate strategic plans into specific, pragmatic objectives and to devise appropriate management systems. Due to the complexity of these tasks the management systems need to be computerised and there are now several computerised management systems available for effective practical use.

This chapter deals with a limited number of property development and valuation topics which demand a good understanding by the facilities manager. The first section is devoted to the decision to develop and project appraisal. Two of the following sections cover the rationale of property investment, rates of return expectations and aspects of value and valuation procedures. A section reviews aspects of taxation and the final section is aimed to explore the long-term aspects of the events in the life of an asset and their appropriate management.

Decision to develop

The decision to develop is the most important decision in the context of the creation and management of operational real estate assets. This decision is really an investment decision usually arrived at as the conclusion of a special evaluation process and in the light of well-defined decision criteria. The decision to develop is a collective term for decision making associated with the development of green field sites, redevelopment of sites occupied by obsolescent buildings and the refurbishment of buildings. This section is devoted to the brief review of the methodology of the appraisal and evaluation of development proposals. Development proposals are evaluated by using one of the following techniques: a special version of investment appraisal called development appraisal, cost-in-use sometimes referred to as the annual equivalent technique, and cost–benefit analysis. The selection of the appropriate technique is essential for the derivation of the right decision indicator. The facilities manager needs to understand the rationale of these techniques in order to participate in the decision-making process.

The decision to develop is concerned with the allocation of resources to create new assets to benefit a private or corporate investor. New assets are also created to benefit the community as a whole and in these cases the public bodies are usually the principal decision makers. After the creation of the assets there is a continuing demand for additional resources to maintain the buildings and facilities to continue to satisfy the requirements of the occupiers of the buildings and to maintain the efficiency of the assets to produce satisfactory investment returns.

It is important to use the appropriate evaluation technique. Development appraisal is most suited for private sector development proposals where the main criterion is the promise of adequate profits. The evaluation of the efficiency of an asset throughout its productive life cycle can be carried out by using the cost-in-use technique, and this technique is probably the most appropriate for the use of the facilities manager. Public sector development projects require a much broader approach and profitability may be a relatively less important criterion. Cost–benefit analysis is an appropriate technique to appraise large developments in the public sector.

All of the evaluation techniques require an understanding of the principles of discounting. Discounting is an expression of the concept of the time value of money. This simply means that money in the hand is now worth more than the same amount of money at some time in the future. The money in hand today could be invested and earn some interest and could accumulate to a larger sum in the future. The calculation of the amount of money to be invested today, earning a specified interest rate, to grow to a specified sum at a specified date in the future is the process of discounting. Discounting is necessary to facilitate the comparison of cost and revenue items which are dispersed in time, and is intended to bring costs and revenues to a common time base.

In all of the above evaluation techniques the projects considered are seen as time series of cash sums, representing costs and revenues. In the widely used technical jargon such cash sums are called cash flows. Cost items are outflows, revenues are inflows while the difference between inflows and outflows at a particular date is referred to as the net cash flow.

The time series of cash flows is called the cash flow stream. The majority of appraisal techniques are designed to examine and analyse the cash flow streams associated with the projects. Even a cursory visual examination of the cash flow stream can yield valuable insights into a project's financial viability and into the likely performance of the asset in terms of the user's requirements and needs. The careful drafting of cash flow streams is extremely important if the right conclusions are to be derived from the appraisals. Discounting is applied to the cash flow streams and is used in, in one form or another, in all above-mentioned evaluation techniques.

Outline of the rationale of development appraisal

This technique is the principal tool of the developer and the development surveyor who must check the financial feasibility and profitability of new development proposals before any monies are invested into the project. All aspects of the proposed development, such as construction costs, legal costs, finance costs, planning aspects and the expected value of the completed project, will be considered before the decision to develop is made. All these aspects are considered in the context of the prevailing economic climate, the state of the property market, finance and investment markets.

27

Development appraisal is usually carried out by using the residual method or an appropriate cash flow method. The residual method is based on the following simple concept:

$$\frac{\text{Estimated value of the}}{\text{completed project}} \quad - \quad \text{The total costs involved} \quad = \quad \text{Residue}$$

The estimation of the value of the completed project involves the use of the appropriate method of valuation. The calculation of the total costs involved is usually done on the basis of the cost information available at the date of the appraisal. The residue is then calculated either as the residual site value or as the profit residue. The decision criterion is as follows:

Develop if residual site value $>$ Asking price for the site

or

Develop if profit residue $>$ Minimum acceptable profit

While the residual method is a simple and powerful decision tool, its main weakness that it does not take the time value of money into account satisfactorily and it is an over-simplified 'snap-shot' of the balance between the estimate of the value generated by the development and the current costs involved.

Cash flow methods produce more precise and reliable indicators for decision making and are either a discounting or a non-discounting type. When discounting is applied, the evaluation is carried out on the basis of, and in the format of, the discounted cash flow technique (DCF). If no discounting is applied then the technique is usually referred to as the rolling account and a terminal value (TV) is computed. The decision criteria are as follows: when the DCF method is used then either net present value (NPV) or the internal rate of return (IRR) or both NPV and IRR are computed.

Develop if NPV $>$ 0

or

Develop if IRR $>$ The minimum acceptable rate of return

When the rolling account method is used:

Develop if rolled up profit or TV $>$ The minimum acceptable profit

Cash flow methods are more satisfactory as they take into account the time value of money properly, although they can be cumbersome computationally. Another weak point is the subjective nature of the forecasting, estimation and drafting of future cash flow streams.

The conclusions of the above evaluation techniques can be further enhanced by testing the effects of uncertainty and risk using sensitivity analysis, or in some cases, sophisticated risk analysis.

Outline of the rationale of the cost-in-use technique

Development appraisal concentrates on the initial costs of development projects, but when the completed project is occupied and in use the maintenance and operational costs will require the estimation and planning of expenditure patterns over the life span of the building. The users of the buildings and the facilities manager will need a reliable tool to plan, monitor and manage the real costs associated with the maintenance and operational use of the buildings. The cost-in-use technique has been developed to address these problems specifically. The technique does not merely consider the cost of using the building but attempts to ascertain, in investment terms, the economic efficiency of a building including the initial capital expenditure. Cost-in-use can give insights into a number of cost relationships which can assist the developer, the investor and the operational manager of the building in making the correct decisions:

1. The relationship between the capital investment of developing a site and the expected return in terms of the income from rents.
2. The relationship between the capital invested in the installation of services and their running costs.
3. The relationship between the costs of finishes and fittings and their maintenance costs.
4. The relationship between the costs of materials and components and their different life spans.

These insights will enable the decision makers to identify the most economical decision alternatives. The cost-in-use technique rests on a number of assumptions and predictions:

1. Future prices.
2. Interest and discount rates.
3. Lives of buildings.
4. Lives of building components, finishes and fittings.
5. Taxation.

As the above assumptions and predictions are subject to uncertainty an appropriate form of sensitivity analysis must be carried out to underpin the decision-making process. The rationale of the technique is the continuing periodic balance of the annual equivalent costs and the annual income. The annual equivalent cost is the sum of the annualised capital costs and all the other annual costs associated with the operating of the building, maintenance costs, refurbishment and repair costs, and the like. The total annual equivalent of all costs are calculated by summing the annualised costs of the initial costs, annual running costs, and various periodic costs forecast for the operational life span of the building. The annual equivalent of the various types of costs are computed by using the appropriate compound interest formulae and annuity tables. The use of these formulae and tables will be briefly outlined below.

The total costs incurring during the operational life span of a building are classified and converted into annual equivalent component costs as shown under the headings below

Initial costs

Site costs
These include the purchase price of the site and the associated legal and transaction costs. Distinction is made between a freehold and a leasehold site. A freehold site is not a wasting asset, i.e. there is no need to set aside a sinking fund to regenerate the capital invested into the purchase of the freehold site. The site costs are converted into annual equivalents as given below.

Freehold site costs. These will be converted into annual equivalent cost by simply multiplying the total cost of the site with the annual interest rate for borrowing that sum, thus:

$$AE_S = [\text{Site costs}] \times [\,i\,]$$

Leasehold site costs. These will need to be regenerated during the operational life span of the building (more precisely during the span of the lease). This is worked out by using annual sinking fund (ASF) formula:

$$ASF = \frac{i}{(1+i)^n - 1}$$

where i = the annual rate of interest and n the operational life span of the building in years. Usually the product of the above formula is found in annuity tables from which the sinking fund factor SF may be extracted:

$$AE_S = [\text{Site Costs}] \times [SF + i]$$

Building costs. These will be regarded as a wasting asset having a limited life span during which the capital spent on the building must be regenerated. Annual contributions to a sinking fund will facilitate this. The annual equivalent of the building costs will be computed thus:

$$AE_B = [\text{Total building costs}] \times [SF + i]$$

Other costs

Annual costs (C_a)

These are the recurring costs associated with the management and running of the building. They are already in an annualised form so do not require any conversion.

Periodic costs

These costs are all the other costs which are not initial costs or annually recurring costs. The types of periodic costs are distinguished below.

Periodic individual sums. These cost items are expected to occur sometime during the operational life of the building and are converted into their annual equivalent by applying the discounting principle mentioned above. The formula to compute the present value factor (PVF) is as follows:

$$\text{PVF} = \frac{1}{(1 + i)^t}$$

where i is the interest or discount rate and t the number of years to the occurrence of the individual cost item. If more than one individual item is to be considered then the present values of the annual equivalents of each item will be added together. Thus:

$$\text{AE}_{Pi} = \Sigma[(\text{PVF}_t \times (\text{Individual item})_t) \times (\text{SF} + i)]$$

Periodic uniform sums. These are recurring identical sums and they are computed by summing their present value factors thus:

$$\text{AE}_{Pu} = [\Sigma\,\text{PFV}] \times [\text{Uniform recurring item}] \times [\text{SF} + i]$$

The **total annual equivalent cost** is the sum of the above:

$$\text{AE}_T = \text{AE}_S + \text{AE}_B + C_a + \text{AE}_{Pi} + \text{AE}_{Pu}$$

The total annual equivalent cost is the decision or monitoring criterion for the decision maker. The decision maker must compare the total annual equivalent cost with the annual revenue from the use of the building and conclude that

> If AE_T < Annual revenue the building is financially viable

or

> If AE_T > Annual revenue the building is heading for financial problems.

The above evaluation technique is virtually tailormade for the facilities manager who must test and monitor the efficiency of his building in terms of economic and financial aspects.

Outline of the rationale of cost–benefit analysis

Cost–benefit analysis is an evaluation technique mainly used for large projects in the public sector. It is aimed at maximising the value to the community of the benefits derived from capital investment. The technique differs from development appraisal and the annual equivalent methods in that it attempts to quantify, measure and incorporate tangible and intangible social costs and benefits, in addition to the financial costs and profits, into the evaluation of projects. Cost–benefit analysis takes a longer-term view of a broader spectrum of social and financial costs and benefits. The main difficulties associated with this technique are those of definition, quantification and measurement of the intangibles. The computational procedures are usually based on the DCF method. Facilities managers are unlikely to be involved with this type of evaluation although they may be asked to supply data and information from their special sphere of activities.

Investment and returns on property

The last four decades saw an unprecedented growth in investment in real property. Powerful institutional and private investors steadily increased the proportion of direct property investment in their portfolios. More recently, major changes have taken place in the Stock Exchange and new investment vehicles emerged through the unitisation and securitisation of property. The 'man in the street' has also increased his commitment to property investment, directly, by purchasing his house and indirectly, through the property investments of his pension fund. The growth in investment activity is based on the belief that property as an investment medium provides a relatively good security of capital and income in an uncertain economic environment. Besides promising relatively attractive returns, property also offers excellent opportunities for diversifying the huge corporate and institutional investment portfolios.

Following the end of the Second World War profits seemed to be assured through the spectacular growth in property values and the regular incomes from let properties, and demand for space to be rented remained steady until recent times, maintaining confidence in property as an investment medium.

The end of the 1960s and the beginning of the 1970s were the halcyon days of ever-increasing demand for space, rocketing property values, huge profits and plenty of capital to be invested. In those days, the systematic analysis of property projects and the careful design of property investment portfolios seemed to be a superfluous academic exercise. The collapse of the property market in the early 1970s, together with the rapidly accelerating economic decline, created an urgent need for the systematic reassessment of the ways property investment decisions were made and portfolios were constructed and managed. It became obvious that the traditional approach and methodology could no longer cope with the alarmingly complex situation.

The investment characteristics of property are significantly different from the characteristics of assets in other investment media. This is the reason why property is so useful and attractive for the purposes of diversification. On the other hand, such different characteristics had isolated property from the other media, in which tremendous strides were made in the development of decision-making methodology and the modernising of investment and portfolio management techniques.

The amount of capital invested in property and diverted away from other investment opportunities, is huge and requires efficient stewardship. The people responsible for planning further capital investments in property and for the continuing maintenance and improvement of the investment efficiency of existing assets, are the managers of property funds or portfolios and their respective expert advisers. Facilities managers have a very important contribution to make in the management of corporate investment assets, their primary task being the management of the operational efficiency of the buildings in their care.

It is accepted that the principal purpose of business activity in general and investment in particular is to generate profits, or returns. Investment is defined as an activity which requires cash outlay with the aim of receiving, in return, future cash inflows. It is assumed that the increase in wealth, as a result of the purchase of financial assets, is the main objective of investment. The return on investment is a measure of the change in wealth resulting from the purchase of these assets. The prerequisite of any analysis is to determine those factors which determine the level of profitability. The return is seen as a reward for committing and exposing to risk some capital in investment projects. The total return has two principal components, the income earned, and the increase in the value of the asset acquired.

The part of the return which comes from the increase in the value of the asset is either **realised** or **unrealised**. This particular part of the return will only be realised on the disposal of that particular asset, and this aspect could lead to some confusion when the investment performance of the asset is being analysed and monitored. Investment returns are usually regarded as gross potential returns although most prudent investors would rather be interested in the **real returns** after allowances for the erosion of money values, taxes and the like.

As investment means the purchase of future earnings, it will be necessary to formulate future return expectations. **Expected returns** are formulated from the examination of historical returns and the consideration of trends. The ranking of investment alternatives is usually carried out on the basis of the expected returns on the various alternatives. The rate of return produced by capital invested over a time period is as follows:

33

$$\text{Per cent rate of return} = \frac{(\text{Change in capital value}) + (\text{Net income})}{(\text{Capital employed over the time period})} \times 100$$

The above definition is a general one and valid over any time period provided that the following conditions are fulfilled:

1. The capital employed remains constant throughout the period.
2. The income is received at the end of the period in one lump.

In reality, assets may receive additional injections of capital and other cash flows, any time during the period over which the rate of return is to be determined. The timing and size of such money movements affect the computed rate of return if the laws of compound interest are properly taken into account.

Since the prime objective of all rational investors is the achievement of adequate and satisfactory returns, the measurement of returns in the past and the assessment of possible returns in the future will always be an important topic. Earnings or returns are the sum of the returns from incomes, such as dividends, interest and rents, and of the returns from the changes in the value of investment assets. There is a variety of measures and indicators of returns and an alarming variety of definitions and computational procedures. It is very easy to become confused and great care must be taken when interpreting the computed results.

Investors need to look further than the plain figures of the rates of return or other indicators of earnings and profitability, and consider cash flow profiles, timings of large capital injections, reinvestments, gearing and many other aspects. It is virtually impossible to compress the effects of such a multitude of factors into a single figure.

Over short periods, rates of returns and other indicators tend to fluctuate widely, while over long terms these measures tend to converge. In order to identify the total return required by investors, an appropriate yardstick or datum will be needed. This yardstick is usually a close alternative investment. The **target return** has two aspects: the return expected from a close substitute investment and the special characteristics, such as risk, liquidity, marketability and tax of the investment in question.

Traditionally, return and yield expectations were based on the yield on gilts which are Treasury stocks, and all other forms of investments were expected to produce an additional risk premium, reflecting their relative riskiness. The rule is that if gilts yield y per cent then:

Expected yield on debentures	$= y + (1 \text{ to } 2)$ per cent
Yield on preference shares	$= y + (4 \text{ to } 5)$ per cent
Yield on ordinary shares	$= y + (3 \text{ to } 5)$ per cent
Freehold property	$= y + (2 \text{ to } 5)$ per cent

These figures are, of course, only a rough guide, and they are the subject of continuous debate.

Location and value of property

The facilities manager in his decision-making role will try to balance the costs against the advantages of his decision alternatives. He will be mainly concerned how much added value, in money terms, will be the net result of his management activity. The measurement of this added value is extremely difficult as the facilities manager's activities may have an insignificant effect on the fluctuations of the value of the asset in his care. Nevertheless, the changes in the value of the asset give an important insight into the investment and operational efficiency of the asset.

In an economic sense an asset has value if there is demand for its use. The principal determinants of value are supply and demand. The value of the asset is the amount of money for which it can be exchanged at a particular point in time. The place of exchange is the market, hence the concept of market value. On the other hand an asset may have a special value to a particular investor or user. The value of property assets is principally determined by the following factors:

1. *Location*: the situation and accessibility of the property in relation to its use.
2. *Position*: the actual site of the property in its environment.
3. *Physical characteristics*: such as the form, quality, layout, structure, design, and decorative state.
4. Local market factors.
5. Investment market factors.

The process of assessment of value or worth is valuation or appraisal. This procedure may be carried out for statutory or non-statutory purposes. These valuations and appraisals could impinge significantly on the work of the facilities manager and therefore he should be familiar with the principles involved.

Investors are concerned with the determination of the market value of the assets traded on the investment markets and they are also concerned with the worth of investment propositions in the context of their individual objectives, financial circumstances and tax status. These concerns inevitably influence their investment decision making.

The distinction between valuation and appraisal can be summarised as follows:

1. *Valuation* is the determination or assessment of the price at which a particular asset would change hands when offered for sale on an open market.

2. *Investment appraisal* is the assessment of the inherent value or worth of an investment asset to a particular investor.

The above definitions are distinct, regardless of which particular section of the investment spectrum, say the stock markets or the property investment market, is the place where the valuation or appraisal procedures are to be conducted. Property assets are valued in order to assess **open market value** as the best price at which a property might reasonably be expected to be sold on a particular date, assuming a willing seller and a reasonable period within which to negotiate the sale without taking into account any bids from a special purchaser.

Property investment appraisal, on the other hand, would be concerned with the worth to a particular investor, taking into account his individual circumstances, his portfolio objectives and assumptions regarding risks and future performance. The appraisal is mainly concerned with future returns in the light of the principal factors which influence and shape such returns. Most of the principal factors, such as rental growth, obsolescence and inflation are subject to uncertainty.

In order to make rational comparisons of alternatives the **values** or **worth** of the alternatives must be assessed. This is the reason why the valuation and appraisal methods and procedures are so intimately related. Valuation and appraisal have distinct purposes and their respective techniques and methodology are expected to reflect their different rationales. However, these differences may not be immediately obvious, particularly in the traditional valuations and appraisals. The traditional approach to the analysis of investment propositions is to use an appropriate valuation method in order to assess the worth of the proposition by replacing the input factors of the valuation model with subjectively determined expected values.

The income capitalisation method

This method is associated with the expectation of an income stream consisting of constant periodic incomes receivable for the foreseeable future, and is often referred to as the years' purchase method. The question is what should be the present value of the perceived income stream if the investor has definite **rate of return** requirements or targets? In other words, what is the present value of an annuity, receivable for perpetuity or for a specified number of years, at a specified rate of interest?

$$PV = \frac{I}{r}$$

where PV is the present value of the income stream, I the periodic income (constant) and r the interest rate which is the investor's required rate of return. The inadequacies of this method for investment appraisal purposes are obvious:

1. Periodic incomes rarely remain constant for ever.
2. The capitalisation factor or years' purchase (I/r) tends to be 'overloaded' with assumptions concerning various risk components.
3. The investor's rate of return requirements tend to alter with the changing circumstances.

The simplest form of the model of the investment method of valuation is that of a freehold, rack-rented property: rack rent is the maximum rental which could be expected and is equivalent to the current market rental value.

$$\text{Value} = (\text{Annual net rent}) \times (\text{Years' purchase})$$

$$\text{Value} = \frac{\text{Annual rent}}{\text{Required yield}}$$

This model may be considered valid only if the property is let at a fixed rent or lettable at full rental value for such a long period as to amount to for ever, i.e. into perpetuity. Usually, investment valuations or appraisals are aimed at more complex cases and a number of complications arise regarding the net income component and also of the yield component of the model.

The investor's net income is derived from the full rental value (FRV) of the property. The full rental value is defined as the maximum rent for which the property could be let in the open market at a particular date on standard letting terms. The assessment of FRV requires a thorough knowledge of the market and professional skills of a valuer. The investor's net income, derived from the acquisition of a property interest, presents the following complications:

1. The level of income is unlikely to remain constant for ever and will vary during the foreseeable future. These variations are either beneficial or detrimental to the investor's interests. Those variations which are the result of the adjustment of the incomes upwards, towards the prevailing FRV at a particular review date, are obviously beneficial to the investor if he is to exploit the benefits of rental growth or at least to protect the real value of his incomes. Any lowering of the income level will be detrimental to the investor. The reductions of income levels are usually associated with the difficulties of reletting after the termination of a tenancy in a difficult letting market or may be attributable to obsolescence.
2. The income stream may not extend into perpetuity and may terminate sometime in the future. This is inevitable if the investment is a leasehold interest, although the termination of the income stream may be due to some other event.
3. The property may be multi-tenanted with each tenancy governed by different leases and rent-review clauses.
4. Taxation will affect the net income levels and if the model is to be used for appraisal this aspect could be particularly important.

Some of the above complications are taken into account by making appropriate adjustments to the yield requirements. Further complications may arise when the capitalisation of the varying net incomes and their deferment is attempted.

Yields

When market value is to be estimated then the yield must be an accurate reflection of what the market considers to be the appropriate yield for the property, taking into account all the uncertainties and risks associated with the rental income, hence the name: **all risks yield**. When the investment worth is to be assessed then the yield is the expression of the investor's required rate of return.

In both cases the selection of the appropriate yield is absolutely crucial. In the case of market valuation, from the careful analysis of the available market evidence the appropriate **market yield** or **all risks yield** should emerge. In order to determine the appropriate yield, recent transactions must be analysed in the relevant sector of the property market. The analysis can prove to be difficult, particularly if there is a shortage of recent transactions of comparable properties. Market imperfections and various unforeseeable factors are likely to limit and reduce the accuracy of the yield thus derived. In most cases a subjective adjustment of the yield, at the discretion of the valuer, is necessary.

The total income derived from a property is shared between all those who have an interest in that property. The different slices of the total income, apportioned to the participants, have different levels of risks and such different risk levels will be reflected in the different yield requirements of the participants. Traditionally, top slice incomes are regarded as most exposed to risk and hence the higher the income slice the higher the yield expectation to compensate for risk. During periods of high inflation the traditional view of the relative riskiness of the various income slices may have to be reversed.

One of the main determinants of the quality of an investment is its **growth potential**. A rational investor would prefer those investment propositions which have the promise of the growth of incomes and the growth of the capital value. When the assessment of investment worth is attempted then the yield is the minimum rate of return expected by the investor in the light of his business expectations and special circumstances.

The investor's yield requirements are likely to be changed to take into account the perceived or anticipated changes in the risk levels during the life of the income stream. The varying risk levels are, of course, the reflection of the changing circumstances in the investment climate. The date of the next rent review or reversion will greatly influence the capitalisation rate used.

Both the income and the yield components are the result of careful and expert analysis of the evidence available to the valuer or appraiser. Their reliability is totally tied up with the availability of comparables, i.e. data from relevant and recent transactions and deals. It is also assumed that the valuer or

appraiser is sufficiently competent to analyse the evidence and able
the most appropriate possible values of income and yield to be us
valuation/appraisal model.

The computational model for the valuation of the rack-rented ‿enold
property as presented above, needs modification when the valuation or
appraisal of **varying incomes** from freehold properties, or **terminable** and
variable incomes from leasehold interests, is attempted. Taking property
investments as an example: the expected cash flows and their present values will
be determined by the following principal factors:

1. Rental value – rental income – rental growth.
2. Yields – discount rates – opportunity costs.
3. Holding period – time horizon – timing of events and actions.
4. Lease structure – rent reviews – length of lease.
5. Obsolescence – depreciation.
6. Liquidity considerations.
7. Inflation.
8. Management costs.
9. Taxation.
10. Legislation.

Due to the inconsistencies caused by the assumption that income streams will
be constant and perpetual, the principal, and increasingly preferred, alternative
to the capitalisation or YP method is the discounted cash flow approach. The
DCF approach regards the value of an investment as the present value of
expected future income. The DCF model of the value of an investment
requires the statement of the anticipated time profile of the cash flows during
the lifetime of the investment and the selection of an appropriate discount rate
with which the periodic cash flows are converted into present values.

During the 1970s and 1980s, property valuation methodology has been the
subject of considerable criticism and heated debate. The issues involved in this
debate will remain unresolved until it is accepted that the mechanics and the
arithmetic of the valuation process are easily sorted out, while the inputs and
assumptions remain for ever subjective.

Operational property management – obsolescence and depreciation

A primary role of the facilities manager is the maintenance and enhancement of
the operational efficiency of buildings. Management decisions must be made in
the light of the needs of the users of the building and the needs and
requirements of the organisation which owns the building. The corporate
business strategy requires careful and expert management of the property
component of the total asset base of the corporation. The property

Management activity may be summarised as follows: a continuous process of reviewing the property component to determine areas where action can be taken with a view to improving the performance of the property assets and therefore the viability of the corporate organisation. The management activity involves:

1. The analysis of each individual property and comparing its actual performance against the expectations on acquisition and its comparison with other assets in the corporate asset base.
2. The search for ways and means of improving the operational performance of a property asset.
3. Disposing, redeveloping or refurbishing the asset where long-term prospects are likely to be lower than expected.

The property management process may be viewed as the continuing interaction of the decisions made on the basis of an appropriate analysis and the results and consequences of the actions carried out by the managers in charge.

As noted previously, property assets are significantly different from other types of assets in many respects, and special expertise is required for their successful management. Property is notoriously difficult to fit in with other investment assets, mainly because of the lack of understanding of its special characteristics and because of the long-term nature of its returns.

Obsolescence and depreciation

As the impact of new technologies has begun to be felt in the property industry, demand has increased for the inclusion of the effects of the rapid technological changes into the appraisal of investments. The main effects of economic and technological change have been manifested in the accelerating rate of obsolescence of commercial and industrial property. This has affected not only the values of older buildings but has also had an impact on the value of new buildings. Rental growth is likely to be adversely affected and refurbishment or redevelopment is going to be required at an earlier date, which really amounts to an acceleration of the depreciation of virtually all investment property.

Depreciation is defined as the decline in the real value of property and the site and the building components of the value of an investment property are both subject to depreciation, albeit at different rates. The site component of the investment depreciates as a result of the changes in supply and demand, the environmental decay of the area and similar factors while the building component of the investment will depreciate as a result of physical deterioration and obsolescence. Depreciation will affect first, and foremost, incomes and expenses, i.e. the cash flows expected from an investment, and it also affects market yields over time.

For practical purposes it is reasonable to assume that site component of the investment will not depreciate while the building component has a limited, and shortening lifetime over which depreciation will occur. After estimating the realistic life span of the building and selecting a suitable pattern of depreciation it is possible to work out the periodic sums necessary to provide a sinking fund to recoup the cost of the building by the end of its useful life. By incorporating these sums into the periodic cash flows at least a part of the problem of depreciation may be addressed, although in practice this aspect may be ignored.

The other part of the problem is how to estimate the terminal or disposal value of the property; there have been a number of suggestions as to how to resolve this issue, some of which are attractive from a theoretical point of view, while others are more pragmatic, although they all attempt to forecast the unknown.

Taxation and VAT

Taxation is an important aspect of the business environment. Some businesses are exempt from at least some aspects of taxation, others are exposed to its full rigour. The 'gross funds', which include approved pension funds, charities, local authorities and friendly societies, are exempt from taxation, but all other businesses are subject to income, corporation and capital gains taxation. For this latter group of businesses, the effects of taxation on their cash flows will be of substantial interest.

Investment returns and profits are liable to income tax, corporation tax and capital gains tax. The tax status of individuals, corporations and institutional investors varies considerably and the details of tax implications for various businesses are outside the scope of this chapter. However, the attempts to reduce the burden and impact of taxation have considerable implications for the setting out of corporate plans and objectives and the planning of investment strategies. It is sufficient to mention here that those businesses which are liable to high rates of income tax must consider very carefully the various options available to them to reduce or defer the tax burden on their incomes. These businesses should seek those operational means which offer some tax relief on taxes already deducted at source. Alternatively they may defer the tax burden by opting for returns in the form of capital gains. As a capital gain is made when the assets are disposed of, the capital gains tax payment will be due after disposal. Future capital gains taxes can be reduced by utilising the annual exemption allowance.

The periodic tax elements are calculated by working out the taxable income and applying the appropriate rates of tax. The various tax-deductible items of the cash flow depend on the prevailing tax legislation.

VAT

The 1989 tax legislation has extended the VAT liability to the supply of land, civil engineering and construction services. The main effect of this legislation is the creation of a new situation with respect to the tax status of the occupiers of buildings. Depending on their new status they may be able to recover some of their tax inputs. VAT liability has been extended to the purchase of freehold interest in property assets. The detail of VAT goes beyond the scope of this chapter particularly as it may change quickly and it is always prudent to seek expert advice on the current situation.

Bibliography

Aldridge 1989 *Letting business premises* 6th edn, Longman

Aldridge TM, Johnson TA 1978 *Managing business property* Oyez Publishing

Avis *et al*. 1989 *Managing operational property assets* University of Reading

Barter 1988 *Real estate finance* Butterworths

Baum A 1991 *Property investment depreciation and obsolescence* Routledge

Brett 1991 *Property and money* Estates Gazette

Britten, Connellan, Crofts 1990 *The cost approach to valuation* Kingston Polytechnic

Cadman D, Crowe A 1991 *Property development* 3rd edn, E & FN Spon

Colborne A 1990 *The profits method of valuation* Bristol Polytechnic

Darlow C 1987 *Valuation and investment appraisal*, 2nd edn., Estates Gazette

Edward Erdman and CBI 1990 *Property* Mercury Books

Grigg J, Jordan A 1993 *Are you managing facilities?* Allied Dunbar Series

Hargitay, Yu 1992 *Property investment decisions* E & FN Spon

Hawkins CJ, Pearce DW 1971 *Capital investment appraisal* Macmillan

Layard R 1977 *Cost benefit analysis* Penguin

Lumby S 1981 *Investment appraisal and related decisions* Nelson

Merrett AJ, Sykes A 1974 *The finance and analysis of capital projects* Longman

Morley S, Marsh C, McIntosh A, Martinos H 1989 *Industrial and business space development* E & FN Spon

Price Waterhouse and CBI 1989 *Tax: strategic corporate tax planning* Mercury Books

Scarrett D 1983 *Property management*, E & FN Spon

Scott H, McLellan D 1992 *VAT and property* Butterworth Heinemann

Sherriff 1989 *Service charges in leases – a practical guide* Waterlow

Stapleton TB 1986 *Estate management practice* Estates Gazette

LEEDS METROPOLITAN UNIVERSITY LIBRARY

Chapter 4

The legal environment

Mark Tyler, Nick Hadley & Tony Kitson

Introduction

This chapter deals with the legal side of the development and acquisition and disposal of property together with leasing arrangements which are very much the field of the specialist or lawyer. It also picks up the legal side of operations of buildings in use where employees and the public have access. Its emphasis is on property-related law, not that relating to the employment of people which is beyond the scope of this chapter. Lists of the main legislation are contained in the appendix to this chapter. The legal requirements described are those as at May 1994.

Part 1: Planning considerations and constraints on development

Planning permission

The definition of development

Development is the central concept in considering whether planning permission is necessary. It is defined as the carrying out of building, engineering, mining or other operations in, on, over or under land or the making of any material change in the use of any buildings or other land. Subject to certain exemptions and variations any proposals involving activity of this type will require planning permission.

General development order

This has the effect of automatically granting planning permission for many classes of activity. It avoids the need for applying for planning permission for a wide range of minor and routine development. For example, it permits the extension of a house within a proportion of its total area, or the operational activities of electricity, gas and telecommunications companies.

Use classes order

This classifies uses of buildings and land, and specifies changes of use which are not to be regarded as involving development and therefore do not require planning permission. This means that if a person has a use falling into one of these classes, he can change to any other use within that class without needing permission. So, for example, a general industrial building can be used for any type of general industry.

Demolition

The law on demolition is complicated. In summary, planning permission is not usually required for demolition of a commercial building, but approval of the method of works will be required for the demolition of a residential building, or a commercial building which has a significant residential element. Further details are given in Table 4.1.

Procedure

Applications for planning permission are made to the local planning authority. The application must be accompanied by a certificate that no one except the applicant owns the land or that the applicant has served notice on the owner or that he cannot discover the identity of all the owners and has given notice by advertisement. An owner is either a freeholder or a leaseholder with more than 7 years unexpired.

Planning authorities

The local planning authority is the district council in the shire counties and metropolitan areas, and the borough council in London. Planning decisions are taken by elected members on the advice of professional staff. In urban development areas the government has transferred some or all of the local authority's planning powers to an urban development corporation (a non-elected government-funded body).

Outline and full application

A full application is an application giving full details of a proposed development. An outline application for the erection of a building enables the applicant to ascertain whether his proposal is acceptable in principle, leaving certain details ('reserved matters') – siting, design, external appearance, landscaping and means of access – for approval at a later stage. The local planning authority may request more information to enable it to determine the application. Conditions may be imposed on the grant of permission; for example, that a scheme of landscaping should be approved and implemented or that particular materials are used on a facade. Development under full planning permission must begin within 5 years. Under an outline planning permission, details of the reserved matters must be supplied within 3 years, with development within a further 2 years after approval of the reserved matters.

Table 4.1 Demolition of buildings (with effect from 27 July 1992)

Planning permission not required	Planning permission deemed to be granted under the GDO	Planning permission required
A.1 The whole or part of any non-residential building, provided that: (a) if it has a part residential use that part is only ancillary to the non-residential use of the building or other buildings on the same site; and (b) it does not adjoin a dwelling house	B.1 A dwelling-house	C.1 Part of a building in categories A.2–5
A.2 A listed building (but listed building consent will be required)	B.2 A residential home	C.2 Part of a building in categories B.1–4
A.3 A building in a conservation area (but conservation area consent will be required)	B.3 A hostel	C.3 Part of a building adjoining a building in categories B.1–4
A.4 A scheduled monument (but scheduled monument consent will be required)	B.4 A building containing a flat which does not fall within A.1–4	
A.5 A building not exceeding 50 m³ measured externally.	B.5 A gate, fence, wall or means of enclosure if it involves building operations (i.e structural alterations or operations normally undertaken by a builder), provided that in each case: (a) the building has not been rendered unsafe or otherwise uninhabitable by the action or inaction of any person with an interest in the land on which the building stands; and (b) it is not practicable to secure safety or health by repairs or temporary support works	
A.6 A gate, fence, wall or other means of enclosure provided that it does not involve building operations (i.e. structural alterations to a building, or operations normally undertaken by a builder)		
A.7 Where demolition is pursuant to a planning permission for redevelopment		

Note: Deemed planning permission for demolition may not be exercised unless an application has been made to the local planning authority (LPA) for a d[...] whether prior approval is required for the method of works. A site notice must be posted for 21 days of the 28-day period beginning with the date on whi[...] was submitted. If the LPA does not respond within 28 days of the application, demolition may proceed. A determination is not required where demolition is:

(a) urgently necessary in the interests of health or safety, but a written justification of the demolition must be given to the LPA as soon as reasonably practica[...]
(b) taking place on land which is the subject of planning permission or deemed planning permission for redevelopment; or
(c) required as a result of a demolition order or a clearance area; or
(d) required under an enforcement notice.

Appeals

If permission is refused or granted with unacceptable conditions or a decision cannot be obtained from the local planning authority within 8 weeks (or 16 weeks if an environmental statement is required), an appeal can be made to the Secretary of State for the Environment. Appeals can be in writing ('written representations'), by way of an informal hearing or at a public local inquiry. Appeals by written representations or informal hearing are usually appropriate for small or straightforward cases. An inquiry is conducted by an inspector whose power is delegated from the Secretary of State. The inspector hears evidence from the applicant, the local planning authority and other parties affected by the proposal. He can either take a decision himself or, in some cases, make a recommendation to the Secretary of State.

Local, regional and national planning policies

The local planning authority (and the Secretary of State on appeal) must determine a planning application in accordance with the Development Plan, provided it is up to date, relevant to the case and it is not outweighed by other considerations. The Development Plan contains the general planning strategy for the area and specific local policies and land-use allocations. The general strategy is contained in the Structure Plan prepared by the county council. Local policies are contained in the Local Plan which is prepared by the district council. In the case of metropolitan districts and London boroughs, the Unitary Development Plan combines general strategy and local policies.

Other considerations affecting the determination may include national and regional development, the impact on people and the environment and the need for the development. National policies are set out by the Secretary of State for the Environment in DoE circulars, Planning Policy Guidance notes and, on occasion, ministerial statements. Regional policy is contained within DoE Regional Planning Guidance notes.

Environmental assessment

Development which is likely to have a significant environmental impact requires an environmental assessment. Disagreement between the applicant and the local planning authority about the need for an environmental assessment can be referred to the Secretary of State for the Environment for determination.

Listed buildings

Certain buildings are included in lists maintained by the Secretary of State as being of special architectural or historic interest. Listed building consent is required for all works affecting a listed building and its setting. The procedure on applications and appeals is in practice very similar to that for planning applications and appeals. It is exceptionally difficult to obtain consent to demolish a listed building or to alter one to any material extent. The essential difference when comparing listed building consent to planning permission is that listed building consent is needed for wholly internal works that would not require planning permission.

Conservation areas

These are areas designated by the local planning authority as being of special architectural or historic interest, and which have a character or appearance which it is desirable to preserve or enhance. Conservation area consent is required to demolish a building in a conservation area. In addition, if development is proposed, the local planning authority are likely to want full details and will not grant an outline permission. Permission is also needed to lop or fell a tree in a conservation area.

Building regulations

The Secretary of State for the Environment makes comprehensive regulations concerning the design and construction of buildings, together with their fittings, equipment and provision of services. These regulations are effected through advance notification of new buildings or alterations to the local authority, approval of plans by the local authority or supervision and certification by approved private inspectors. (See also the section on Building Regulations on p. 64.)

Tree preservation orders (TPOs)

A local planning authority is under a duty to make a TPO if it believes it should do so in the interests of amenity. The TPO will generally prohibit the cutting down, topping, lopping, wilful damaging or wilful destruction of trees without the consent of the local planning authority. Exceptions to the measures include trees that are dying or dead or those that are dangerous.

Planning enforcement

Local planning authorities have a variety of powers to prohibit or restrict unauthorised development.

Enforcement notices

An enforcement notice may be issued if the local planning authority considers that there has been a breach of planning control – an unauthorised operation, an unauthorised material change of use or breach of a planning condition. The notice specifies the breach, the steps to remedy it and the time within which the steps are to be carried out and the reason why it was expedient to issue the notice. The time limits during which enforcement can take place are: 4 years in the case of an unauthorised operation; 10 years for unauthorised change of use; and 10 years for breaches of operational conditions. The notice can be challenged by appeal to the Secretary of State. Until the appeal is determined the notice does not take effect. If there is no appeal, or the notice is upheld on appeal, failure to comply with it can render the owner or occupier liable to criminal prosecution.

Stop notice

As the enforcement notice does not take effect until any appeal against it has been settled, the local planning authority can, once the enforcement notice has been served, if it believes the continuation of the breach until that time will cause serious problems, serve a stop notice which will prevent the breach continuing until any appeal has been withdrawn or determined. If the stop notice is withdrawn by the authority or the enforcement notice to which it relates is quashed, the authority may have to pay compensation.

Breach of condition notice

This can be served by the local planning authority on a person who fails to observe the conditions attached to a planning permission. There is no right of appeal and failure to comply could lead to criminal prosecution. The only defence is that the recipient had taken 'all reasonable measures' to comply with the steps to remedy the breach set out in the notice.

Court injunction

The local planning authority may use this remedy in addition to or instead of other enforcement powers. The local planning authority must have strong grounds for seeking an injunction; they must be able to prove a major breach of planning control has occurred or is about to occur, such as the demolition of a listed building.

Planning contravention notice

This seeks information concerning the use, operations or activities carried out on land where the local planning authority suspects a breach of planning control has occurred. If the recipient does not respond, he is liable to criminal prosecution and further enforcement action. He is given the opportunity to make positive suggestions for regularising the position. The notice is, in effect, halfway between informal action by the local planning authority and the full rigour of an enforcement notice.

Right of entry

If there are reasonable grounds, a person authorised by the local planning authority can enter land or premises without warrant to see if there is or has been a breach of planning control, to decide if the local planning authority's powers (as outlined here) should be exercised.

Part 2: Acquisition, ownership and disposal of property

Introduction

English land law has grown up over many hundreds of years and was the subject of a major overhaul in 1925. Since that time, it has been possible to categorise the main interests in land as freehold and leasehold and also to draw a distinction between titles which are registered at the Land Registry and those which are not.

Freehold and leasehold interests

The distinguishing feature of a freehold estate is that for all practical purposes it represents absolute ownership and it is the 'best' estate capable of existing at law.

A leasehold estate is distinguished by the fact that the duration of the interest is limited to some specific time, for example 25 or 99 years. There will always be an estate which is superior to a leasehold one, whether that be another leasehold or a freehold one. The practical effect of this in the case of business leases is that the consent of the person holding the superior estate is likely to be required in a number of different instances, for example if the leaseholder requires to transfer the lease to someone else or wishes to carry out alterations. At the end of the leasehold term the leaseholder will be responsible for vacating the property and handing it back to the person who has the superior estate.

Registered and unregistered land

Unregistered land means any land which has not become registered at the Land Registry; registered land is by definition that which is so registered.

The system of land registration now applies to the whole of England and Wales, although it is only in the comparatively recent past that this has been the case since the system has been expanded gradually since 1926. In general terms, any freehold interest which is sold and any leasehold interest which is granted for more than 21 years or, in the case of unregistered land when transferred has more than 21 years left to run, is now registrable at the Land Registry on the occasion of the grant or transfer.

Acquisition and disposal of freehold property

In many cases the procedure which is adopted for the acquisition of freehold or leasehold property is the same, save in circumstances where it is a new lease which is being granted. This section gives an outline of a typical series of events in a straightforward acquisition of a freehold interest in a commercial property; the procedures applicable in the case of residential property are slightly different.

Procedure

Searches and enquiries

Once preliminary negotiations have been completed between the parties, the purchaser will receive a draft contract from the vendor's solicitor. On receipt of that contract or upon receipt of a plan sufficient to identify the property in question, the purchaser's solicitor will carry out a variety of different searches, the exact number and type being dictated by the particular property in question. These are likely to include some or all of the following:

- *Local authority*. This will reveal, for example, the planning history for the property and whether or not there is any outstanding enforcement action which is being taken, whether any compulsory purchase orders have been made, whether the property adjoins a road which is adopted and maintained at public expense and certain information regarding other roads and drains.
- *Commons registration*. This will reveal whether or not the property is subject to any entries relating to common land and town or village greens.
- *British Coal*. This will normally show land where some form of coal working has taken place.
- *National Rivers Authority and British Waterways Board*. These give details of responsibilities for the repair of banks and liability to flooding in the case of rivers, streams and canals respectively.
- *Railtrack*. This search is directed primarily towards ascertaining responsibilities for the maintenance of boundary fences.

Other searches commonly made are those of electricity, gas and water companies to ascertain the location of services. More specific searches are sometimes made depending upon the locality of the property, for example in relation to brine working in Cheshire and mine working in Cornwall.

In addition to making searches of third parties, the purchaser's solicitor will usually also raise a number of preliminary enquiries of the vendor's solicitor which are directed partly towards ascertaining the legal position relating to the title to the property and partly towards practical issues such as whether or not there have been any notices or disputes, means of access, planning, maintenance of boundaries and contamination.

Surveys and reports

Where appropriate a surveyor should also make investigations into the state and condition of the property and, for example, in the case of development land, more detailed investigations by surveyors and environmental consultants are also likely to be undertaken.

It is also now common for the purchaser's solicitor to be supplied with details of the vendor's title to the property at the same time as a draft contract is supplied and this will therefore be investigated at the same time as all of the searches and enquiries are being raised and carried out. The title investigation is likely to involve the purchaser's solicitor in carrying out other searches of the Land Charges Registry or the Land Registry, and the Companies Registry.

At the conclusion of all of these investigations the purchaser will receive reports from his solicitor, surveyor and other consultants to advise him fully of all matters affecting the property before he is committed to its purchase.

Timing

Once all of the surveys and searches have been carried out and reports submitted, the purchaser will be in a position to exchange contracts for the acquisition. This will bind the purchaser and, save in limited circumstances, he will thereafter not be able to avoid paying the balance of the purchase price (there normally being a 10 per cent deposit paid on exchange) to the vendor and becoming the owner of the property. It is vitally important that all appropriate enquiries and searches are raised before this point in time is reached.

Following exchange of contracts, which commits all parties to the transaction, there is usually then a gap of between 2 and 4 weeks before completion of the transaction takes place. This gap may be due to the financing requirements of the purchaser, or simply the desire of the parties to be committed to the transaction in advance of the date on which the vendor wishes to leave the property or the purchaser to take occupation of it. There is, in law, no reason for there to be any such period and it is possible for exchange of contracts and completion to be simultaneous.

Contracts

Types

The contract may either be unconditional in which case it will take immediate effect, or be conditional upon some specified matters being satisfied before the vendor and purchaser become committed to sell and buy the property. These might include the results of surveys, other properties being acquired or roads being diverted. The most common form of conditional contract relates to a planning permission being obtained for the future development of the property being acquired.

Requirements

A contract for the sale or other disposition of an interest in land must be in writing. The written document must be signed on behalf of the parties to the transaction and must also contain all of the terms which have been agreed. The law relating to the requirements for a valid contract was made more rigorous in 1989 and it has become much more difficult for a contract to arise by means of an exchange of correspondence. It is, nevertheless, still common for the phrase 'subject to contract' to be used on correspondence passing between the parties or their advisers prior to a written document being signed and dated. If any form of side letter is intended to be used to deal with matters which the parties do not wish to set out expressly in the contract itself, the contract must refer to and incorporate the side letter otherwise it will not be binding.

There are limited exceptions to these requirements, of which two concern sales by public auction and the grant of short leases not exceeding 3 years.

Content

A contract will typically incorporate by reference standard conditions which are published in printed form. The conditions deal with a wide variety of 'technical' issues relating to the vendor's title to the property, the parties' obligations and responsibilities between exchange and completion, how any income from the property is to be enjoyed and what is to happen should either party default on their obligations, among other things. It is very common for some of these standard conditions to be varied by additional express terms of a contract.

The contract will also ordinarily provide for payment of part of the purchase price, typically 10 per cent, on exchange. It will also specify the matters subject to which the property is sold and the date on which completion is to take place. If, for example, the purchaser fails to complete on the due day, there will be a machinery provided for the service of a notice by the vendor making time of the essence so that at the expiration of this further period the purchaser will forfeit any deposit paid and the vendor may resell the property.

The contract will also deal with the responsibility for insuring the property between the date on which the contract is exchanged and the date on which completion takes place. Most commonly, it is the purchaser who will accept this responsibility and in most cases it is important that the purchaser takes out the insurance, whether or not the vendor's insurance is being continued at the same time.

Breach of contract

A breach of the contract may be caused by a number of different circumstances, for example because the purchaser claims that there has been a material misrepresentation made to him, perhaps in the replies made to pre-contract enquiries, upon which he has relied in entering into the contract. A more typical situation arises where the purchaser fails to complete and the vendor determines the contract.

Remedies for breach can be divided into two separate categories, claims for damages and claims for specific performance. The latter is a decree forcing the parties to carry out their obligations.

Conveyances and transfers

Completion procedure

After contracts have been exchanged and prior to completion, unless there has been any substantial delay it would not be usual to renew the general searches, enquiries and surveys referred to under 'Procedure' on p. 50. The purchaser's solicitor will, however, make searches of the Land Charges Register (in the case of unregistered land) and of the Land Registry (in the case of registered land) to ensure that there have been no matters registered subsequent to the details of title which have been provided by the vendor's solicitor which either prevent the vendor from transferring the property or affect in some way the interest which is being transferred. These searches confer periods of priority for the purchaser so that he will not be affected by any other transactions completed within the same period.

Where the vendor is a company, a search of the Companies Registry will ordinarily be made immediately prior to completion in order to ensure that no undisclosed charges or mortgages have been registered and from which a release is required, and also to ensure that the ability of the company to sell has not been affected by the appointment of a liquidator or one of the categories of receiver.

It is also usual practice for the purchaser's solicitor to send 'requisitions' to the vendor's solicitor prior to completion. Apart from questions relating to the vendor's title to the property, now more commonly dealt with prior to exchange of contracts, these requisitions will deal with practical matters such as the account to which the completion monies should be sent if completion is taking place by post, how the release of any mortgages or charges is to be dealt with and which documents will be handed over at completion.

The deed by which legal title to a property is transferred from a vendor to a purchaser is known as a **conveyance** in the case of unregistered land, and as a **transfer** where the land is registered at the Land Registry. Both deeds serve the same purpose. A transfer is more simplistic in form and avoids the use of the more traditional wording which is still retained for the purposes of conveyances. It is possible to use a transfer in the case of land which is registrable at the Land Registry on completion of the document, and this has become common practice.

The mechanics of completion are now most frequently achieved by completion monies being sent via the banking system and the parties' solicitors making the appropriate arrangements by telephone.

Post-completion matters

Once completion has taken place, the conveyance or transfer must usually be presented to the Inland Revenue for registration and, in the case of transactions where the value exceeds £60,000, stamp duty at the rate of 1 per cent on the amount of the consideration must also be paid at the same time. Where the consideration is not more than £60,000, a certificate to this effect can be incorporated within the document itself and if this is done no stamp duty is payable. The conveyance or transfer will then be sent with an appropriate application to the Land Registry for registration of the purchaser as proprietor of the property in question, such application being made within the priority period conferred by the appropriate searches made prior to completion taking place.

Mortgages

Where the property being purchased is subject to a mortgage, it must be released on completion. This will be done by means of a vacating receipt being endorsed on the mortgage deed itself or some other form of deed of release being entered into, depending upon whether the property is unregistered or registered.

Leases

Leases of commercial premises can vary in scope from comparatively short-term arrangements of less than 12 months, to leases granted at a substantial premium with payment of a ground rent for terms in excess of 100 years. The most common form of lease which will be encountered, however, is one for a term of somewhere between 10 and 25 years with an initial market rent being reviewable at specified intervals, commonly every 5 years. In this section it is therefore proposed to take such a lease as an example for discussion, and assume also that it is a lease of part of an office block as this brings into account service charge considerations which would not be present in leases of other types of property where there are no areas the ownership of which is retained by the landlord and the enjoyment of which is common to all of the occupiers in the building. These are features shared by any type of property with such 'common parts', for example a factory unit on an estate, and in those cases the lease will follow the same basic pattern.

The content of business leases

Format

Most business leases follow a similar form of layout, starting with a list of definitions used throughout the document and followed by clauses dealing with the length of the term and the amount of rent payable, covenants by the tenant, landlord and any sureties, agreements and declarations concerning a variety of matters including forfeiture, rent review and service charge calculation and administration. Clauses which deal with the extent of the property being demised will also address the question of rights which are granted to the tenant and those which are reserved for the benefit of the landlord and the other occupiers. The tenant's covenants will typically occupy about one-third of the whole document.

The term of a lease may also be brought to an end in advance of the contractual expiry date by a number of ways, for example due to a surrender agreed between the parties, the operation of a break clause by either the landlord or the tenant which has been agreed to be operable at a certain time, by the merger of the leasehold interest in the immediately superior interest in the property, by disclaimer in the event of the tenant becoming insolvent, by frustration in rare circumstances where a fundamental purpose of the lease has ceased to exist and by forfeiture in the event of breach of covenant by the tenant or other event affecting the tenant such as liquidation or the appointment of a type of receiver.

There are important restrictions on the landlord's right to forfeit a lease and in certain cases it is also possible for a landlord to waive a right to forfeit if he knows that certain types of breach have occurred and has nevertheless still accepted the existence of the tenancy. The most usual illustration of this is the acceptance of rent after the particular breach complained of has occurred.

Term, demise and rents
In the type of lease under discussion the term of years granted will be for a fixed period. It is possible for leases to be granted for periodic terms, for example from year to year, and also for a period which can be brought to an end by either the landlord or the tenant at any time. Most business tenancies do not end at the expiry of the contractual term, but are continued by statute; this is dealt with under 'Security of tenure' on p. 59. It is also important to remember that as the law stands at present, a landlord or a tenant remains liable upon the covenants which they give in the lease notwithstanding any subsequent disposition of their respective interests. This is an issue which is particularly acute for tenants who may be called upon to pay large sums of rent some years after they might have thought that they had no further responsibilities. This doctrine of privity of contract, as it is called, has been under review for some time and is almost certainly going to be altered in the near future, possibly during the latter part of 1994.

In a lease of part of an office block, the property demised will ordinarily exclude exterior walls and structural features and include simply internal non-structural parts and finishes. This is because the landlord wishes to retain control over the remainder for the purposes of uniformity throughout the building and also in order to ensure consistency of repair. The costs which the landlord incurs in carrying out repairs to these retained parts will be recovered from the tenants via the service charge.

It is usual to find various sums in a lease reserved as rent, for example service charges and insurance payments, and the effect of doing so is to render the tenant liable to the remedy of distress in the event of non-payment. 'Distress' is an ability on the part of the landlord to seize the tenant's goods in certain circumstances in order to recoup sums due to the landlord. Rent strictly so called, however, is limited to the amount of the annual payment due to the landlord for the benefit of the lease, such sums usually being payable in the type of lease under discussion by means of four equal payments in advance on the usual quarter days. Failure to pay within a certain specified period will usually attract an interest penalty. The annual rent will almost certainly be subject to review by means of provisions which, over the years, have steadily become more of an art form.

The intention of rent-review clauses is to increase the amount of the annual rent payable on the specified dates from that previously payable to the market rent applicable to the premises at the date of review. They have become the subject of considerable litigation and expertise and in large measure have attempted to put forward a hypothetical situation for the purposes of assessing the revised market rent. In clauses which are initiated by service of a notice by the landlord, the fact that such a notice may be served after the time envisaged, for example after the review date in question, will not ordinarily disentitle the landlord to a review of the rent unless there are special circumstances which apply to make time of the essence in the lease in question. It is now usual for rent review clauses to provide that on the relevant date of review, the rent may go up, but not down.

Landlord's covenants
The typical lease will contain a covenant on the part of the landlord to allow the tenant to use the premises without hindrance for the purposes of the use permitted by the lease, and in the case of a property of the type under discussion further covenants dealing with insurance and service charge payments allied to an obligation on the part of the landlord to carry out repairs to those parts of the building which are not let to the tenant.

The landlord's covenant for 'quiet enjoyment' applies only to the landlord causing any interruption to the tenant's use of the property by an unlawful act; it does not prevent interference by anyone with a title superior to that of the landlord unless the clause is modified to include this protection.

Tenant's covenants
The covenants of a tenant contained in a typical lease of business premises will be extremely wide ranging and will include obligations relating to statutory provisions including planning requirements, allowing the landlord to have entry to the premises for specified purposes and indemnities for the benefit of the landlord. If a surety is to be provided for the tenant, then further clauses will be added obliging the surety to ensure that the tenant performs the obligations with indemnities in default and obligations on the part of the surety to take up a lease in the event of the original term being disclaimed by a liquidator of the tenant.

Specific provisions
There are certain critical areas to be dealt with in a lease of commercial premises and these are outlined in this section.

Repair. The landlord will accept responsibility for repairing and maintaining any items the use of which is common to the tenant and other occupiers of the relevant building, including any retained parts, for example the main structure of the property, which are not demised to tenants. This section concentrates on the repairing obligations of the tenant.

The usual requirement will be for the tenant to keep the property demised in a good and substantial repair and condition. In so far as the property is out of repair at the date of the lease, then there will be an obligation implied on the tenant to put the property into good repair. This must be considered in the context of a proviso that a tenant is not responsible for putting the property into a better state of repair than it was in at the date of the lease. The consequence of these seemingly conflicting obligations is that if the property has deteriorated from a state in which it was once in, the tenant must carry out repairs, but if the property has always been out of repair, for example because there has been an inherent defect in its construction which does not cause further damage, then the tenant will have no such obligation.

In the context of a lease of part of an office block these concepts are not likely to be as material as they would be if the whole of the building were let to the tenant and became the tenant's responsibility. The principles are, however, relevant to the landlord's obligations in the context of recovery of costs via service charge provisions. In leases of property where the responsibilities are divided between the landlord and the tenant, it is particularly important that the drafting of the lease deals adequately with the division of those responsibilities and identifies precisely those parts of the building which are to be maintained by the tenant and the landlord respectively.

In the event of any breach by the tenant of its repairing covenants, the landlord may seek forfeiture of the lease, or the performance of the obligation by the tenant or damages. The lease will usually contain a provision enabling the landlord to enter the premises and carry out the repairs at the cost of the tenant in the event of the tenant failing to comply with a notice requiring the repairs to be done. The amount of damages which are recoverable by a landlord is limited by statute and is related to the diminution in the value of the landlord's interest caused by the breach of the repairing covenant by the tenant.

Service Charge. Where a service charge is payable the lease will contain detailed clauses dealing with the machinery for payment and the costs which are recoverable by the landlord for the services which the landlord carries out. There will usually be provision for on-account payments to be made by the tenant during the course of the year with a balancing account drawn up at the end of that period. The list of services to be provided by the landlord will commonly be divided into those which must be provided, and those which may be provided in the landlord's discretion. The landlord will often try to avoid liability for any failure to provide any of the services in question. From the point of the tenant, it is important to ensure that all essential services are contracted to be provided, that the landlord's discretion is qualified and that it is not possible for the landlord to improve the property at the cost of the tenants.

Assignments. Restrictions will be placed upon the ability of the tenant to assign or underlet its interest. Typically, assignments will only be allowed with the consent of the landlord and underlettings will either be placed on the same basis or restricted altogether. Restrictions on the ability on the part of a tenant to underlet parts of the property let are also common, together with provisions enabling a tenant to share occupation with other companies within the same group. There has been statutory intervention in this area to provide some measure of protection to tenants in relation to the manner in which a landlord may exercise a discretion to grant or refuse consent and in relation to the time which is taken in this process.

User. Apart from the provisions of the lease itself, the ability of the tenant to use the premises will be limited by the general law applicable to town and country planning. Even if a use is permitted by the lease, the ability of the tenant to use the property for that purpose is not warranted by the landlord and in all cases the tenant must ensure that the premises may lawfully be used for the intended purpose. The fact that the premises cannot be used for such purpose will not frustrate the lease or give the tenant any redress against the landlord.

Very restrictive user covenants will affect the tenant's ability to assign or otherwise deal with its interest in the building, but may also have an effect on the amount of rent which the landlord may claim on the occasion of any rent review. It is common for obligations to be imposed upon the tenant not to use the premises for illegal, immoral and other specified purposes and in the case of retail premises to remain open during usual trading hours.

Alterations. Restrictions on the ability of the tenant to alter the premises will be included. Minor internal alterations may be permitted without consent. A landlord is usually concerned to have control over structural alterations and the external appearance of the building. Where a particular alteration cannot be carried out without the landlord's consent, statute has provided that such a consent cannot be unreasonably refused and in certain cases involving alterations which are classified as improvements, by use of a statutory machinery a tenant can override an absolute prohibition against alterations.

Insurance. It is important that the lease contains suitable and adequate provisions to deal with the insurance both of the premises and of the building of which the premises may form part. If the landlord accepts this responsibility, as will commonly be the case with a multi-let building, it is important that all usual risks are insured against and that the insured sum is adequate. The difficulties caused by lack of insurance for certain risks has been highlighted by concerns over terrorist damage. In the event of damage or destruction by an insured risk rendering the premises let to the tenant unusable, the annual rent payable under the lease will usually be suspended until whichever is the earlier of the date on which the premises are again rendered usable and the expiry of a specified period, commonly 3 years. From the perspective of a tenant, it is important that where a landlord has accepted the responsibility for insurance, then the landlord should be responsible for making good any deficiencies in the insurance monies at his own cost.

Security of tenure

Leases of business premises are affected in a number of areas by statutory provisions, as has been seen already. The principal and most important area in which protection has been afforded to a tenant concerns the entitlement to remain in occupation at the expiry of the contractual term of the lease.

Tenancies which are affected

Arrangements which do not create tenancies, such as licences which do not involve the creation of an interest in land itself, tenancies at will which are determinable by the landlord or the tenant at any time, and residential accommodation provided to an employee for the purposes of that person's employment, do not enjoy statutory protection in this context. Leases granted for an express period in excess of 6 months and periodic tenancies which continue, for example, from year to year, do enjoy protection. Protection is also only enjoyed by a tenant who occupies premises for the purposes of a business carried on by him, but has now been extended to licensed premises.

Effective protection

The concept of the statutory provisions is that at the expiry of the contractual term, the lease does not end but simply continues unless and until determined by the landlord or the tenant in accordance with the legislation. The basic entitlement of the tenant is to be granted a new lease on substantially the same terms and conditions as the one which is being continued, subject to an increase in the rent to the market level then applicable. A landlord may require the lease to be in a modern form, but may not impose any major new burden upon the tenant in doing so.

The statutory protection will not apply if the landlord is able to establish one or more specified grounds which disentitle a tenant from being able to renew his lease. Some of these grounds involve defaults on the part of the tenant and others include, for example, a desire on the part of the landlord to demolish and reconstruct the premises which would not be possible if he cannot obtain possession of the property. Where a tenant is not entitled to a new tenancy through no fault of his own, the tenant is entitled to compensation assessed according to a statutory formula. By agreement between the parties made before the original lease is granted *and* by the sanction of a court order, it is possible to exclude the statutory provisions relating to security of tenure.

Procedural requirements

The scheme of the legislation envisages that either the landlord will serve a notice upon the tenant bringing the original contractual term to an end, or that the tenant serves a notice on the landlord requesting the grant of a new tenancy. In either event, the old lease continues until either the new lease is granted or the proceedings for renewal are discontinued or determined. After the service of the original notice by either the landlord or the tenant, certain other notices have to be given.

From the tenant's point of view, it is vitally important that the statutory timetable for the giving of any notice by the tenant is adhered to strictly; courts do not have a discretion to extend some of the dates by which notices have to be served and a failure to adhere to the time limits is a frequent cause of tenants losing their rights to the protection of the legislation.

While the statutory procedure is being followed and until the new lease is granted at the revised rent, the landlord is entitled to payment of an interim rent assessed by the court at a reasonable level somewhere between that payable under the old lease and the revised market rent payable under the new one.

The procedural requirements are technical and complicated and it is essential for a tenant to take prompt and immediate action in order to safeguard his rights. While the statutory procedure should be followed in all cases for this purpose, most new leases are granted by agreement between the parties and the legislation is therefore used most commonly simply in order to protect the bargaining position of the tenant. This and other deficiencies in the legislation have been acknowledged and certain reforms proposed.

Compensation

A tenant of business premises may be entitled to compensation from a landlord in two circumstances, the first being where the tenant is not entitled to renewal of a lease through no fault of his own as mentioned under 'Security of tenure' on p. 59. The other circumstance is where the tenant has carried out improvements to the property.

'Improvements' in this context is not a clearly defined term but has been construed generally as alterations carried out by and at the cost of a tenant which increase in some way the value of the interest of the landlord. The difficulty with the legislative provisions is that they call for the service of notices before the works are carried out. The landlord has the opportunity of carrying out the proposed works at his own cost in consideration of an increased rent. The compensation is payable only at the expiry of the tenancy in question, which may be some years after the works themselves have been carried out to the property. The amount of the compensation is related to the increase in the value of the landlord's interest caused by the improvement in question. Consequently, if there is no addition of value or, for example, if the landlord proposes to demolish the premises, no compensation will be payable. In addition, business leases will ordinarily contain provisions requiring a tenant, at the request of the landlord, to remove at the expiry of the tenancy any alterations which the tenant has carried out and this may have the effect of circumventing the statutory provisions, although it should be noted that the statutory provisions are stated to apply notwithstanding any contract to the contrary.

Part 3: Health, safety and welfare: aspects of buildings in use

Duties under statute and common law

Health and Safety at Work, etc. Act 1974 and duties of management

The Health and Safety at Work, etc. Act 1974 (HSWA) is the principal statute regarding this area. It lays down broad obligations (called **general duties**) on all employers and businesses and establishes a framework in which more specific health and safety regulations are implemented to address particular risks. There are also statutory requirements for certain types of premises, the most important being the Factories Act 1961 and the Offices, Shops and Railway Premises Act 1963, although these statutes are gradually being superseded and their provisions replaced by more up-to-date health and safety regulations, made under the scheme of the 1974 Act. The statutory requirements are supplemented by a number of Approved Codes of Practice. These codes are not mandatory, but failure to observe the guidelines is admissible in evidence and will lead to a presumption that statutory duties have been contravened.

The HSWA has a very wide scope and applies to facilities managers in a number of ways, as detailed below.

Duties to employees
The Act provides that 'it shall be the duty of every employer to ensure, so far as is reasonably practicable, the health, safety and welfare at work of all his employees'. This includes in particular the provision and maintenance of safe plant and safe systems of work; safety in the use, handling, storage and transport of articles and substances; provision of information, instruction, training and supervision, maintaining a safe place of work, including entrances and access and providing a safe working environment.

Duties to persons other than employees
In addition to these duties, every employer is obliged 'to conduct his undertaking in such a way as to ensure, so far as is reasonably practicable, that persons not in his employment who may be affected thereby are not thereby exposed to risks to their health or safety'. Thus all businesses have obligations

61

not to put at risk members of the public, visiting contractors, and anyone else who might be endangered by activities of the business.

Duties relating to control of the premises

It is recognised in the Act that more than one person may be involved in controlling the premises. There is a duty on each person who has, 'to any extent', control of non-domestic premises to ensure they are safe and without risk to health. The Act specifically provides that where the person has, by virtue of a contract or tenancy, an obligation in relation to maintenance and repair of the premises or safety from plant or substances of said premises, that person shall be treated as a person having a duty for these purposes.

Complying with the duties – management requirements

Compliance with these duties requires knowledge of the relevant statutory requirements and the application of principles of good health and safety management. The legislation lays down certain mandatory tasks.

The HSWA requires any employer with five or more employees to have a written statement of policy with respect to health and safety in the organisation and the arrangements in force for carrying the policy out. This statement has to be drawn to the notice of all employees. Under the Management of Health and Safety at Work Regulations 1992 additional management duties were created. There are now requirements to carry out formal assessments of risk, which need to be documented (as with the safety policy). Formal arrangements must be devised (and recorded) for effective planning, organisation, control, monitoring and review of safety measures.

Every employer is now obliged to appoint one or more 'competent persons' to advise and assist in undertaking the necessary measures to comply with the statutory requirements. These may be employees or outside consultants. Information and training must be provided to staff about the risk assessment, and safety measures.

There are obligations under these regulations particularly relevant to facilities management which concern workplaces shared by employees from more than one organisation, and persons working at a host employer's premises. When people from outside organisations are present to do work they, and their employers, have to be provided with appropriate information on risks, and the necessary precautions to be taken. Temporary staff and those with fixed term contracts, as well as employees, must be supplied with health and safety information before starting work. Where a workplace is being used by the staff of two or more employers, whether on a temporary or permanent basis, the employers have to cooperate and coordinate their safety measures.

There are various additional duties to assess risks under specific regulations (see 'Miscellaneous requirements for business premises' on p. 69).

Civil liabilities and other duties

Breach of the statutory requirements is a criminal offence. In some circumstances (in particular breach of regulations under the HSWA, but not the general duties under the HSWA itself) civil liability may arise to pay compensation to a person who has been injured in some way. Any entitlement in this respect has to be pursued by the individual concerned.

Liability for the condition of buildings is mainly governed by other principles, in particular the Occupier's Liability Act 1957 and the common law. The 1957 Act applies to unsafe premises causing injury or damage to property (e.g. slippery or uneven floor surfaces, dangerous electrical wiring and unstable structures). Under this Act occupiers have the 'common duty of care' which is described as a duty to take such care as is reasonable in all the circumstances of the case to see that visitors will be reasonably safe when using the premises for the purposes for which they are permitted to be there. In the view of the courts, anyone who has a degree of control over the premises, such that it ought to be realised by him that a failure to take care may result in injury, can be treated as an occupier. Because of this very wide interpretation of occupation, liability can arise from temporary or shared occupation, as well as actual ownership or permanent occupation.

In cases where the Occupier's Liability Act might not apply (e.g. because the injury or damage occurs *outside* the premises, or because the defendant is not deemed to be within the legal definition of an occupier) common law liabilities would still arise, most probably under the law of negligence which involves an enquiry into whether the defendant took reasonable care. Vendors and landlords of premises may also be liable, in some circumstances, to persons injured as a result of faulty buildings or maintenance work (Defective Premises Act 1972).

Where there is damage to adjoining premises, or interference with their use, an action might also be brought under the common law of nuisance which differs from negligence mainly in the absence (in most instances) of a requirement on the claimant to show that there has been carelessness by the defendant. Such cases can also sometimes be classified as 'statutory nuisances' which would enable the local authority to serve an abatement notice on the person responsible. Examples of statutory nuisances are noxious fumes and gases, noise and dust.

Persons responsible for premises cannot exclude their liabilities for death or personal injury merely by posting warning notices or imposing contractual requirements on injury in the premises; disclaimers of this type are void by virtue of the Unfair Contract Terms Act 1977. Disclaimers as to other types of damage (e.g. in relation to damage to personal property or vehicles) are not prohibited although the courts may not always permit these to be enforced, if they are deemed to be unreasonable.

Carrying out work on premises, alterations, repair, maintenance and cleaning

Building Regulations

The Building Regulations 1991 impose requirements ensuring that the premises themselves are constructed in such a way that they do not endanger the occupants. They are not an exhaustive list of design and construction requirements; rather they represent a basic level of safety deemed suitable for most buildings. The requirements of the regulations are explained in the official 'Approved Documents' issued on behalf of the Secretary of State. They cover fourteen main issues:

- materials and workmanship
- structure
- fire safety
- site preparation resistance to moisture
- toxic substances
- hygiene
- drainage and waste disposal
- heat-producing appliances
- Stairs, ramps and guards
- conservation of fuel and power
- resistance to the passage of sound
- ventilation
- access and facilities for disabled people
- glazing – materials and protection

Construction Regulations 1961–1966

These regulations contain detailed requirements for undertaking construction work. It should be noted that construction for these purposes is defined in very wide terms as meaning 'building operations' and 'works of engineering construction'; this extends to structural alteration, repair or maintenance of a building (including repointing, redecoration and external cleaning), demolition and laying foundations. The regulations contain a great many requirements ranging from supervision and inspection of work to fencing, edge protection, lifting equipment, use of scaffolding and lifting gear, and various other matters. (These regulations may be updated and republished to be made consistent with EU requirements for safety precautions in construction.)

The Construction (Design and Management) Regulations 1994

These new regulations that take effect in October 1994 will impose additional management requirements where construction work is undertaken. Again, the definition of construction is wide and these rules are expected to extend to alterations, repairs, maintenance and cleaning, except when these are minor works in existing premises.

Where work subject to the regulations is to be carried out the 'client' for whom the work is done will have to appoint a competent person or organisation to undertake the statutory roles of 'project supervisor' and 'principal contractor'. The client will also have duties to allow adequate time and resources for the work, and to provide information about the premises. The project supervisor will have to draw up a 'health and safety plan', to be developed further and applied by the principal contractor. Ultimately a 'health and safety' file of safety information will have to be produced and passed on to subsequent owners. The project supervisor and principal contractor will have various other duties regarding safety measures at the design and execution stages respectively.

Rules on the workplace environment

New rules were introduced recently in the form of the Workplace (Health, Safety and Welfare) Regulations 1992. Workplaces in use before 1 January 1993 are subject to older rules which continue to apply until 1996, when these regulations will take full effect. In fact, the old and the new rules do not differ greatly in relation to the matters described here.

Room dimensions and space requirements

Suitable arrangements for safety and comfort have to be made in rooms where people work, including sufficient height, floor areas and unoccupied space.

The Approved Code of Practice (*Workplace health safety and welfare*) gives the advice that, as a rule of thumb (there are exceptions), the total volume of a room when empty, divided by the number of people normally working in it, should be at least 11 m^3. Careful space planning may be needed to allow sufficient unoccupied space when rooms are in use.

Ventilation

Ventilation must be effective in enclosed areas, comprising a sufficient quantity of fresh or purified air. Any plant used for this purpose must incorporate warning devices to signal a breakdown which might endanger health or safety. Guidance is available in various HSE and CIBSE publications.

Indoor temperatures

During working hours temperatures in all workplaces inside buildings have to be reasonable. The methods of heating or cooling must not cause escapes of fumes, gas or vapour that might be injurious to health. The Approved Code of

Practice says that a 'reasonable temperature' for these purposes should normally be at least 16 °C, but factors such as draughts and humidity need to be taken into account, as must the practicality of maintaining temperatures in hot or cold process areas and rooms which of necessity open to the outside.

Lighting

Lighting must be 'suitable and sufficient', and should, as far as possible, be naturally light. Emergency lighting is required where features in artificial lighting would pose a danger. The HSE Guidance Note *Lighting at work* contains recommendations on installation and maintenance of lighting.

Noise

Under the Noise at Work Regulations 1989 employers are required to safeguard the hearing of their own employees and other workers. The basic duty is to reduce the risk of damage to hearing to the lowest level reasonably practicable. In addition, assessments of exposure to levels of noise likely to be above 85 dB(A) are required. At certain higher levels of noise positive steps have to be taken to reduce exposure, and to make ear protection available. There are various other requirements in the regulations dealing with supplemental protection measures and information for staff.

Specific workplace hazards

Fire precautions

Rules on fire precautions and fire certificates for certain premises are laid down principally by the Fire Precautions Act 1971, although there are various other relevant Acts and regulations. 'Designated premises' may require fire certificates. These are chiefly hotels and boarding houses, and workplaces, i.e. factories, offices, shops and railway premises. Certificates can specify means of escape, fire-fighting equipment, fire alarms and various other requirements. Premises which are exempt from certification nevertheless must have adequate means of escape and fire-fighting equipment. The statutory requirements are being reviewed by the Home Office and new regulations are expected in 1994 which would introduce a duty to carry out fire risk assessments in virtually all workplaces, preparation of evacuation plans, statutory fire drills and various other requirements.

Electricity

The Electricity at Work Regulations 1989 lay down general principles of electrical safety and apply generally to all workplaces and electrical systems (both high and low voltage). Under the regulations there is an overriding duty to provide and maintain a proper safe system of work on electrical systems, whether live or if made dead, and to ensure that any work activity carried out on or near an electrical system is safe. All electrical systems must be constructed and maintained so as to prevent danger, so far as is reasonably practicable. This includes design and selection of electrical equipment. Staff engaged to work on electrical equipment must also be competent. The regulations also impose a series of specific duties governing (among other things) the siting of electrical equipment in hazardous environments; insulation and earthing; cutting off supply and isolation of electrical equipment and precautions for equipment made dead.

Detailed advice on the meaning and application of these regulations is contained in HSE Guidance Notes.

Chemicals

The Control of Substances Hazardous to Health Regulations 1988 (COSHH) apply to chemicals, dusts and micro-organisms, and lay down requirements on all employers both as regards their own employees and anyone else who may be affected by their operations. These rules apply not just in industrial settings, but to office premises, building works and anywhere else where exposure can occur. (Exposure to lead and asbestos are the subject of separate regulations.)

The principal requirement is that exposure to substances hazardous to health must be either prevented, or where this is not reasonably practicable, adequately controlled. The regulations and associated guidance notes lay down occupational exposure limits for many substances. There are further requirements regarding the use of control measures, monitoring exposure levels, and (as is required in some circumstances) health surveillance of people who are exposed to substances. Information and training on safety precautions and use of protective equipment must be provided.

There is an obligation under COSHH not to carry out any work that may give rise to exposure to substances hazardous to health unless a 'suitable and sufficient assessment' of the risk has been carried out. This entails a full investigation of the likely exposure, and will often require reference to the safety data sheets supplied by producers of the materials in question.

Asbestos

The sale of asbestos products is now greatly restricted by legislation, and its current use in buildings is limited. However, there are various requirements in the Control of Asbestos at Work Regulations 1987 that apply where there may be exposure to asbestos, including identifying the type of asbestos involved and carrying out risk assessments before work is done. A written plan of work has to be drawn up, and in some circumstances the HSE or the local authority must be notified of the work in advance.

Under the Asbestos (Licensing) Regulations 1983 work with asbestos insulation or coating may require the person concerned to obtain a licence from the HSE unless certain conditions are met for an exemption.

Legionnaires' disease

The Notification of Cooling Towers and Evaporative Condensers Regulations 1992 lay down the requirement that local authorities must be notified of premises with wet cooling towers and evaporative condensers. This is to assist the authorities in carrying out inspections. There are no health and safety regulations laying down specific measures for the control of legionella, but there is an Approved Code of Practice entitled *The prevention or control of legionellosis (including Legionnaires' disease)* which is supplemented by a Guidance Note called *The control of legionellosis*. These contain recommendations for cleaning and monitoring regimes. If these recommendations are not followed the courts are likely to regard maintenance as inadequate and insufficient to meet the obligations imposed by the general duties under the HSWA.

Display screen equipment

The Health and Safety (Display Screen Equipment) Regulations 1992 set out standards to be met by VDUs and other display screen equipment, furniture and surrounding work areas which may require modifications to some premises by the end of 1996. Workstations put into use for the first time from the start of 1993 are subject to the requirements straightaway. They also impose new obligations for the care of employees and others using display screens, including assessments of workstations, the provision of rest breaks and, in some circumstances the supply of eye-tests and spectacles where needed for this type of work.

Provision and use of equipment

A range of new requirements applying generally to equipment used in workplaces have been introduced by the Provision and Use of Work Equipment Regulations 1992, with the aim of gradually replacing older legislation in this area. These rules concern physical dangers such as unguarded moving parts, high temperatures, instability and a variety of other matters. The new rules apply specifically to equipment first provided after the start of 1993. They will affect *all* equipment by the end of 1996. There are also requirements (which came into effect immediately) concerning the selection of *suitable* equipment, proper maintenance and adequate instructions and training for persons operating the equipment.

Use of certain very dangerous equipment (e.g. circular saws, packing equipment and guillotines) is covered by the Prescribed Dangerous Machines Order 1964 and is subject to the user first having received full instructions and training.

All lifts and hoists used in workplaces have to be of sound construction and properly maintained. Legislation applying to factories, offices and shops requires periodical (usually 6-monthly) examination of lifts and hoists by a 'competent person', and a record has to be kept. There are more stringent design requirements for lifts used specifically for carrying persons (as opposed to goods and equipment). (See the Lifting Plant and Equipment (Record of Test and Examination etc.) Regulations 1992 and the Offices, Shops and Railway Premises (Hoists and Lifts) Regulations 1968.)

Pressure systems

Current statutory requirements relating to pressure systems (e.g. steam boilers and pipework) are largely contained in the Pressure Systems and Transportable Gas Containers Regulations 1989 which impose duties on users, designers, manufacturers, importers and suppliers of pressure systems or transportable gas containers. Duties are also imposed on the users of pressure systems who are required to maintain the systems and provide instructions on how to operate them. A written scheme for the periodic examination of the pressure system by a competent person must also be prepared and safe operating limits established for the system. Separate provisions apply to transportable gas containers. The regulations are only partly in force and the provisions relating to schemes of examination, operation and maintenance of pressure systems are due to come into force on 1 July 1994.

Miscellaneous requirements for business premises

Notification requirements

As described above, notice has to be given for specific types of activity (e.g. building work, work with asbestos and use of cooling towers). In addition, there is a duty to give advance notice to either the HSE (or the local authority if appropriate, see further below) of the fact that premises are to be used and persons are to be employed in factories, offices, shops and railway premises. There are prescribed forms to be used for this purpose.

The Health and Safety Information for Employees Regulations 1989 require employers to display approved posters containing details on health and safety and the local enforcement authority, or to provide approved leaflets to staff. (This is in addition to information to staff required under other regulations.)

Safe working conditions

In addition to the provisions on the working environment outlined above the Workplace (Health, Safety and Welfare) Regulations 1992 cover a variety of hazards which need to be addressed. These cover the following:

- cleanliness and waste materials
- workstations and seating
- floors and traffic routes
- falls and falling objects
- windows, translucent doors, gates and walls
- accommodation for clothing and changing facilities
- facilities for rests and eating meals
- ability to clean windows safely
- escalators and moving walkways
- sanitary conveniences
- washing facilities
- drinking water
- skylights and ventilators

Maintenance

Most of the more recent health and safety regulations now include specific provisions for carrying out maintenance work. Requirements are found, for example, in the Workplace Regulations on maintaining equipment devices and systems 'in an efficient state, in efficient working order and in good repair' and similar obligations arise under the COSHH Regulations, the Noise at Work Regulations and the Work Equipment Regulations. The courts have taken a very broad view of what constitutes a 'risk' for the purposes of laying down duties to take reasonable precautions under the HSWA, and consequently the *absence* of properly organised and implemented maintenance arrangements as a precaution against a risk is, by itself, capable of constituting a breach of health and safety legislation – regardless of whether or not people were *actually* exposed to the danger in question. Thus, maintenance systems have become a critical aspect of such monitoring, and achieving, compliance with the statutory obligations.

Other legislation

This chapter has only outlined the major considerations for facilities management. A fuller list of relevant Acts of Parliament and regulations is contained in the Appendix to this chapter. Reference should be made to the HSE's current edition *Publications in series – list of HSE publications* which contains details of all relevant Approved Codes of Practice, formal Guidance Notes and other advisory literature.

Enforcement and penalties

The enforcing authorities

The HSE is the central enforcement body. Its inspectors cover industrial premises, construction and some public authority owned buildings, and they are the recipients of statutory notifications and accident reports, etc. Local authorities, acting through their environmental health officers, have responsibilities for enforcement in retail, storage, catering and offices premises.

Enforcement notices

The means of enforcement most commonly used by inspectors are improvement notices, which require the recipient to remedy contravention of the duties within a specified time, which must be at least 21 days. In more serious cases – where the contravention is deemed to involve a risk of serious personal injury – a prohibition notice may be served, and this can order the immediate suspension of an activity or, in an extreme case, complete closure of operations or a building. Failure to comply with either type of notice is an offence. The legislation provides rights of appeal against such notices. An appeal can suspend the effect of an improvement notice until the determination of the proceedings in the Industrial Tribunal. A prohibition notice is unaffected by an appeal unless the tribunal gives a direction specifically suspending it.

Prosecutions

Inspectors have a discretion to prosecute in the event of the duties being contravened, irrespective of whether or not an accident has occurred or someone has been injured. Prosecutions are normally brought against the company or other organisation employing the persons working in the premises, or which has control over the matters where the breach has occurred.

The fines can be up to £20,000 in the magistrates' courts. If the case is regarded as a serious one it may however be dealt with by the Crown courts where there is no limit on the fine. Directors, officers, managers and employees can also be prosecuted in their personal capacity if they can be shown to have been individually to blame for a contravention of the health and safety requirements. In such cases the penalties are the same as those described above, except that an individual may be imprisoned for certain offences (notably breaching an enforcement notice) and directors may (although this is still rare) be disqualified from holding office in a company.

Appendix

Planning legislation
Building Act 1984
Planning and Compensation Act 1991 Sections 1–11
Planning (Listed Buildings and Conservation Areas) Act 1990
Town and Country Planning Act 1990

Building Regulations 1991 SI 1991 No. 2768
DoE Circular 36/78
DoE Circular 21/91
DoE Circular 17/92
Planning (Listed Buildings and Conservation Areas) Regulations 1990 (and
    DoE Circular 8/87)
Town and Country Planning Appeals (Determination by Inspectors) (Inquiries
    Procedure) Rules 1992 (and DoE Circular 24/92)
Town and Country Planning General Development Order 1988
Town and Country Planning (Applications) Regulations 1988
Town and Country Planning (Assessment of Environmental Effects)
    Regulations 1988 (and DoE Circular 15/88)
Town and Country Planning (Inquiries Procedure) Rules 1992
Town and Country Planning (Use Classes) Order 1987 (and DoE Circular
    13/87)

Property legislation
Access to Neighbouring Land Act 1992
Land Charges Act 1925
Land Registration Act 1925
Landlord and Tenant Act 1927
Landlord and Tenant Act 1954
Landlord and Tenant Act 1988
Landlord and Tenant (Licensed Premises) Act 1990
Law of Property Act 1925
Law of Property Act 1969
Law of Property (Miscellaneous Provisions) Act 1989
Leasehold Property (Repairs) Act 1938

Health and safety legislation
Health and Safety at Work, etc. Act 1974
Factories Act 1961
Fire Precaution Act 1971
Offices Shops and Railway Premises Act 1963

Asbestos (Licensing) Regulations 1983
Building Regulations 1991
Construction (Design and Management) Regulations 1994
Construction (Head Protection) Regulations 1989

Construction (General Provisions) Regulations 1961
Construction (Lifting Operations) Regulations 1961
Construction (Health and Welfare) Regulations 1966
Construction (Working Places) Regulations 1966
Control of Asbestos at Work Regulations 1987
Control of Industrial Major Accident Hazards Regulations 1984
Control of Lead at Work Regulations 1980
Control of Substances Hazardous to Health Regulations 1988
Electricity at Work Regulations 1989
Examination of Steam Boilers Regulations 1964
Fire Certificates (Special Premises) Regulations 1976
Fire Precautions (Application for Certificate) Regulations 1989
Fire Precautions (Factories, Offices, Shops and Railway Premises) Order 1989
Gas Safety (Installation and Use) Regulations 1984 and 1990
Health and Safety (Dangerous Pathogens) Regulations 1981
Health and Safety (Display Screen Equipment) Regulations 1992
Health and Safety (Emissions into the Atmosphere) Regulations 1983
Health and Safety (Enforcing Authority) Regulations 1989
Health and Safety (First Aid) Regulations 1981
Health and Safety Information for Employees Regulations 1989
Health and Safety (Training for Employment) Regulations 1988
Highly Flammable Liquids and Liquefied Petroleum Gases Regulations 1972
Ionising Radiations Regulations 1985
Ionising Radiations (Outside Workers) Regulations 1993
Lifting Plant and Equipment (Records of Test and Examination, etc.)
   Regulations 1992
Management of Health and Safety at Work Regulations 1992
Manual Handling Operations Regulations 1992
Noise at Work Regulations 1989
Notification of Cooling Towers and Evaporative Condensers Regulations 1992
Notification of Installations Handling Hazardous Substances Regulations 1982
The Offices Shops and Railway Premises (Hoists and Lifts) Regulations 1968
Personal Protective Equipment at Work Regulations 1992
Pesticides Regulations 1989
Power Presses Regulations 1965
Prescribed Dangerous Machines Order 1964
Pressure Systems and Transportable Gas Containers Regulations 1989
Protection of Eyes Regulations 1974
Provision and Use of Work Equipment Regulations 1992
Reporting of Injuries, Diseases and Dangerous Occurrences Regulations 1985
Safety Representatives and Safety Committees Regulations 1977
Safety Signs Regulations 1980
Sanitary Conveniences Regulations 1964
Washing Facilities Regulations 1964
Workplace (Health, Safety and Welfare) Regulations 1992

Chapter 5

Design in practice – planning and managing space

John Worthington

Managing design

Design is too often conceived as the marzipan that is added to provide glitter after the cake is baked. Nothing could be further from the reality. Design provides the coordinating vision which structures and directs a myriad number of small-scale individual decisions. Design decisions are made at many scales, from that of the form of the building to day-to-day design decisions by the facility manager of how most effectively to lay out a conference room for a specific event. Design in its broadest definition is the meaningful and imaginative allocation of physical resources.

The role of the facility manager is to understand the organisation's needs and expectations, and match these to the most appropriate design solutions, using external consultants as appropriate. This chapter will focus on the management of the briefing, design and planning of buildings and space to meet most effectively an organisation's building objectives.

Briefing and design as an iterative process

Design decisions are made at a variety of levels, each with different time horizons, and requiring various intensities of detail. Four distinct levels of decision making have been identified, each reflecting a different stage of permanence, and requiring a separate briefing and design process. (Figure 5.1):

1. *Building shell*. The structure and skin which endure for the full life of the building, i.e. 50 years plus, and for which the key design decisions concern shape, size and the ability to adapt to organisational and technical change, particularly floor-to-floor heights, structural and planning modules. These

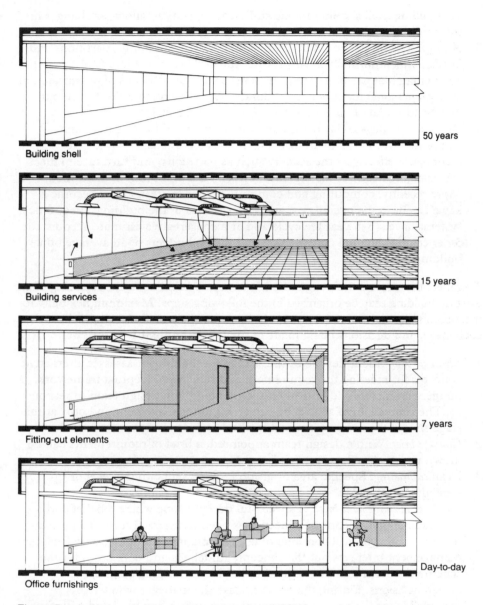

Figure 5.1 Layering design decisions (*source*: DEGW)

are long-term decisions which are difficult to change through the life of the
building, and have major impact on future adaptability.
2. *Building services.* Principally include heating, ventilation, lighting and cable
   distribution which may last for 15–20 years and for which the design
   challenge is to provide adequate cooling, cabling and power capacity for
   accommodating increasing levels of information technology. The capacity of

75

the building shell should provide sufficient capacity to allow for changes in the provision and technology of services over time.

3. *Scenery.* The fitting-out of interior elements such as ceilings, partitions and finishes which normally have a shorter life cycle than services (7–10 years). These match detailed user requirements and address issues of organisational change, personal identity and corporate style. The briefing for fitting-out may be formulated independently of the building shell.

4. *Settings.* The day-to-day design and management of the furniture and equipment within the building shell. The facility manager's role is to reconfigure effectively the scenery such as partitions, and furniture to meet the changing needs of the organisation with the minimum of disruption. More recently, computing and communications **systems** have become a key element in the overall cost and effectiveness of the building. Electronic systems have a 3–5 year life cycle and at a conservative estimate account for 5 per cent of the total construction and fit-out budgets of an average office building.

To reflect these layers the design briefing for a new building or the replacing of an existing building may be organised in the following steps. Maximum flexibility for the organisation is ensured by only the essential information being collected at each stage, and decisions being made at the **last responsible moment.**

1. *Strategic brief.* Identifies the business case for the design, assesses alternative concepts for meeting the requirement and sets the conceptual framework, budget parameters and critical requirements for the design team to respond to. The strategic brief should be agreed by top management and only at this stage should the design team and method of procurement be selected.

2. *Concept brief.* With a design team appointed, a brief of requirements can be drawn up which reflects servicing and fit-out requirements.

3. *Detailed briefing.* Specific area or group requirements, to the level of individual staff needs.

4. *Facilities management brief.* A successful design is one where a belief and understanding of the initial concept has been transferred from the project team to those who will continue to use and manage the space. The facilities management brief sets out the concept, guidelines and data bases for the scheme in a form that can be used to inform continuing planning and design decisions. During the project phase the manager who will be responsible for the project after completion should be associated with the team, preparing operating briefs for specific areas and establishing management data bases (computer-aided facilities management – CAFM) drawing on project data.

Projects whether they are for a new building or a small-scale fit-out have two distinguishable paths, which require to be separately identified, but managed to provide a coherent single solution. The facility (project) manager's role is to integrate:

- *User interests* (demand) which will continue to change so that options are kept open until the last moment, to ensure maximum business flexibility.
- *Building team* (supply) who will be assessed on keeping within budgets and meeting the programme. They will aim to fix their requirements at the earliest possible moment to reduce risk.

Effective design management is finding a cost-effective balance between these two interests.

Managing change

In current management literature there is much discussion of achieving change through participation. Similarly, in design, many would argue for involving the user. Twenty years of office planning have shown that, like the briefing process, decision making can be similarly layered, and issues identified according to whether they are for decision, discussion or information. Three layers of decision making are identified, corporate (board), departmental, individual:

1. *Corporate*, concerned with choice of site, form of building, type of interior layout, space standards, allocation of space to departments (stacking plan) and budgets. It may wish to discuss these issues with staff groups, but the final decisions are long term and corporate.
2. *Departmental*, within the building form, stacking plan and standards set by the board, departmental heads may have control over decisions of how their area is organised, furniture allocation and relationships between groups, allocation of space budgets between individual workplace and ancillary functions.
3. *Individual*, within the group, individuals may have the flexibility to vary the planning of their workplace, amount of screening and selection of furniture accessories.

Effective projects rely on managing inevitable change. The process will be made easier by:

- Layering the briefing and design process and continuously reminding yourself, the team and users, of which decisions are appropriate to the shell, services, scenery or settings.
- Clearly separating organisational issues (demand) from the building solutions (supply) (Figure 5.2).
- Ensuring that during the decision-making process, or in managing day-to-day changes, there are clear **levels of decision making** (Figure 5.3).
- Spending time at the early stages of project planning and testing options to **save costs later** (Figure 5.4).

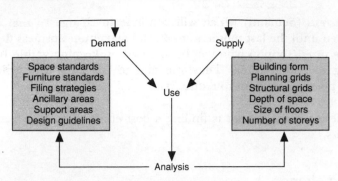

Figure 5.2 Operating and cost reduction in office buildings – understanding demand and supply (*source*: DEGW)

Corporate
- Space standards (space budget)
- Layout concept
- Allocation of space (stacking plan)
- Distribution of support
- Budget and priorities

Department
- Allocation of space between departments/ business units (blocking)
- Layout of areas
- special areas/equipment
- Furniture allocation

Individual
- Selection of furniture accessories
- Amount of screening within guidelines
- Workplace arrangement

Figure 5.3 Clarity in decision making (*source*: DEGW)

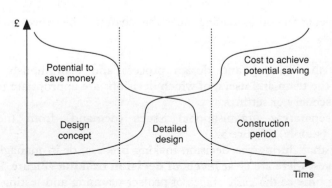

Figure 5.4 Planning to save costs (*source*: DEGW)

Spending time at the early stages of a project design identifying needs, and assessing options, is time well spent. This is a small expenditure compared with the budget at risk once contractors are on site. Changes of mind at the implementation stage can result in heavy cost penalties.

Identifying requirements

The design and planning process is concerned with matching organisational characteristics to building requirements (Figure 5.5). Organisations can be described according to their degree of homogeneity or separation, number of staff, patterns of work, assimilation of technology or corporate style. Similarly, building requirements can be described according to the need for spatial continuity or dispersal, floor area, depth of space, complexity of servicing and style of design and quality of specification.

Understanding your needs
- Roles – services to be delivered
- Centralised or decentralised
- Projected manpower
- Speed of change
- Degree of interaction
- Take up of information technology
- Size of working groups
- Interaction with public

Building implications
- Location, accessibility, image
- Size, number and independece of buildings
- Amount of floor space required
- Size of buildings and floors (number of floors)
- Size of floor, depth of building
- Ease of servicing
- Depth of building
- Number of entrances
- Zoning of building

Figure 5.5 Delivering the service – matching needs to buildings (*source*: DEGW)

Building requirements

To ensure the appropriate building shell whether designing a new building or selecting from the existing stock the issues listed in Table 5.1 should be reviewed in establishing building requirements.

Interior layouts

The facility manager in identifying requirements should recognise the economic, technological and social pressures that are changing the patterns of work and the impact this may have on physical layouts. The office environment is faced with radical change as we move from the processing function to the model of the office as a focus for collaborative work (Figure 5.6). Key organisational questions to be addressed and their layout implications may be as listed below.

Table 5.1 Building requirement issues

Criteria	Organisation issues	Design decisions
Size	How many staff will the organisation have now and in the future? Staff numbers, equipment, future plans	Is the building big enough? How can it allow for growth and change?
Shape	What relationships are required between staff? What degree of access should be allowed for the public?	Is the building the right shape?
Growth and change	What technological, organisational and marketing changes occur?	Can the building meet new organisational demands?
Servicing	How well does technology impact on work processes? Speed of take-up of IT. Environmental expectations of staff	What technology and environmental services are required to support the work?
Quality	What are the corporate values? Should resources be distributed equally?	What messages does the building broadcast to staff and outsiders?
Maintenance	How will the building be managed? What are the lines of responsibility for change?	What patterns of facilities management and maintenance will be established?

Organisational characteristics
- Amount of interaction required between staff.
- Time staff spend in the office and at the desk.
- Range of functions undertaken, degree of interactive work.
- Degree of interaction with the public, and staff from other locations.
- Speed of organisational change, and sensitivity to technological innovation.
- Importance of status, and degree of hierarchy.

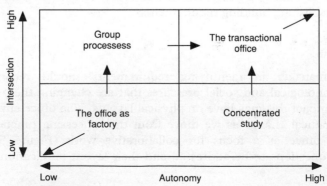

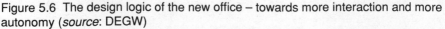

Figure 5.6 The design logic of the new office – towards more interaction and more autonomy (*source*: DEGW)

Layout implications
- Proximity of workstations (density of use) and amount of enclosure.
- Allocations of space to shared activities, relative to individual workplaces. Management and sharing of workplaces.
- Range of work settings, and flexibility of environmental systems required.
- Zoning of areas for security, range of meeting spaces provided, varying choice of fit-out and quality.
- Adaptability of building shell and services, degree of uniformity of workstations to allow for interchangeability.
- Staff space standards, number of different workplace types, distribution of fit-out budget.

Defining space needs
The size of the building may be calculated by assembling a space budget (Figure 5.7) for present and future requirements. For the future needs of a company with a moderate, say approximately 4 per cent, annual increase in staff, it is normal to allow space sufficient to take into account growth for 2 years after move-in. In rapidly growing organisations, say approximately 15 per cent increase in staff per annum expansion space may be provided for by a policy of moving groups out of the building, to make room for the expansion of those that remain.

	Total = 20.5 m²	20.5 m²/person gross external area	
0.5	External walls	20 m²/person gross internal area	Core
4.0	Core, structure, plant, etc.	16 m²/person net internal area	
3.0	Primary circulation	14 m²/person maximum usable area 13 m²/person designed usable area	
3.0	Support	10 m²/person designed office area	Support
3.0	Ancillary	7 m²/person workplace area	
7.0	Workplace		Workplace
	Secondary circulation		

Figure 5.7 Trends in space standards – total space budget (*source*: DEGW)

A total space budget for a building is composed of the following elements:

1. *Workplace areas.* The space required by each grade of staff to undertake the work, plus the immediate area required to circulate between equipment and workplaces. Individual workplace requirements are normally generalised as

a set of workplace standards which form the basis of calculating the overall size of a building. Depending on the hierarchical character of an organisation the number of grades of workplace may vary dramatically.

2. *Group requirements.* In addition to the area allocated for each individual, additional space may be required for the storage of group files and reference materials, special equipment such as terminals and informal meeting areas.
3. *Secondary circulation.* The space required to move within and between groups is approximately an additional $12\frac{1}{2}$ per cent of elements 1 and 2. For ease of calculation this area is normally included within the workplace standards.
4. *Common amenities.* Facilities provided for use by all staff, such as canteen, reception, print and mail room, and break areas.
5. *Special facilities.* Computer area, training rooms, laboratories and the like. In many organisations today 30–40 per cent of the total area may be occupied by special facilities.
6. *Primary circulation.* The space required for access between department and primary and secondary cores is approximately an additional 15 per cent of elements 1 + 2 + 3 + 4 + 5.
7. *Building core and plant.* Lifts, escape stairs, lobby and WC facilities. In a well-designed building this accounts for 20–25 per cent of the total area. In air-conditioned buildings between 8–12 per cent of the total area is taken up by space for plant and vertical ducts.
8. *Area of structure and perimeter construction.* Additional area included in arriving at the gross overall size for the building.

When planning interior layouts, allocation of space per person will need to be agreed according to:

1. *Amount of time spent at the workplace.* In consultancy, marketing and product service organisations the emphasis is increasingly on staff members being at the client's premises or with suppliers, with the result that workplaces may be occupied for only 30–40 per cent of a typical week. Consideration in these cases should be given to a free address system of workplaces where space is shared and space allocated on an as-required basis.
2. *Functionality.* The type of work being undertaken and the need for confidentiality, or to concentrate, or for one to one meeting, and storage and layout.
3. *Status.* Also the need through the allocation of space and quality of furniture to provide signals to outside visitors and colleagues.

The information collected during interviews on future staff numbers, pattern of work, relationships, amount of storage and special equipment needs is formulated as a space budget for working groups. Within the total space required for a group, the allocation of space to individuals or common activities may vary depending on the style of management.

Assessing options

Design is the thoughtful matching of physical form to organisational requirements. The process for a new building is in the designer's mind, while as a day-to-day occurrence for facility managers it may be the matching of existing buildings, layout patterns or equipment to match effectively an organisational demand. Building form can be described according to the following:

1. *Depth of space* (glass to glass):
   (a) Narrow (up to 15 m) and allowing for natural light or ventilation.
   (b) Medium (15–20 m). Mixture of natural and mechanical servicing.
   (c) Deep (20 m+). Mechanical servicing.
   Various depths of buildings can be assessed against organisational demands as in Figure 5.8.

	Space efficiency (usable to gross for typical floor, excluding plant)	Layout options	Ease of communication	Adaptability	Staff satisfaction - perimeter aspect - local control	Adaptability to IT	Total occupancy cost - construction - operating	Ease of management
Narrow	79%	Cellular, small group	Minimum	Maximum	High	Natural vent heat gain	Capital: low Revenue: medium high	Good
Medium	84%	Cellular, small group, large group	Intermediate	Maximum	High	Local plant Adaptable	Capital: medium Revenue: medium	Good
Deep	90%	Large group	Maximum	Minimum	Low	Central plant Inflexible	Capital: high Revenue: high	Poor

Figure 5.8 Comparison of building types by depth (*source*: DEGW)

2. *Location of cores*. Will impact on efficiency of space, and ease of sub-letting.
3. *Floor plate configuration* (linear, continuous or mat). Influences ease of communication, flexibility of planning, ease of sub-leasing.
4. *Building rise, number of floors*.
5. *Structure* – frame, load-bearing walls, load-bearing facade and internal columns.
6. *Servicing*:
   (a) *Perimeter dependent* – relying on light, air and cable management from perimeter walls or partitions.

(b) *Planar dependent* – using artificial ventilation, lighting and cable distribution from the floor or ceiling.

(c) *Hybrid* – a combination of natural (perimeter) servicing and artificial (planar) servicing.

Within the building shell depending on the depth of building and its configuration a number of interior planning options are available to reflect particular organisational needs. Layout types will vary according to degree of enclosure, density of workplace distribution, and the mix of functions. Table 5.2 assesses six alternative layout configurations against a variety of organisational criteria. Some layouts are illustrated in Figure 5.9.

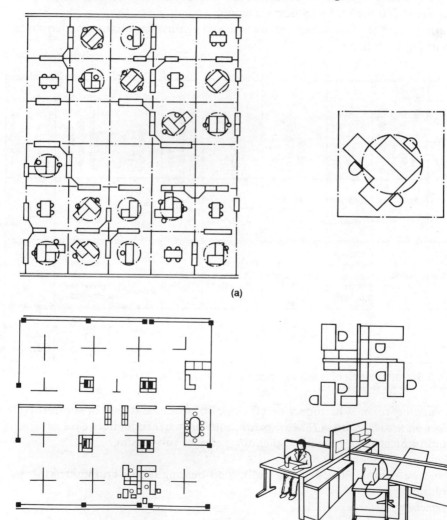

(a)

(b)

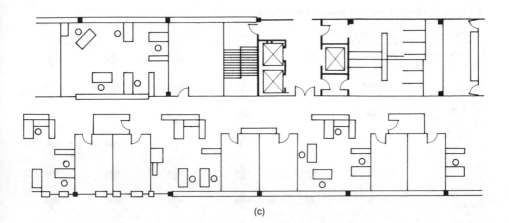

(c)

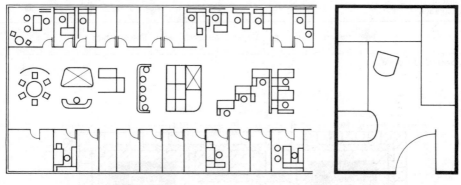

(d)

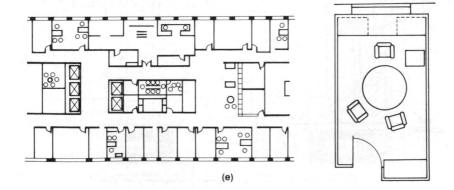

(e)

Figure 5.9 Some styles of layout: (a) open plan; (b) structured; (c) group; (d) combi-office; (e) enclosed. (*Source*: DEGW)

85

Table 5.2 Comparison of layout types

Criteria	Open plan	Screened	Group	Self-regulatory	Combi	Cellular
Individual staff satisfaction	—	●	+	+	+	+
Absorb IT	—	●	+	+	+	+
Allow for rapid change	●	●	+	+	●	●
Meet alternative work patterns	—	—	+	+	—	—
Enhance communication	●	+	+	+	+	—
Increase density	●	●	+	+	—	+
Cost of installation	—	●	+	●	—	+
Cost of adaptation	—	—	+	+	+	●

+ Performs well   **●** Depends on spec   **—** Disadvantage

(*Source*: DEGW)

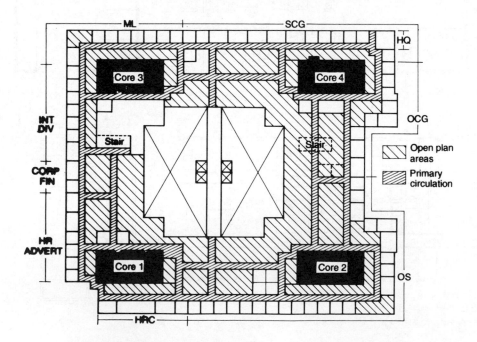

Figure 5.10 Planning concept (*source*: DEGW)

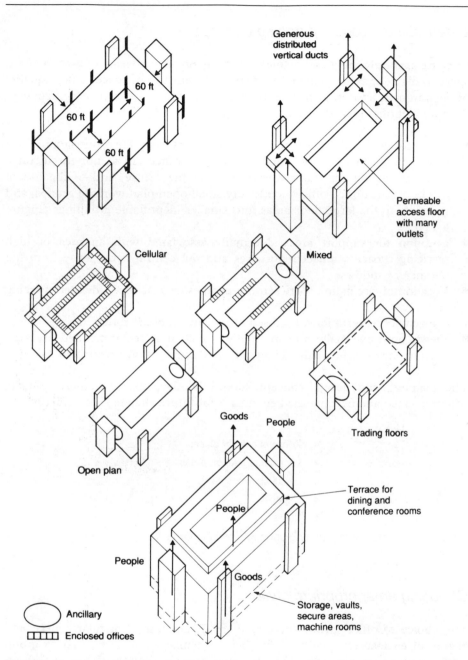

Figure 5.11 Concept diagram for Broadgate, showing options for cellurisation (*source*: DEGW)

Establishing a robust planning concept

Effective space planning and management rely on a clear vision of how the floor space available may be planned to ensure efficient use of space, a high quality of environment and an attractive aesthetic appearance. The planning concept diagram identifies for a typical floorplate (Figure 5.10):

- Zones for enclosed offices, and the potential capacity for cellurisation. Care should be given to the location of enclosed offices so as not to cut off a perimeter aspect for those workstations in the centre, and to the use of blocks of partitioned offices to identify small open plan working groups, and to break up the large floor areas into smaller identifiable groupings (Figure 5.11).
- Location for support areas. Normally associated with an area of high servicing capacity, adjacent to cores and the central zone, away from the perimeter windows.
- Location of circulation, between fire escapes events, cores, defined working areas.
- Capacity of workstations, enclosed offices and support zones.
- Views, both externally and internally, which it is recommended are kept open to enhance the quality of layouts, and to help staff orientation.

The planning and design concept should be developed together, formally communicated and become the benchmark for future change (Figure 5.12).

- Zones of cellular offices
- Location of support areas
- Location oif circulation
- Capacity
- Views

Figure 5.12 Approach to planning concept (*source*: DEGW)

Choosing an appropriate style

The choice of office layout (density of staff, amount of ancillary space and degree of enclosure), quality of finishes, and mixture of individual to group activity space, directly reflect the character an organisation wishes to project. Corporate style is a balance between corporate expectations and individual aspirations (Figure 5.13). Open plan layouts reflected strong corporate demands for greater communication, ease of change, reduced operating costs and ease of supervision. Greater enclosure reflects individual demands for

Coprporate	Individual
• Accommodating change	• Status
• Interaction/communication	• Privacy
• Ease of management	• Aspect
• Cost in use	• Personal control
	• Worksurface

Figure 5.13 What style of layout? – corporate versus individual (*source*: DEGW)

status, privacy, 'a room with a view', personal control and autonomy. Recent layout concepts such as the Scandinavian combi office aim to satisfy the need both for individual personal space and group interactive areas.

Typical issues to be addressed by organisations when agreeing an appropriate style of layout are given under the headings below.

The degree of diversity

Most organisations today encompass a wide variety of functions and different patterns of work. Should one layout style and standard of furniture and space distribution be applied to all working groups? The company should address issues such as:

- Centralised or decentralised space management and budget control.
- Degree of flexibility within the planning concept.
- Number of workplace sizes and variance of equipment allocation.
- How change is managed.

The need to establish a creative business environment

Office work is shifting from information processing with isolated, continuous patterns of work, to group work which tends to be intermittent and collaborative. The layout expectations are given in Table 5.3.

Table 5.3 Comparison of layout expectations

Criteria	*Office factory*	*Collaborative group space*
Space standards	Imposed-elaborate	Irrelevant
Layout	Ganged and dense	Diverse, complex
Boundaries	High articulated	Differentiate between settings
Servicing	Integrated	Independent of layout
Ergonomics	Critical	Less important
Style	Corporate	Varied

A collaborative business environment will generate a large range of spaces for events, formal and informal meetings, business support functions and supportive facility management systems.

Allocation of capital budgets

The size and allocation of the project budget is a direct reflection of corporate aspirations:

- Should quality be allocated evenly, or to the 'front of house' public areas?
- Should there be one or several standards of specification depending on grade and departmental function?
- Should the main expenditure be on staff amenities or business support?
- What investment should be made in allowing for change and future adaptability?
- How important are capital costs in relation to ongoing operating, adaptation and maintenance costs?

All these questions will need to be addressed by the facility manager and his board. Table 5.4 provides an example of how the final interior fit-out budget was agreed for a corporate headquarters. A low, medium and high budget cost was provided for the main functional areas, and photographs and specifications provided to explain the different qualities. The top management committee then made decisions on quality levels for each function, reflecting the importance they attached to each environment to meet the company, human resources, marketing and human objectives. The final budget (those costs in bold type) was a balanced decision for each element close to the overall previously agreed budget of 3.5 million French francs.

Table 5.4 Allocating capital budgets (000s of French francs)

Function	Low	Medium	High
Closed offices	381	**630**	890
Open offices	805	**1117**	1117
Central zone	547	**341**	753
Conference room	50	101, **125**	172
Meeting rooms	**117**	135	237
Cafeteria	289	332	**387**
Training special	**374**	615	860
Other	**230**	1108	1479
FF total	2793	4379	5895

(*Source*: DEGW)

Planning for information technology

Information Technology (IT) is a fast changing field. Over the last 20 years we have seen dramatic changes, from the mainframe of the late 1960's, through mini computers, to the personal computer (PC) established by the introduction of the IBM (PC) in 1980 to the mobility of lap top and palm top computing of the 1990s. A conservative estimate of typical total costs for 1980s and 1990s commercial office buildings shows that the greatest relative increase in expenditure is IT equipment which has increased from 2 to 5 per cent of the total construction costs.

When planning for IT in buildings, three layers of decision making are involved (Figure 5.14; Table 5.5 gives constructional implications):

1. *Primary infrastructure.* The vertical direct space required within the building, which should be up to 2 per cent of the floor plate area, and distributed to reduce congestion at connection points.
2. *Secondary distribution.* The distribution across the floor, which may be conduit ducts, raised floor or flat wiring. Interfaces will be achieved through floor boxes.
3. *Tertiary wiring.* The wiring routes from the floor to the individual equipment. It is at this stage that the greatest flexibility is required, and the most disruption and visual clutter can be caused.

Each element of distribution should be planned for separately and interfaces carefully considered.

Table 5.5 Constuction implications of wire management systems

Criteria	Raised floor	Floor trunking	Suspended boom	Suspended ceiling	Perimeter trunking
Wire capacity	+	●	●	+	—
Wire routeing	+	●	●	+	—
Density of outlets	+	+	●	●	—
Adaptability	+	+	●	●	+
Capital cost	—	—	●	—	+
Cost of adaptation	●	●	●	—	+
Visual impact	+	+	—	●	+
Maintenance	+	+	—	●	+
Compatibility with existing shell	—	●	+	●	+
Cable management	●	+	+	●	+

+ Performs well   ● Depends on spec   ▬ Disadvantage

(*Source*: DEGW)

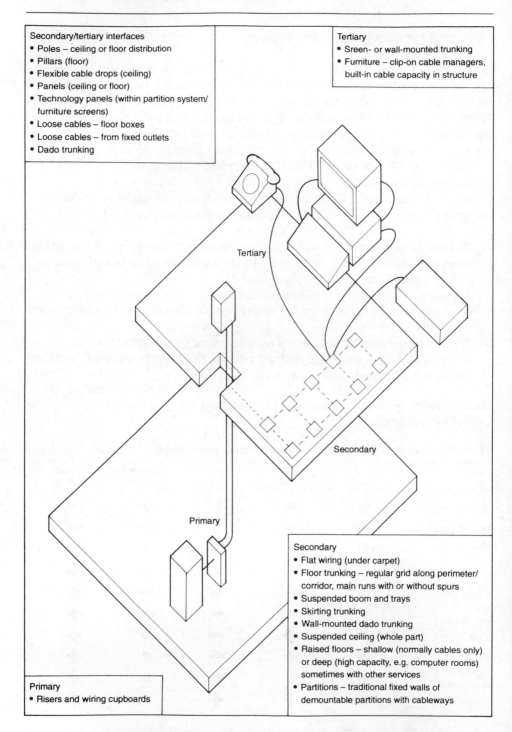

Secondary/tertiary interfaces
- Poles – ceiling or floor distribution
- Pillars (floor)
- Flexible cable drops (ceiling)
- Panels (ceiling or floor)
- Technology panels (within partition system/ furniture screens)
- Loose cables – floor boxes
- Loose cables – from fixed outlets
- Dado trunking

Tertiary
- Sreen- or wall-mounted trunking
- Furniture – clip-on cable managers, built-in cable capacity in structure

Tertiary

Secondary

Primary

Secondary
- Flat wiring (under carpet)
- Floor trunking – regular grid along perimeter/ corridor, main runs with or without spurs
- Suspended boom and trays
- Skirting trunking
- Wall-mounted dado trunking
- Suspended ceiling (whole part)
- Raised floors – shallow (normally cables only) or deep (high capacity, e.g. computer rooms) sometimes with other services
- Partitions – traditional fixed walls of demountable partitions with cableways

Primary
- Risers and wiring cupboards

Figure 5.14 Categories of cable distribution – generic types (*source*: DEGW)

Managing the design and planning process

If intelligent buildings are to achieve their full potential, it is essential that they provide an infrastructure to support new working patterns that challenge the conventional use of time and space at the workplace. To date IT has often been viewed as a panacea overlaid on old working habits. In future, successful firms will be those that absorb technology into the culture of the organisation, and are prepared to rethink work processes to generate a new culture of intelligence.

New roles are emerging for the developer, building owner and IT supplier. As firms move away from the long-term inflexibility of buildings designed to suit only one organisation, we may expect to see partnerships formed between users and suppliers to provide robust building shells, which can be tailored to varied user requirements through the fit-out, equipment and day-to-day management provided. The developer and owner may be expected to provide the intelligence infrastructure and value added services. IT suppliers will increasingly take the central role in the intelligent building market as they shift from hardware suppliers to services integrator. Spanning, as they do, both product and services, they are the natural candidates to identify requirements, specify solutions, purchase products and services, install systems and ensure continuous management.

The emphasis will be on total organisational effectiveness rather than merely on building automation efficiency. A holistic long-term approach is emerging which integrates building, space and business concerns to meet corporate objectives. This will require:

- Better user briefs.
- More responsibility for suppliers to convince users of the benefits of intelligence.
- Better comparative performance data on both efficiency and effectiveness.
- Better understanding of user and building life cycle interactions.
- New forms of procurement and delivery of buildings and intelligence.
- Redefinition of facility management towards organisational goals.

Chapter 6

Life cycle appraisal

Roger Flanagan & Laurence Marsh

Introduction

As will be seen, this chapter is about a technique which is useful in respect of appraising designs, as well as in appraising buildings in use. It therefore provides a bridge between the strategic property management, property development, and design chapters and the following chapters on data acquisition, performance and management.

One of the techniques which can help the facilities manager to make facilities more efficient and effective from a cost viewpoint is the area of life cycle appraisal. A wide range of terminology is in use:

- *Whole life cycle cost.* The generic term for the costs associated with owning and operating a facility from inception to demolition. Whole life cycle costs include both the initial capital cost and the running costs.
- *Life cycle cost analysis.* Involves analysing the running costs and performance data for a facility in use.
- *Life cycle cost planning.* Involves forecasting future running costs for a facility.
- *Life cycle cost management.* Techniques used by the facilities manager to aid effective management.
- *Cost-in-use.* Used less in practice now; the forerunner of the whole life cycle cost appraisal.

For the purposes of this chapter the term whole life cycle cost (LCC) appraisal will be used.

Whole life cycle cost appraisal of buildings in use

It may seem rather obvious to suggest that the decision maker should examine the total cost implications of any decision. All consumers apply this concept in a more or less formal fashion when considering expenditure on consumer durables such as cars, freezers or houses. The consequences of not doing so are clear. Nevertheless, it is probably true to say that within the UK, whole LCC appraisal has not been generally implemented either at the design stage or occupancy stage of a project.

Several reasons for this apparent failing can be suggested. Firstly, in the past, budgeting the operation and maintenance costs have not been considered to be as important as the budgeting of the initial capital cost. We are living in times of capital rationing and most owners focus solely on the initial capital investment. As a result, some of the buildings that were erected in the 1960s and 1970s have become very inefficient from the viewpoint of owning, operating and maintaining. Owners and professionals within the construction industry were slow to recognise that the changes in the economic climate have upset the balance between capital and running costs of facilities. As long as running costs were relatively low, there was little, if anything, to be lost by using minimum capital costs as a selection criterion. The changes in relative costs now being experienced are sufficiently great so as to demand a change in perspective. It is reasonable to expect that real incomes and energy costs will continue to rise, further increasing the importance of running costs relative to capital costs.

Secondly, initial costs and running costs have been treated as separate budgets whereas the starting point of a whole LCC appraisal approach is that capital and operating costs are intimately linked and should not be treated separately. It follows that if management decisions and control systems are to be compatible with LCC output and recommendations, there must be at least some, if not complete, integration of capital operating budget procedures.

Thirdly, the feeling is often expressed that since whole life cycle appraisal deals with the future, and since the future is uncertain, the results of any whole LCC appraisal will inevitably be inaccurate. While there is some truth that any forecast about the future can only be accurate within the bounds of a best guess, hunch or forecast using the past as a benchmark, 'it's better to be almost right than precisely wrong'.

Fourthly, buildings are durable assets and while new buildings are continually being added to the existing stock, the majority of building users will be making decisions regarding existing buildings. At the same time, the durability of buildings implies that design decisions made during their initial construction, while perhaps correct at the time, may well need to be altered to adjust for unforeseen changes in economic conditions. In an era of low energy costs it would have been difficult to justify double or triple glazing solely on cost grounds, whereas it might now be sensible to change existing glazing systems. The move towards materials that are easy to clean and maintain is driven at least in part by labour costs relative to other costs. A whole LCC appraisal will identify the potential for such changes.

Fifthly, the problems of collecting and analysing data are often referred to as being a major shortcoming of applying life cycle appraisal. It is true that life cycle appraisal does require data, but the facilities manager will, in any event, need to collect and analyse data on the operating and maintenance cost of the facility as an important element of overall cost management. Such data will identify in detail major areas in which an organisation incurs cost, and also point to ways in which potential cost savings can be achieved.

Lastly, while undertaking whole LCC appraisal there is considerable uncertainty. The most obvious point to make about the uncertainty issue is very simply that all decisions are based upon uncertain information, whether these decisions refer to estimates of initial costs or estimates of future costs. All that changes is the degree of uncertainty. More importantly, techniques now exist that allow us to use uncertainty in order to improve decisions. Whole LCC appraisal techniques can be used in conjunction with risk analysis techniques. An overriding priority of most owners is to avoid surprises: indeed, this will often be more important than searching for the lowest cost option. Risk analysis techniques identify the primary sources of potential surprises and identify their likely impact.

The idea that whole LCC appraisal produces scientific answers that leave little scope for managerial decision making is undoubtedly based upon the belief that any calculations that involve some degree of mathematical manipulation must be accurate. It remains the case, however, that whole LCC appraisal is merely a guide to those making decisions, an additional piece of information that can be fed into the process of arriving at a final choice of options, whether it be in respect of a component maintenance programme and so on.

The mathematical techniques involved are straightforward and will be familiar to anyone who has undertaken investment appraisal, the primary technique involving discounting cash flows. All of the manipulations can be performed on modern microcomputers and indeed, it is recommended that this is the way which calculations should be performed in order to reduce the tedium and to allow those doing the calculations to get on with the interesting questions of determining the final choice!

While whole LCC appraisal looks at the balance between the initial and future expenditures, the basic idea is that spending additional sums now may well reduce expenditures in the future. In addition, more intangible benefits may flow from increased initial capital expenditures, in terms of improved aesthetic quality, reduced disruption during refurbishment or planned (or panic) maintenance, or increased income-generating power of the building. Many of these intangible benefits are difficult to quantify in any objective way. Nevertheless, they are important and should be allowed to influence the design process. The concept of tangible and intangible benefits will be discussed later.

Whole life cycle cost appraisal and the facilities manager

An effective facilities management strategy will capture much of the data on the operation and running costs of the project. However, there are a number of general items that have to be considered on the building's running costs and performance. Listed below are some of the items which will be relevant to the facilities manager when considering the data issue:

- Source of the data.
- Reliability of the data. (Where did they come from? Were they from a published source?).
- Conversion of the data into a meaningful structured format.
- How can the data be held on record?
- How old are the data? Do they relate to one year, or a number of years? How should they be averaged? How should they be updated?
- How does the age of the building and the main components affect the maintenance cost? Do we know the conditions of the various items?
- What performance figures are available, how much electricity, gas, water, oil, etc. has been used? What is the cleaning programme and how are the data recorded?
- How has the maintenance been managed and how are future budgets derived?
- What is the condition of the building, when was the last condition survey undertaken and what did it show?
- How has the building been used/abused? What are the occupancy terms and types of activities undertaken?
- If the building is rented what are the service charges payable by the tenants?
- What is the superficial floor area and breakdown of the space use?
- What is the glazed external window area (this is needed to help assess energy performance and the cleaning costs)?
- What are the forecasts about the future life expectancy/obsolescence/decay in materials and components?
- What are the forecasts for planned/preventive/unplanned/corrective maintenance?
- What are the forecasts about modernisation/refurbishment/adaptation/retrofit in the future?
- How has the building and parts of the building been depreciated in the company accounts for balance sheet purposes?
- How has taxation been handled?
- What information is reported to management by the facilities manager?

As can be seen from the list above, there is reliance upon using running cost and performance data gathered from the facility, together with forecasts of future events. Despite the progress in forecasting techniques, the fact remains that there is no infallible way to predict the future as forecasting is not an exact science.

The motivation of owners

Certain costs may be of much greater concern to some owners than to others, because owners are very different in their expectations. Everybody wants to reduce their operation and maintenance costs, but in the case of an investment company who are letting the building to a tenant, their main criterion is to maximise rental income and to show a return for their investors.

Owners will differ in whether they are looking for short-term profit, or long-term returns, or satisfying a public need. The time-scale for the facility will also have an impact on how long a time horizon the owner sees for the use of the facility. Furthermore, whether the capital is borrowed or retained profits are used will influence the method of funding work being undertaken. For example, there may be considerable gains to be achieved by installing a building energy management system. However, if the client is only looking at an occupancy period of 4 years, it is unlikely that on a simple pay-back basis the investment will be warranted. Few clients are likely to praise their advisers or managers for spending more money today that 'might' show a saving in 10 or 15 years' time.

Maintenance expenditure can be an emotive subject for many clients. When budgets become tight, it is frequently the planned maintenance expenditure that is reduced. Crisis maintenance is a reality of everyday life. It can be predicted that certain types of mastics will start to fail from 10 years old, yet frequently adequate provision for their renewal is not made. Deferred maintenance has become a fact of life. The picture is not all bleak because many owners are recognising that the high investment cost in a facility has to be safeguarded by spending money on planned maintenance. Plenty of warning needs to be given for any items of major expenditure. The facilities manager has to maximise the performance of the building for the owner, the investor and the user. With property investment the property is the machine that generates the income, and that investment has to be managed rather than merely monitored.

Owners have become aware that the total cost of a project will vary between building types; the hours of use and the occupancy profile of the building are important factors. For example, if the total discounted cost of an elderly persons' home is considered over a 40-year time horizon, studies have shown that about 70 per cent of the cost is in the operation and maintenance cost phase, while 30 per cent of the cost is the initial capital cost. Schools are used less intensively than hospitals or airports and when these are considered over a 40-year time horizon the initial capital cost can be nearer 50 per cent. Similarly, in a hospital building essential maintenance cannot be deferred to ease pressures on the maintenance budget, because safety and reliability will always be the prerequisite.

Although some of the costs occur on an annual basis, maintenance expenditure is both annual and intermittent, and all facilities require maintenance expenditure. Lack of adequate maintenance causes an exponential deterioration as the maintenance needs increase, and an unpainted window today means replacement of a rotten window tomorrow.

Discounting and LCC

The discount rate has two important functions. Firstly, it enables future costs over a time horizon to be equated with their present value; in effect it is an exchange rate converting tomorrow's costs and revenues into today's. Secondly, by converting future costs which occur at both regular and irregular intervals to today's equivalent it is possible to directly compare different options. Discounted net present value or net present costs should not be confused with real monetary value. If an item has an initial capital cost of £50,000 and a net present cost of £430,000 this does not mean that the owner must have £430,000 to afford the £50,000 investment today.

When preparing a whole LCC appraisal it is essential that all costs associated with the particular option are identified. These data may be usefully represented in the form of a cash flow; in this way both the magnitude and timing of future expenditure can be addressed. When considering such a flow of costs it is essential that allowance is made for the 'time value of money' as dealt with in Chapter 3. A simple example is of a periodic maintenance cost of £105 envisaged to arise one year after component installation. If the return on investment (interest rate) is 5 per cent, a sum of £100, set aside at the beginning of the component life as an initial investment, would be worth £105 after one year. Therefore, it can be seen that in order to cover future costs of a given value, only money of a lesser value need be set aside.

The basis for appraisal is that all costs are represented in the form of discounted cash flow (DCF), in which costs are converted into present value. As noted previously, the present value (PV) of a sum £x received/spent in t years time with an interest rate of i per cent is given below.

$$PV = £x \frac{1}{(1 + i)^t}$$

In the above equation the rate i used to calculate PV is referred to as the discount rate. Figure 6.1 illustrates the effects of discounting £100 at various rates over 30 years. From Figure 6.1 it can be seen that the impact on the PVs of various discount rates is significant. It should be noted, however, that the aims of an LCC appraisal is to provide a comparative study of costs over time rather than to predict costs with absolute accuracy. Although the discount rate used should not greatly affect the relevance of the cost plan, this does not relieve the decision-maker of the duty of predicting a realistic value. The use of an excessively high rate will lead to the favouring of projects where the operating and maintenance costs are seen as being of less importance. In general, the rate chosen should not be less than the anticipated long-term market interest rate.

When preparing an LCC appraisal the discount rate which should be used is the 'net discount rate'. This represents the real return on money invested

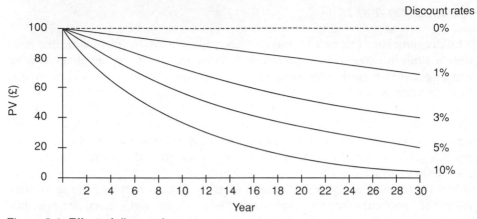

Figure 6.1 Effect of discounting rates

allowing for the fall in value due to inflation. This is sometimes called the real discount rate. The nominal discount rate does not take inflation into account. Inflation will increase costs over the life of the building and therefore increase the required PV investment. Calculation of the net discount rate (NDR) is shown below (D = discount rate, IR = inflation rate).

$$NDR = \frac{(1 + D)}{(1 + IR)} - 1\%$$

Selecting a discount rate is not easy – variations in economic conditions make interest rates highly volatile. Since costs must be accounted for over the life of the building, it is more prudent to take a rate which more accurately reflects the relationship between interest and inflation rates over time.

By substituting the discount rate in the first equation with the net discount rate it is possible to calculate the net present value (NPV) of costs which occur during the life of the building. The addition of capital outlay and NPV running costs will then give the total NPV cost of the option. This figure represents the amount of money which, if set aside today, will exactly cover all required expenditure.

In calculating the total NPV cost of a given option, the above methodology relies primarily on the assumption that the owner will invest the required sum in order to cover all future expenditure. However, in reality costs are largely financed by future earnings. Although the total NPV cost will not reflect the true cost to the client, LCC appraisal does allow valid *comparison* between options under consideration.

In the commercial environment, a company will take account of a number of factors when selecting the discount rate. A company's cost of capital is the weighted average of the cost of debt and the cost of equity with due regard of long-term interest rates and any risk premium that would be expected. The risk premium reflects the additional percentage that might be added to cover 'risk investments'. A nominal discount rate for a proposed hotel development pre-let to an operator in 1994 might be 9 per cent plus 2 per cent risk premium. Assuming an inflation rate of 3.5 per cent, the real discount rate would be 7.5 per cent.

When it is predicted that certain project items will inflate at a rate different from the retail price or building cost index (for example fuel costs) the use of different discount rates for the components is recommended. This produces an adjusted present value (APV). Calculating the NPV is an appraisal technique. Similarly, calculating the internal rate of return (IRR) and payback for projects are also appraisal techniques; be careful not to confuse the three methods.

The attitude of the decision-maker of the company will affect the choice of discount rate used in the whole LCC appraisal; inevitably, we are all subject to bias. The facilities manager will be dealing with upgrading, refurbishment and retrofitting and the same rules apply regarding choice of discount rate for these types of projects.

The time horizon

The time horizon relates to the period over which the LCC appraisal is to be carried out. It is extremely rare that the time horizon will be equal to the physical life of the building, and the following factors may be of relevance in determining a suitable period for study:

1. *Physical life.* This includes expected service life and design life taking due account of maintenance requirements.
2. *Economic life.* This is 'the period over which the occupation of a particular building is considered to be the least cost alternative for meeting a particular objective'. Therefore, the economic life of the building extends until a cheaper alternative can be found to serve the same purpose. It should be noted that use may continue after this period for reasons other than those of a purely financial nature.
3. *Functional life.* This is often closely linked with the economic life of the building and relates to the period over which the building is occupied by the client for the purposes for which it was built. Where the functional life is less than the physical life of the building, the building may be sold when the functional life expires. This will provide the client with a residual value of sale.
4. *Social and legal obsolescence.* This will occur either when social factors result in the client rejecting the building or legislation renders its use impossible. Such factors are difficult to predict but may include comfort, safety, appearance, aesthetics or technological factors.
5. *Technological life.* Technology is moving at a very fast pace; many items are

becoming technologically obsolete after only a short life. For example, lifts now have a technological life of 10–15 years, whereas this used to be over 30 years. They still work effectively and are still safe, but the users demand better controls and faster speeds.

6. *Locational obsolescence.* Locations become unfashionable and choosing a time horizon/period of analysis is difficult. There is no text book answer for the 'correct' period of analysis – account has to be taken of the owner's needs. Equipment choice will often be based on the expected service life, whereas building lifespan may be considered to be 10 years (the developer's opinion) or 25 years (the owner's).

Clearly the determination of a suitable time horizon will depend on the client's expectations and the nature of the project to be undertaken. In practice, however, it is not necessary to take very long time horizons, to say 100 years, even if the economic life of the building is expected to reach this. One obvious reason for this is that the reliability of data used to make calculations of costs, say 100 years into the future, is likely to be low. Economic conditions, technology and expectations are all likely to change. Secondly, the PV of costs incurred so far into the future will become insignificant within the overall cost plan – providing little credibility.

Identification of costs and benefits

The cost implications of a particular choice of component will fall into two categories, tangible costs and intangible costs.

Tangible costs

Such costs, as the name suggests, can be readily quantified. Tangible costs are divided into the initial capital costs of installation and subsequent operating and maintenance costs. The running costs associated with the various components of the building design fall broadly into the following categories:

- replacement
- annual and periodic maintenance
- cleaning
- fuel charges
- insurance
- taxes
- water and sewerage charges
- porterage
- security
- administration and management

The facilities management database will have details of the cost under various sub-headings. The costs need to have performance data recorded, e.g. how much fuel was used and at what charge. The LCC appraisal for a given component must allow for replacement within the overall life of the building. When analysing the **expected service life** of a component it will be dictated, in part, by the frequency of maintenance. In order to reliably predict future replacement/maintenance costs of the component the rate of deterioration must be forecast. Some components will deteriorate slowly and demand minimal attention, while others will have significantly shorter replacement lives and require frequent maintenance, depending upon factors such as the overall design and usage of the building. For example, it can safely be assumed that the deterioration rate of a given floor finish will be significantly higher in a main corridor than in an office.

Intangible costs

Although difficult to measure, the intangible costs associated with an option may have a major role to play in the decision process. Such costs may be applied equally to the overall design or a specific design or a specific component of design. For example, a private sector client in his choice of surface finishes to a shop may decide on an option with low initial capital costs. This reduction in tangible costs may be offset by an intangible cost if a loss of prestige results in reduced custom. Another intangible cost is the disruption cost incurred during installation, maintenance or replacement which may result in a loss of profit, custom or productivity. For example, the selection of a particular low-cost plant item may give rise to a frequent requirement for maintenance. In this case the service down-time associated with such an option may be considered as an important intangible cost.

Unfortunately there is no easy way to calculate intangible costs. A fair assessment can only be made by those professionals and owners who have an intimate working knowledge of the situation.

Due to the inherent uncertainty associated with calculating intangible costs, it would be imprudent to include them directly in the LCC appraisal. The separate analysis of such costs should address the question, 'how big would these intangible costs have to be before they would influence the final decision?' If the magnitude of intangible costs associated with any option are considered insufficient to affect the overall position they may be ignored. However, if they are considered to be sufficiently large further examination will be required.

Benefits

As with costs, benefits may be either tangible or intangible. Careful consideration of benefits is necessary in order that 'double counting' does not occur. For example, the tangible benefits associated with low maintenance will have been reflected in tangible running costs. If double counting does occur the cost of an alternative may appear lower than it really is. As is the case with intangible costs, intangible benefits are not easily quantified.

Whole LCC appraisal – a case study

Introduction

This section is designed to illustrate the practical application of whole LCC appraisal methodology. The case study chosen deals with the specification of curtain-wall based glazing during the design stage of the project. However, the principles illustrated are equally applicable to a situation in which facilities manager may be required to specify a similar system as part of a refurbishment or retro-fit programme. This case study examines the factors which determine the selection of suitable options, the identification of costs and the way in which they are evaluated as part of the LCC appraisal.

The project

The building design utilised for this case study comprises an eight-storey office block of square floor plan. The gross floor area for each storey is 929 m^2 – giving an overall gross floor area of 7432 m^2. The overall structural system is based around *in situ* concrete reinforced columns and beams. All external faces are 100 per cent glazed with curtain walling. A roof plant room provides an extra storey and provides necessary services to all main storeys.

The choice of glazing for this hypothetical building must be considered both in terms of thermal insulation and environmental comfort factors. Due to the nature of the external wall construction (100 per cent glazed), building designs of this type invariably employ solar control glazing. The reflective nature of such products allow for enhanced control over building heat gains over standard glazing as well as affording a greater degree of 'privacy'. This case study focuses on the specification of solar control glazing within the building design outlined above.

Selection of glazing options

The choice of glazing for any building design must reflect thermal insulation requirements of the current Building Regulations. With reference to Section L of current regulations, it was determined that the maximum allowable U-value (heat loss rate) for glazing used in the building was 2.3 W/m^{2}K. Recognising this fundamental requirement, three glazing unit options were considered. In order to achieve the necessary level of insulation all units were double glazed (solar control outer pane/clear glass inner). Three options were selected for analysis in the appraisal (see Table 6.1). The options selected display varying technical performances within the two areas detailed below.

Thermal insulation
The U-value represents the rate at which heat is lost/gained through the unit. The higher the U-value the poorer the insulation capability of the unit.

Solar control
This concerns the ability of the unit to shield the building envelope from heat gains due to solar radiation. The transmittance of the unit represents the proportion of incident radiation which is allowed into the building. It should be noted that both solar heat gain and fabric insulation will affect the demands placed on the building air-conditioning system (1.0 would represent clear glass; 0.1 would be a tinted glass).

Table 6.1 Performance criteria

Option	Unit	U-value (W/m²K)	Solar transmittance	Capital cost per m² (£)
A	Antisun/'K' glass	1.9	0.45	62
B	Suncool/clear float	2.3	0.16	77
C	Suncool/'K' glass	1.8	0.14	100

Cost identification

The costs in this case study fall into the following areas:

- initial capital costs
- periodic intermittent maintenance costs
- annual fuel costs (air conditioning)

There are other running cost items associated with the glass wall, such as cleaning and annual maintenance, but these are not dependent upon the type of glass chosen. The calculation of all costs of each glazing option was undertaken using a computer spreadsheet. The following section describes briefly the method by which such costs were calculated and draws on data contained in Tables 6.A.1–6 in the appendix.

Initial capital cost
Calculated by multiplication of the option unit cost (Table 6.1) and the building glazed area.

Periodic maintenance cost
The calculation of periodic maintenance costs were based on a standard pane area of 3.2 × 2.4 m and the assumption that, on average, one pane will be replaced every 2 years as a result of wear and tear.

Building fuel costs

As previously described, the choice of glazing will affect both thermal insulation and solar heat gains. In order to address the effect which these factors will have upon the annual fuel costs, the cost model incorporates a complex set of calculations designed to predict energy demands under each option. Tables 6.A.5 and 6.A.6 detail the calculation of annual fuel costs under option A and the following gives a brief description of the methodology adopted.

The basis of calculating annual fuel costs is the assumption that initially, before the consideration of casual gains, the building will be at a temperature equal to that of the average external temperature. This is considered on a monthly basis in order to take account of seasonal temperature variations. Total casual gains are then calculated in order to represent the power (kW) that the building will absorb from the building occupants, internal lighting system and solar radiation. This value is based on data contained in Tables 6.A.1, 6.A.3 and 6.A.4 relating to the number of occupants, lighting units, their respective power outputs and the average intensity of solar radiation. It should be noted that an important factor in determining solar heat gain is the transmittance of the glazing option.

Consideration is then given to the internal temperature change produced by casual gains. An important factor in calculating this value is the ventilation rate shown in Table 6.A.1. This represents the frequency with which the air contained within the building is replaced by means of ventilation in order to remove contaminants. Since 2.25 air changes per hour will occur in the building the heating period will be approximately 27 minutes. After this time the entire building air volume will be effectively exchanged with air from the external environment. The internal temperature change is calculated by considering total casual gains over a single heating period. This calculation also includes data contained in Tables 6.A.2 and 6.A.3 relating to the volume and specific heat capacities of both the air contained within the building and structural components.

The simple addition of external temperature and the subsequent change caused by casual gains then gives the theoretical internal building temperature. The temperature change required is then calculated as the difference between this figure and the standard required internal temperature (Table 6.A.1).

The net energy requirement includes the energy which must be supplied/removed in order to achieve the temperature change required (the basic energy requirement). In addition it also includes the energy that will be lost to/gained from the external environmental at the required internal temperature (the fabric heat loss/gain). The net energy requirement represents the energy which must be supplied by means of heating (positive figures) or removed by means of cooling (negative figures) over a single heating period.

By reference to the period of monthly occupancy (Table 6.A.1), all net energy figures are then converted into the standard unit of fuel measurement (kWh). For the purposes of this case study it has been assumed that the building will be heated by means of gas-fired boilers and that cooling will be by means of electricity powered plant. Therefore, all positive power requirements (heating) are expressed in terms of gas costs with negative figures converted into electricity costs. In carrying out these calculations reference is made to current unit fuel costs as well as the overall operating efficiency of the air conditioning systems within the building (assumed at 70 per cent). Table 6.2 shows the capital and running costs calculated for each option under the cost model detailed above.

Table 6.2   Capital and running costs

Option	Capital (£)	Replacement (£ biennual)	Electricity (£ p.a.)	Gas (£ p.a.)
A	205 592	467	71 922	79 522
B	255 332	591	43 745	86 830
C	331 600	768	42 174	85 829

LCC appraisal considerations

Having identified the costs associated with each option it was then necessary to consider the manner in which they were to be analysed in the LCC appraisal. The principal issues involved in LCC appraisal relate to the period of analysis and the rate at which future costs are discounted.

The time horizon
For the purposes of this case study the period of analysis was set at 30 years. It was considered that this represented a reasonable assumption as to the economic life of the building and would therefore be of most use to the decision maker.

The discount rate
As previously discussed, the discount rate which should be used is the net discount rate, representing the real return on money after allowing for the fall in value of that money due to the effects of inflation. In this case study a rate of 4 per cent was taken to represent the overall relationship between interest rates and inflation over time. It was assumed that all calculated maintenance costs would rise in line with the general rate of inflation. Therefore, all such costs could be discounted at the general net discount rate of 4 per cent.

By contrast, it is widely considered that fuel prices may rise at a rate above that of the general inflation rate. Predictions regarding future energy costs were compiled by the Department of Energy to be used as evidence in the Sizewell B public inquiry. This study concluded that the increase in fuel costs would be affected primarily by general world market conditions and GDP, rather than by the domestic inflation rate. The study predicted the likely growth rates of both gas and electricity prices under a range of possible conditions. For the purposes of this case study three possible scenarios were selected as shown in Table 6.3. It can be seen that under scenario 1 low world prices accompanied by a 2.5 per cent growth in GDP result in a real growth rate in gas prices of 3.5 per cent (the rate of growth above general inflation). The resulting discount rate is obtained by subtracting the real growth rate from the general net discount rate of 4 per cent. Although this calculation is not strictly correct, it is sufficiently accurate for this situation. The fuel discount rates given under scenario 1 were selected as a basis for primary LCC appraisal – with scenarios 2 and 3 used in a subsequent sensitivity analysis.

Table 6.3 Growth rate scenarios

Scenario	GDP growth %	Gas		Electricity	
		Real growth rate	Resulting discount rate	Real growth rate	Resulting discount rate
1	2.5	3.5	0.5	1.7	2.3
2	1.5	2.9	1.1	1.4	2.6
3	0.5	3.7	0.3	1.6	2.4

The LCC appraisal

Primary analysis

Discounted cash flows were drawn up for each option to include all associated costs, as identified in Table 6.3. The general net discount rate of 4 per cent was applied to maintenance costs with the appropriate rates for fuel costs under scenario 1. The cash flow for option B is shown in Table 6.A.7 and the total NPV cost of each option is displayed in Figure 6.2. From this analysis it was concluded that B was the lowest-cost option of the three considered with a total NPV cost of £3,614,000.

As previously discussed, LCC appraisal should also consider intangible costs/benefits. Within the context of the options considered in this analysis, it was considered that no intangible costs or benefits will be afforded by any of the glazing units. All glazing options are of similar design and therefore demand the same methods of installation. Each was assumed to have the same replacement periods and therefore would incur equal disruption throughout the life of the building. All options are similar in style and specification and are likely to induce the same 'prestige' factor.

Sensitivity analysis

In order to establish the effects of a variation in the future cost of both gas and electricity on total NPV costs, revised cash flow calculations were produced to reflect the differing relative inflation rates of fuel under scenarios 2 and 3. Although the discount rates used under these scenarios caused variations in

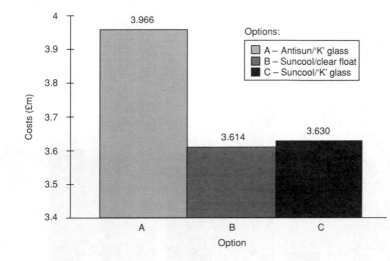

Figure 6.2 Total NPV costs – scenario 1

total NPV costs, the overall ranking order of option costs remained unchanged. This effect is illustrated in Figure 6.3.

Generally when NPV costs are calculated under differing rates from those used in the primary analysis. If the ranking order does change this will normally mean that there is so little difference in the cost of the options affected by using the two rates, that for all practical purposes the difference should be ignored and they should be treated as equal in ranking order.

Under this analysis it was demonstrated that the ranking order between options is unaffected by changes in the discount rates used for fuel. Quite obviously very large changes in the discount rate for fuel would affect the ranking of options. However, the assumptions made in this analysis regarding future fuel cost projections are believed to represent reasonable expectations and thus provide a sound basis for comparisons.

It was therefore concluded that option B is the most attractive of the options analysed by virtue of the lowest NPV cost under all scenarios.

Summary and conclusions

Whole life cycle appraisal, whether of new building proposals or refurbishment, can assist facilities managers and the design team to make comparisons of the likely long-term cost consequences of alternative design choices. Although the technique is not, as yet, widely used in the UK construction industry, there are mounting pressures on running and replacement costs in buildings which should lead to its greater use.

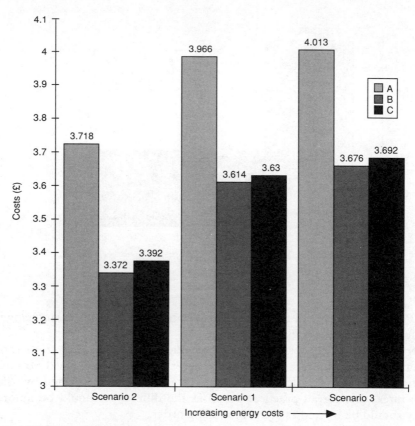

Figure 6.3 Total NPV costs

A facilities management view of operating buildings must include the element of forecasting which will require the consideration of a range of future cost possibilities. Clearly, no one can forecast the future accurately, as finance, labour and fuel costs will change in relation to maintenance and replacement costs. Nevertheless, owners who are investing large sums of money over long periods of time will be familiar with the DCF and sensitivity analysis techniques used in the development feasibility and valuation calculations referred to in chapter 3.

Therefore the reader should bear this in mind when referring to the next chapters, because in the future, long-term forecasting of maintenance and running costs will need better data than most organisations currently have available.

Appendix

Table 6.A.1 Building data

GFA*	7 432 m²	Number of occupants	1800
NFA†	7 200 m²	Hours of daily occupancy	10 hours
Storey height	3.4 m	Yearly occupancy	252 days
No. storeys	8	(assume 210 hours per month)	
Roof/floor area	929 m²	*U*-values: Floor	0.45 W/m²K
Glazed area	3 316 m²	Roof	0.25 W/m²K
Internal volume	25 269 m³	Lighting: No. lamps	1000
Required internal temperature	20°C	Power	80 W
Ventilation rate (no. air changes per hour)	2.25/hour		

* GFA = gross floor area
† NFA = net floor area

Table 6.A.2 Building components

Element	Area (m²)	Thickness (m)	Volume (m³)	Density (kg/m³)	Mass (kg)	SHK (J/kgK)	SHC (kJ/K)
R.C. structure			1 202.00	2 000	2 404 000	1 000	2 404 000
Blockwork	3 184	0.102	324.77	1 400	454 675	1 000	454 675
Plaster	7 464	0.013	97.03	600	58 219	1 000	58 219
Floor screed	7 200	0.05	360.00	1 200	432 000	840	362 880
Suspended ceiling	7 200	0.013	93.60	950	88 920	840	74 693
Carpet	7 200	0.005	36.00	950	34 200	840	28 728
Insulation	929	0.135	125.41	25	3 135	1 400	4 390
Total structural volume			2 238.81				3 387 585
Total internal volume			25 269.00				
Air volume			23 030.19 m³				

Table 6.A.3 Standard data

Power output per person		110 W
SHK of air		1.012 kJ/kgK
Density of air		1.173 kg/m³
Volume of air		23 030.1 m³
SHC of air		27 338.5 kJ/K
Fabric heat factor		0.05
Fuel costs:	Gas	£0.01508/kWh
	Electricity	£0.0749/kWh
	A/C system efficiency	0.7

Table 6.A.4   Monthly sunshine and temperature data

Month	Duration bright sunshine (h)	Average intensity over day (W/m²)	Mean external temperature (°C)	Maximum external temperature (°C)	Average external temperature (°C)
Jan.	1.5	67.5	4	7	5.5
Feb.	2.5	112.5	4.5	7.5	6
Mar.	4	180	6.5	10.5	8.5
Apr.	6	270	9.5	14	11.75
May	7	315	12.5	17.5	15
June	7.5	337.5	16	21	18.5
July	7	315	17.5	22.5	20
Aug.	6	270	17.5	22	19.75
Sept.	5	225	15.5	19.5	17.5
Oct.	3.5	157.5	11.5	15.5	13.5
Nov.	2	90	7.5	10.5	9
Dec.	1.5	67.5	5	8	6.5

Table 6.A.5 Fuel costs, Option A

Month	Net energy req. (kJ)	Power per month (kWh)	Quarterly fuel consumption (KWh) Gas	Quarterly fuel consumption (KWh) Electricity	Fuel cost (£) Gas	Fuel cost (£) Electricity
Jan.	2 488 286	134 822				
Feb.	2 330 647	688 269				
Mar.	1 730 471	511 030	2 763 030		41 666	
Apr.	999 516	295 169				
May.	218 360	64 485				
June	−535 936	−153 268	513 791	226 098	7 748	16 935
July	−820 834	−242 403				
Aug.	−725 547	−214 263				
Sept.	−193 799	−57 231		734 139		54 987
Oct.	718 136	212 075				
Nov.	1 733 990	512 069				
Dec.	2 280 447	673 444	1 996 554		30 108	

Total annual gas cost   £79 522
Total annual electricity cost   £71 922

Table 6.A.6 Annual energy requirements, Option A

Month	Average external temperature (°C)	Solar gains (kW)	Occupant gains (kW)	Lighting gains (kW)	Total casual gains (kW)	Internal temperature change (°C)	Internal building temperature (°C)	Temp change required (°C)	Basic energy requirement (kJ)	Fabric heat loss/ gain (kJ)	Net energy requirement (kJ)
Jan.	5.5	50.36	198	80	328.36	2.67	8.17	11.83	2 327 030	161 256	2 488 286
Feb.	6	83.94	198	80	361.94	2.94	8.94	11.06	2 174 951	155 696	2 330 647
Mar.	8.5	134.30	198	80	412.30	3.35	11.85	8.15	1 602 578	127 893	1 730 471
Apr.	11.5	201.45	198	80	479.45	3.90	15.40	4.60	904 986	94 530	999 516
May	15	235.02	198	80	513.02	4.17	19.17	0.83	162 755	55 606	218 360
June	16.5	251.81	198	80	529.81	4.31	22.81	−2.81	−552 617	16 682	−535 936
July	20	235.02	198	80	513.02	4.17	24.17	−4.17	−820 834	0	−820 834
Aug.	19.8	201.45	198	80	479.45	3.90	23.70	−3.70	−727 772	2 224	−725 547
Sept.	17.5	167.87	198	80	445.87	3.63	21.13	−1.13	−221 601	27 803	−193 799
Oct.	13.5	117.51	198	80	395.51	3.22	16.72	3.28	645 849	72 287	718 136
Nov.	9	67.15	198	80	345.15	2.81	11.81	8.19	1 611 658	122 332	1 733 990
Dec.	6.5	50.36	198	80	328.36	2.67	9.17	10.83	2 130 312	150 135	2 280 447

Table 6.A.7 Cash flow, Option B

| Capital cost | 255332 | Fuel costs | Gas | 86830 |
| Replacement | 591 | | Electricity | 43745 |

General net discount rate	4%		
Real gas inflation rate	3.5%	Period	30 years
Real electricity inflation rate	1.7%		

Discount rate	*Capital*	*Replacement* 4%	*Gas* 0.5%	*Electricity* 2.3%
Year				
0	255332			
1			86 398	42 762
2		547	85 968	41 800
3			85 541	40 861
4		505	85 115	39 942
5			84 692	39 044
6		467	84 270	38 166
7			83 851	37 308
8		432	83 434	36 469
9			83 019	35 649
10		400	82 606	34 848
11			82 195	34 064
12		369	81 786	33 299
13			81 379	32 550
14		341	80 974	31 818
15			80 571	31 103
16		316	80 170	30 403
17			79 771	29 720
18		292	79 375	29 052
19			78 980	28 399
20		270	78 587	27 760
21			78 196	27 136
22		250	77 807	26 526
23			77 420	25 929
24		231	77 034	25 346
25			76 651	24 777
26		213	76 270	24 220
27			75 890	23 675
28		197	75 513	23 143
29			75 137	22 622
30		182	74 763	22 114
Total NPV		5 013	2 413 362	940 505

Capital costs	255 332	NPV gas costs	2 413 362
NPV replacement costs	5 013	NPV electricity costs	940 505
Total capital/replacement	260 345	Total fuel costs	3 353 867

Chapter 7

Construction procurement

Alan Park

Introduction

In the course of normal working activities every facilities manager responsible for premises will be faced with the need to procure building works. This procurement can be new construction or adaptation of existing structures and both of these will be reviewed in detail later in this chapter.

Throughout the chapter references are made to the terms 'client', 'facilities manager', 'premises, building and facility'; these are adopted generally to mean respectively:

- *Client*: the building occupier who generates the need for new, altered or extended premises and enters into the contracts to create the revised space.
- *Facilities manager*: can be a professional consultant or in the direct employment of the building occupier and performs the function of premises or estate manager with the added responsibility of liaising with the occupancy departments and management.
- *Premises, buildings and facility*: refers to any structure, storage yard, or land used for the purposes of the occupier's core activities.

Construction procurement starts with proper identification of the need to be fulfilled as without this it is impossible to instruct the design process properly in order to generate the enquiry to the construction industry. The need will be defined in terms of an architectural or engineering brief and it will be possible in general to establish if it is reasonable to adapt existing buildings or whether a new structure is required. In the latter case a further choice must be addressed and that is site availability. The chart in Figure 7.1 shows the typical operational flow of the decisions through the early stages of seeking professional advice and then briefing the selected professionals. As an example which helps

115

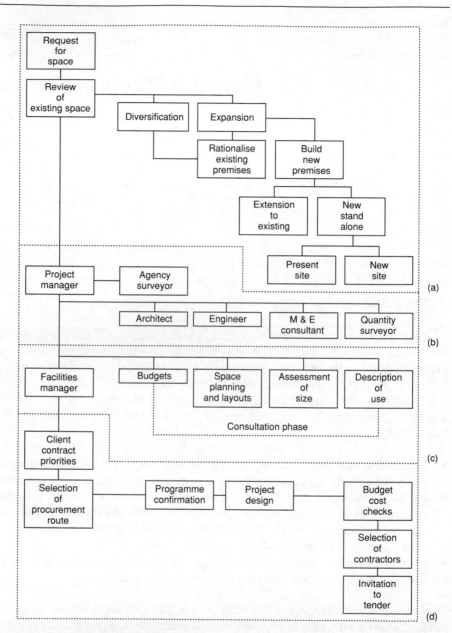

Figure 7.1   Procurement of space

to illustrate the application of the flow chart, suppose you are managing an industrial manufacturing facility and a market opportunity influences the company board to manufacture a new product. A request for space will be raised by the production engineering department which, in this case, shows that the need is for a new building standing alone from the existing facility. A site is therefore necessary, and perhaps the existing location is fully committed or there are communication or grant benefits that suggest that a new location is desirable. The most appropriate decision requiring a search for a new site will be prompted by the route highlighted in Figure 7.2.

Whatever the best route determined by the steps described, any procurement other than works of minor maintenance scale will require some level of professional advice. The traditional approach to the appointment of the professional construction consultants, requires the client to select and engage each of the disciplines. Currently this method is said to be cumbersome, and some clients prefer to adopt a 'one stop shopping' route of appointing a lead consultant, either a project manager or the architect, who in turn engages and pays the other consultants. This method clarifies the responsibility routes and coordinates the interchange of information. Figure 7.1(b) shows the relationships graphically.

Once the professional team is assembled a design brief can be developed in consultation with the lead consultant. The purpose of the brief is to define the end requirements of the development in enough detail to constrain the design team without stifling their scope to create imaginative solutions. A successful brief will ensure that the client receives a building that matches the occupational performance expectations, is on time in relation to the overall programme and is at a final cost that does not exceed the project budgets. The consultation phase of brief development as in Figure 7.1(c) considers all the priorities to be met and each project will have its own specific list which will need to be anticipated at this stage. The flow of information during this stage is active in both directions from the facilities manager through the project

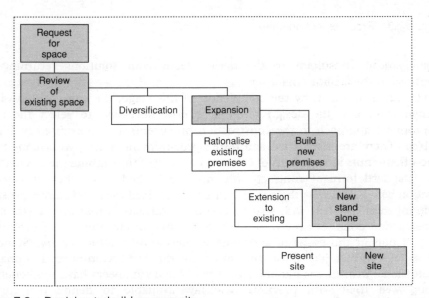

Figure 7.2   Decision to build on new site

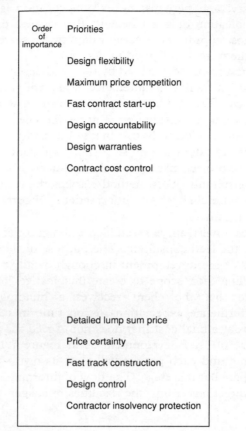

Figure 7.3   Procurement priorities

manager/lead consultant to the design team with solutions returning for approval to the facilities manager.

Having established, by the completion of this stage, the composition of the design team and the design brief, it is now necessary to select the most appropriate approach to the construction procurement as illustrated in Figure 7.1(d). There are many tried and tested procurement routes, with many more one-off attempts at variations of contracts which try to combine the strengths of one standard form of contract with those embodied in another. A word of caution here is to advise the use of well-tried standard forms whenever possible. The inherent problem with writing bespoke contracts is that unless you are a construction contract expert, or are able to engage one, the risk of protracted legal action in the event of a dispute is high and therefore costly. Standard forms of contract like those sponsored by the Joint Contracts Tribunal or professional institutions like the Institute of Civil Engineers have the benefit of being well tried with previous case law available to define the current interpretation of most contentious clauses.

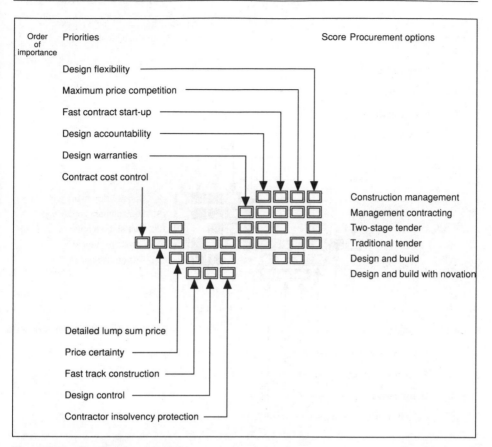

Figure 7.4   Procurement options

The selection of a form of contract is partly dictated by the type of construction. For example, a design and build contract can be ideal for a detached new factory or warehouse buildings, but is totally inappropriate for difficult cut and carve type operations encountered in altering old buildings. The design team, through the lead consultant, will advise on the most appropriate form, but for them to do this successfully they need to be briefed on the risk priorities. All contractual arrangements have an element of risk for the parties and as a rule in a normal market the cost of the construction contract is in inverse proportion to the risk imposed upon the contractors at tender stage. The greater the risk a contractor assumes within his tender the more money he will require to ensure he does not finish up with a loss.

The list in Figure 7.3 suggests a series of universal priorities that must first be numbered in order of importance. This numbering is done prior to considering procurement options, then the three or four most important selections are marked up on the matrix in Figure 7.4 which guides selection towards the most suitable contractual option. In the example shown in Figure 7.5 the priorities of

119

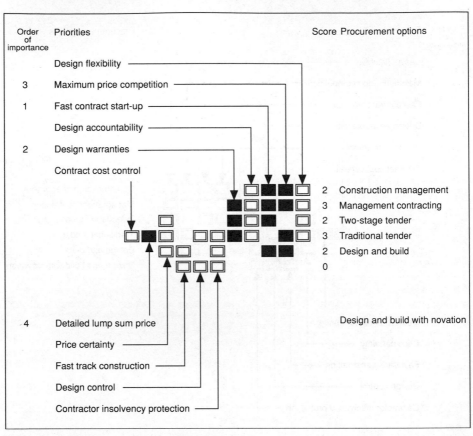

Figure 7.5   Choosing a procurement route

fast start-up, with design warranties and a competitive lump sum price with a detailed build-up, indicate a traditional tender route and management contracting tied on three boxes each. A detailed lump sum price is preferred here to the alternative option of overall price certainty as perhaps the nature of the project cannot exclude variations during the contract that will require negotiated price adjustments. The choice of the design team in this case would probably be directed towards management contracting as this offers marginally more scope for the first priority of fast start-up. Had lump sum price been the first priority then the traditional approach of design drawings supported by rapidly produced tender documents would have scored highly.

New construction

This is probably the easiest form of construction to procure as the required building is free of the constraints imposed by existing structures and so allows a free approach to design solutions. There are other constraints, such as planning consents, site conditions and shape, exposure and geographical location. The priorities that dictate contract choice shown in Figures 7.3 and 7.4 are obvious in their content and are a guide to help the facilities manager to ask the relevant questions of the design team. Each project has its own peculiarities so this list cannot be considered complete; it will need to be reviewed on a project-by-project basis. Follow a logical approach, think about the achievements that on completion, and in retrospective analysis, would make this an ideal project and write the list down. Think also about events during or on completion of the project like late completion, cost overrun and poor internal design, which would qualify as a criticism of you or the project, and write them down too. Now review the matrix priority list and mark it according to your first 'wish list' and use the second list to confirm that your selection is the best choice to avoid problems.

Contracts fall into a series of categories:

- design and build or package deal contracts
- traditional lump sum contracts
- management contracts
- negotiated contracts

Each of these categories have varying degrees of risk and the following paragraphs will outline the basic principles of each type.

Design and build contracts

This procurement route has a number of variations like develop and construct, but in all cases the maximum risk is transferred to the contractor. In this case contractors are invited to tender, assuming responsibility for not only the construction of the building but also its design. The success of the completed building depends largely on how well its performance requirements may be defined at the time of inviting tenders. It is difficult to write the operational requirements of the building into a watertight specification that will both brief the contractor, and ensure his subsequent design provides the desired quality.

There is a fundamental long-term risk that must be controlled and it is that the contractor, who is to be entrusted with the design of the building, can enhance his profit at the expense of quality by instructing his designers to downgrade their solutions and lower the standard of materials and components specified for the construction.

It is normal in design and build contracts for the contractor to engage professional practices of architects, engineers, surveyors and services consultants to prepare the design on which his lump sum tender is based. If the enquiry to the contractor allows too much latitude then there will be disappointment related to the finished building, and there can also be a heavy burden of maintenance and repair in the years to come.

121

Design and build is often championed as a fast track procurement route allowing a rapid start on site, which is true, but it is not an exclusive benefit as other procurement methods can also establish a rapid start on site.

The nature of the project has a bearing on the choice of design and build, as the more complex the building the greater the care that must be exercised in writing the enquiry. There are many successful contracts through this route, particularly those where the performance requirements of the building can be detailed at the outset with the expectation that changes will not be necessary during the contract period. Design and build provides a lump sum price that, so long as the goalposts are not moved once the contractor is appointed, requires the contractor to deliver the building to specification, on time and for that lump sum. It is difficult to establish this rigid discipline as buildings are normally a compromise, and the facilities manager will be expected to react to market forces, departmental arguments and other external pressures to modify the requirements.

Consider the example of a bottling plant where the design and build contract was placed on a requirement to bottle mineral water in plastic bottles and the contractor designed and priced on this basis. A large trade supply order is won that must use glass bottles and so dictates a second bottling line plus increased storage and access for bottle delivery. The plastic bottles are being blown on site from bulk delivered chips. This is a major variation to the contract that will require skilled negotiation with the contractor to ensure a fair price adjustment and no excessive penalty to the programme.

A problem in the current low tendering market is the decision by contractors to price low to win contracts, and then to seek to enhance the return and to extend the construction programme. An example like the bottling plant would let such a contractor off the contractual hook.

The purpose of these warnings is not to discredit design and build but to make facilities managers aware of the pitfalls. Take account of the risks, define and fix the design requirements and do not make fundamental changes once contracted and the project will be successful. If the likelihood of significant variations is high then an alternative procurement route that allows design flexibility and maximum price competition should be considered before finally embarking on design and build.

Develop and construct is a variation on the design and build concept where the initial design is worked up by a design team appointed by and working for the client. The design so created is then used as part of the invitation to tender documentation, and the contractors assume responsibility for the design, and also work up the details needed for construction working drawings. The variation on the theme helps to avoid the principal risk of design and build, by placing the concept design under the client's direct instruction, which limits the contractor's scope for deviation to suit commercial purposes.

Whenever members of a design team are appointed in this way by a client, a clear understanding of any future roles they are to play once the construction phase commences must be established. In the simplest arrangement the design professionals will have no further interest in the project once the concept design is completed, but if the building is anything other than simple, novation, or reappointment, of all or part of the design team to the contractor is worth considering. With novation the client will have the power to require the successful tendering contractor to assume the continuing services of the chosen consultants. The benefit to the client is that of design continuity, in that the people responsible for the concept now have to ensure the contractor turns it into a reality. This may be the approach to design and build with the best probability of success all round.

Traditional contracts

In this case the client will appoint a design team, either individually or through a project manager, to administer the project from first identification of needs through to handover on completion, and beyond, to the end of the defects maintenance period (the guarantee). The team provides the client with design solutions, construction advice and cost control.

The main risk in this method lies in the lack of a contractual obligation between the design team and the contractor. This separation of the parties can lead to an adversarial project where the client assumes the risk for the consequences of design failures, and lack of a team approach. One must remember, however, that traditional contracts are so named because of their very successful operation over many decades of producing good buildings and satisfied users. The contractual links in this form are illustrated graphically in Figure 7.6 and the missing link between the designers and the contractor is obvious.

It is usually argued that traditional tenders take longer to start on site as the priority is to finalise as much of the design before inviting tenders from contractors. The tender documentation is intended to provide identical

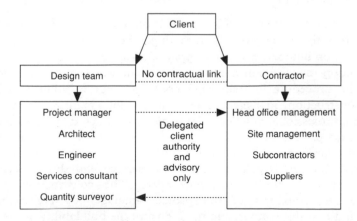

Figure 7.6   Contractural links

documentation for the contractors to price and can be based on drawings and a specification of components, materials and workmanship, or more usually, on drawings and bills of quantities. The bills of quantities are measured listings of the materials and labour needed to construct the building and are priced by all tendering contractors. The final total price so established by the bills becomes the lump sum inserted in the form of tender.

Because of the great amount of pricing detail available to the quantity surveyor from the successful tender, it becomes much easier to control the cost of any variations to the contract. Whenever variations occur, the quantity surveyor can readily assess the cost by applying the prices tendered by the contractor and ideally should agree these costs as the contract progresses.

Much of the cost risk to the client is avoided by the quantity surveyor performing this task quickly, and accurately, with regular cost-reporting procedures that advise on the anticipated final project cost. Like all forms of procurement, whenever a shortcoming is perceived, modifications are devised to eliminate it. The criticism of traditional contracts, of slow start-up on site, are addressed at least in part by adopting a two-stage tender approach. In this case simplified bills of quantities are prepared on initial design information and used as the competitive tender selection document. A contractor is selected and the more detailed quantities are priced as soon as the design permits, often while the early stages of construction are under way.

The problem here is that although the client retains complete control over the design of the building the client is committed to a contract without a confirmed final price. The price at commencement will be a budget figure based on the first-stage tender plus the quantity surveyor's estimate of the cost of the remaining works. Success here depends on the skill of the quantity surveyor in judging the market and in negotiating the second-stage tender within the budget limits.

Management contracts

There are two main variations on this type of contract, one is called construction management the other management contracting. The similarity in the names is a source of confusion but their respective approaches are as follows.

In construction management contracts the client will engage a design team rather like the procedure in traditional contracts, but in addition will also engage a construction manager. The construction manager may be an individual or a professional practice. The project is broken down into the trade groups and these packages of work are tendered individually. The construction manager then coordinates these activities both to meet the project programme and the overall budget, is paid a fee for this service and should receive no financial benefit from the construction costs. The construction manager assumes the responsibilities of the project manager by controlling the programme and cost throughout, and must ensure the buildability of the design while liaising closely with the client. This is in effect a combination of the project manager's role, and the administrative one of dovetailing subcontractors, the latter function which is undertaken within other forms of contract by the main contractor.

This form of contract is seen to be advantageous, enhancing the design team's advice by a practical input from the construction manager on the construction methods, or buildability, while incorporating a high degree of price competition. In other forms of procurement the client will receive an overall competitive price for the building, whereas in this method the client will be able to choose from competitive prices in all the trade packages. In other forms of contract arrangement it is usually only the main contractor who has access to this benefit.

While there are benefits, there are also drawbacks to construction management. The main one is lack of overall price certainty at the start of the project as each trade package is only tendered whenever it is needed for the project. The budget is based on the construction manager's judgement, usually advised by the quantity surveyor, and any errors that result in package tenders exceeding the budget allowance will increase the client's risk, as the project will already be under way on site. Clearly problems on later packages, like finishings, decorations or furnishing could be impossible to resolve without incurring an overspend.

Construction management is viewed as a 'fast track' approach to projects, and if the need for the building is pressing, then the financial risk may be balanced out by the ability to start up faster and complete earlier. If this is to be the justification for adopting construction management, then it is recommended that the overall financial benefits of fast track construction are quantified. This will involve a study of the financial benefits to the client of having the building in use early. For example, suppose the client is in the food industry and revised legislation demands a new processing hall in order to retain a core export market. If the deadline for conformity would be overrun by using other building procurement methods, and consequently a loss of market would occur, it is realistic to set that cost against the price risk of construction management, assuming it is capable of meeting the deadline.

Management contracting requires the client to engage a contractor on a fee basis to organise the building process. The management contractor carries out the role of obtaining trade prices and organising the work on site rather like the construction manager, except that in this case the financial risk is passed to the contractor. This method is also fast track, as the design will not be complete before work commences on site, but of course it is the management contractor that receives the ultimate competitive trade pricing benefit, as he is not obliged to pass on any savings in relation to the overall contract price.

Negotiated contracts

Whenever circumstances dictate the selection of a single contractor, a negotiated contract offers better protection than entering into an open-ended

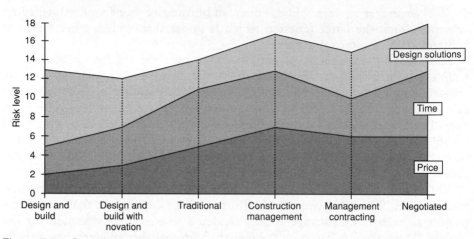

Figure 7.7 Cumulative risk analysis

commission in terms of price, quality and time. Various reasons can suggest that only a single contractor is considered for a project, such as specialist ability, security clearance and familiarity with the site. Without a contract the contractor would simply be instructed to carry out the necessary works and submit his bill at the end. This provides no security and many unpleasant surprises can happen. The best approach is to select the contractor, and, in the simplest method, ask for a lump sum quotation. Of course, an estimate is an opinion and can be worthless in controlling the final cost, whereas a quotation is a commitment to carry out the defined works for that price.

On more complex contracts, the price can be broken down into sections and negotiated with the contractor. Agreement on section prices helps to produce realistic stage payments for work done and avoids the risk of overpayment that would be embarrassing should the contractor become bankrupt. More detailed breakdowns include schedules of rates to be applied to items of work measured on completion by the quantity surveyor. Rates like the price per square metre of concrete floors and brick walls, in fact all components in a completed building, can be quantified by lengths, areas, volumes or numbered items and all can be priced per unit.

The chart in Figure 7.7 gives a visual portrayal of the price, time and design risks in the contracts discussed.

Work to existing structures

Working in existing buildings and structures presents special problems, as design solutions can be limited, the layout or existing construction may be less than ideal, access to the building for contractors may be restricted and the client may need to continue in occupation and use the building throughout.

All the forms of procurement available for new construction can be used in alteration and refurbishment projects in existing structures but some are less satisfactory than others. Before considering the procurement options let us look at the various types of projects that may be encountered.

The scale of alteration works ranges from simple small works, like forming new door openings or building lightweight partitions, through to major repair projects that substantially alter the existing structure to suit new uses. As a rule one must consider the completeness of design, of the finished alteration, which can be achieved prior to involving a contractor. The principle is that the better the definition the more contractual risk can be devolved to the contractor, and only in the most detailed cases should design and build options be considered. It should be remembered that with design and build there is a considerable amount of multiple effort across the tendering contractors who each need to develop the design for their tender, although only one contractor will be successful. This multiple effort is wasteful and costly, and while in times of cut-throat competition it does not show as a price penalty to the client, the role is reversed in a buoyant contracting market, with design and build becoming less attractive.

Generally, therefore, the procurement options are those of the traditional and the management contracts which allow best for the unexpected problems that always occur whenever working with existing structures. The facilities manager will be engaged in managing workspace while it is in active use, so the procurement of building alteration works is potentially an enormously disruptive event. The choice here is to disrupt the contractor in his activities or cause inconvenience to the business while the works are carried out. The only way to adjudicate on this choice is to research and evaluate the total impact of the proposed works, establish how and where business activities will be unacceptably affected, and set about constraining the disruption.

The biggest irritations caused by building works are mess on the site, dirt on the contractor's access route and dust downwind from the site. Many business activities may be severely affected by mess, such as food processing, electronics assembly, hospitals, and even commercial offices where staff are inconvenienced, and equipment malfunctions. In such circumstances, the facilities manager will seek to keep the disruption within acceptable levels by use of contract conditions imposed on the contractor, such as wetting demolition works to reduce dust. The worst situation is working on a building that must remain in operation throughout. Here, in addition to considering the design and procurement options, the creation of temporary screens to contain dust and the reduction of noise are fundamental.

Containment of the contractor must be defined otherwise any available space will be used for material storage, fabrication and parking. Screens, hoardings and the like become a physical boundary that segregates construction from core business with the added benefit of establishing a line of security. It seems obvious to keep contractor's operatives from unauthorised entry to premises, but construction sites are dangerous places that also must be secured from public access.

CONTRACTOR QUESTIONNAIRE (tick the appropriate boxes)

1.00 Name _____

2.00 Address _____

_____

_____

3.00 Telephone no. _____

Fax no. _____

4.00 **COMPANY DETAILS**

	£1–10m.	£10–25m.	£25m.+
4.10 Show annual turnover in last 3 years	☐	☐	☐

	3 years	2 years	1 year
4.20 In last 3 years was company profitable in	☐	☐	☐

	Yes	No
4.30 Registered under BS 5750 for this type of work	☐	☐
4.40 Has formally documented safety policy	☐	☐
4.50 Will provide design warranty	☐	☐
4.60 Part of a trading group	☐	☐
4.70 If yes to 4.60 parent guarantee available	☐	☐

	Attached	Not attached
4.80 Attach details of directly employed resourcing in management, supervision and operatives	☐	☐

	yes	no
4.90 Experience of this type of project	☐	☐

	10 miles	20 miles	20 miles +
4.10 Distance of permanent office from site (radius)	☐	☐	☐

4.11 Level of employers' liability insurance £ _____

4.12 Level of third-party cover £ _____

4.13 Level of design liability insurance £ _____

NOTE: All details entered on this questionnaire are subject to verification

Figure 7.8 Typical questionnaire

The selection of contractors to tender for any works should be carried out against predetermined parameters. The use of a questionnaire highlighting the strengths which are sought in the successful contractor, together with some questions which, when answered, would exclude certain contractors from invitation, will help to identify those capable of satisfying the client's requirements. A typical questionnaire is shown in Figure 7.8, showing the general financial and resourcing questions, with space to add specific enquiries relating to the project.

It is a fundamental part of good competitive tendering policy that only contractors which the client is prepared to accept on the project are invited to tender. Tenders are expensive for contractors to prepare and selection should be done at a pre-qualification stage. This approach is supported by the *Code of procedure for single stage selective tendering* published by the National Joint Consultative Committee for Building. The benefit of adopting this approach not only saves abortive tendering costs but ensures all the tenders received are worthy of consideration, as there is little point in inviting six contractors to tender, only to reject three on grounds of, for example, financial stability. The matching of contractors to the scope of the proposed works is important, as large contractors with overheads will find it impossible to compete with small or medium-sized ones on local small and medium-sized projects. It is a matter of matching the contractors' resources, financial backing and experience to the project.

Larger estates often have either direct labour organisations, or term contractors, engaged to carry out routine building operations like maintenance or minor alterations. This method of procuring building works has a number of advantages for the facilities manager, and, as with all other contracting forms, some counterbalancing disadvantages.

Let us look firstly at the purpose of direct labour, and secondly, let us examine the alternative of term contractors. Direct labour departments have been operated by many local government organisations for years and the departments employ tradesmen and building managers as full staff members. Some larger commercial estate occupiers adopt the same system, particularly if an adequate and constant workload is available to keep the department fully occupied. A benefit is perceived to be the convenience of having a permanent building department instantly available on the estate to react to the occupiers' and management's demands to repair, maintain or alter the buildings. The inherent weakness in direct labour is that it is often impossible to maintain the constant workload necessary to make the department economical as it takes only a small amount of 'standing time' to raise unit costs. Attempts to avoid this problem include the principle of staffing the department to cope only with the mean workload, either delaying additional demands until they can be programmed into the mean level in the future, or, if early action was essential, by bringing in top-up labour from external contractors. This addresses the peaks of activity.

The drive towards increased competitiveness in industry, and tighter budget controls imposed on local authorities, brought about analysis of the cost-effectiveness of direct labour organisations. Market testing of proposed building works, by competitive outsourcing, brought in the current popular method of competitively tendered term contracts. In this method, suitable maintenance, or specialist external contractors are invited to price, by submitting hourly rates for tradesmen, and fixed prices for predetermined work items valid over a period of time, usually at least a year. As a result the facilities manager has a contractor in place who is bound to provide adequate labour to carry out any reasonable workload, and it is no longer necessary to juggle resources. This therefore reduces the risk of causing disputes internally between departments over the priorities of their requests.

The term contractor may also be approached to undertake minor building works even if they are outside the scope of his contract. Minor alterations, like forming new door openings, or building small ancillary structures, can be negotiated with the term contractor who is familiar with the site and its restrictions, has the labour and materials available and will be able to react much faster than the alternative of selecting new contractors to tender for the works. It therefore becomes a matter of balancing the urgency of the proposed works, and the convenience of using an already engaged contractor, against the sharper competitiveness of price in inviting specific tenders.

Performance specification contracts

This is a method often favoured for services installations. With the proper use of this method the client, as the building user, gains the best of design advice from the services engineering consultant, together with the installing contractor's expertise on buildability. In this approach, the client prepares a brief for the services consultant, who, in consultation with the client, works this up into a definitive performance specification covering, for example, building temperatures, number of air changes, demand for the supply of hot water, steam power and the like. The design at this stage is only indicative but will have noted any features the client wishes to be included or avoided in the completed installation. Services contractors have a long tradition of providing design solutions to definitive performance specifications. On receipt of the client's enquiry to tender for the works, specified on the client's behalf by the services consultant, the contractor designs the best solution in detail. The contractor has a wealth of experience, not only of the current equipment and component options available on the market, but also on equipment delivery times and the types of installation that are currently performing best in practice. This practical experience gained from ordering and installing services is the buildability input into the design solution.

The key to success is in writing a definitive performance specification that allows the contractor the scope for design input but restricts him enough to ensure a quality end product. In this instance, performance specification contracts, which involve the sharing of design between the services consultant and the contractor, are vulnerable to the problems of design and build contracts. There is an incentive for any contractor driven by commercial pressures to provide the minimum product for the maximum price and to use his design opportunities to this effect. An inadequately defined performance specification will therefore leave the client at some risk.

While commonplace in services contracting, performance specification contracts are successfully used in many sectors of building procurement. Any major element of a building, requiring specialist design skills which can be found within a contractor's organisation may benefit. The design of cladding and curtain walling, acoustic ceilings, computer access floors, and lifts, are but a few examples. The ultimate application of performance specifications is to complete buildings, but this can only be justified as being in the client's interests if the building is highly specialised, and the invited tendering contractors can be expected to produce enlightened and radical solutions.

Control systems

Every successful project needs to satisfy the client's requirements on cost, time and quality so effective control systems must be set up to monitor these aspects. As this section is intended to be only an introduction to project planning, further reading is recommended at the end of this chapter.

Cost control

This may range from price certainty on simple projects in respect of fixed lump sum contracts or quotations, through to price-adjustable contracts which require detailed budgeting at the outset, involving prices relating to milestone stages in the construction process. Milestones may be completion of substructures, completion of structural frame and all of the other 20 or so recognised elements in a new building. The final cost of each element needs to be agreed promptly with the contractor as soon as possible after the element completion, to make the cost control effective. In practice, the elemental cost forecast is compared with the finalised costs, and a running variance report is maintained in order to prompt corrective action to keep the final cost in line with the budget. The example in Figure 7.9 shows a typical elemental budget with the variance report attached. In this case the high-risk element of substructure works, where unforeseen problems in the ground caused extra cost, and floors where a late decision to install full access floors also caused extra cost, can be accommodated partly by allocating from the contingency fund and partly from savings found from later elements. The object of cost control is to try to ensure that the final cost agrees with the total amount the client is willing and able to pay, and it is always best to assume that there is no additional money available to pay for an overspend.

131

PROJECT TITLE: XXXXXXXXX
PROJECT COST STATUS REPORT no: three
Datapoint 10/93

Elements		Contract cost	Final cost	Budget variance over(+)/under(−)	Remarks
Substructure	Element sub-total	**212 000**	263 000	51 000	Remeasurement of foundations
Superstructure	Upper floors	190 000	187 000	−3 000	
	Roof	217 000	224 000	7 000	
	Stairs	107 000	105 000	−2 000	
	External walls	263 000	242 000	−21 000	Reduction in facing brick features
	Windows and external doors	261 000	274 000	13 000	
	Internal walls and partitions	234 000	269 000	35 000	Occupancy changes
	Internal doors	110 000	97 000	−13 000	
	Element sub-total	**1 382 000**			
Internal finishes	Wall	55 000	61 000	6 000	
	Floor	68 000	82 000	14 000	
	Ceiling	51 000	48 000	−3 000	Full access panels
	Element sub-total	**174 000**			
Fittings and furnishings	Element sub-total	**118 000**	132 000	14 000	
Services	Sanitary and plumbing	470 000	*455 000*	*−15 000*	Estimated savings on fittings
	Electrical	330 000	*320 000*	*−10 000*	
	Ventilation	73 000	*75 000*	*2 000*	
	Gas	0	*0*	*0*	
	Lifts	80 000	*82 000*	*2 000*	
	Communications	22 000	*15 000*	*−7 000*	Change to combined telephone and pa
	Builder's work	26 000	*18 000*	*−8 000*	
	Element sub-total	**1 001 000**			
External works	Element sub-total	143 000	116 000	−27 000	Ommission of prov sum
Preliminaries		622 000	*595 000*	*−27 000*	
Contingencies		**200 000**	*192 000*	*8 000*	
	Overspend			*−8 000*	
Total contract sum		**3 852 000**	*3 852 000*	*0*	

Figure 7.9 Typical elemental budget (estimated figures in italics)

132

PROJECT TITLE: XXXXXXXX
PROJECT TIME STATUS REPORT no: three
Datapoint 10/93

Work stage	Programme stage	Critical activity	Within alloted time	Delayed	Time adjust (weeks)	Cumulative adjust (weeks)	Remarks
C	Outline proposals	□	■	□	0	0	
D	Scheme design	□	■	□	0	0	
E	Detail design	■	□	■	4	4	Project financing option studies
F–H	Tender action	■	□	■	2	6	Late design changes
J–K	Contractor mobilise	■	■	□	–1	5	Accelerated start-up on site
	Substructure	■	■	□	0	5	
	Superstructure	□	■	□	0	5	
	Internal finishes	□	■	□	0	5	
	Fittings and furnishings	■	■	□	0	5	
	Services	■	□	■	7	12	Extended lead times on equipment
	External works	□	■	□	0	12	
	Time float in programme				–8	4	All time float used
L	Handover	■	□	■		4	Overall delay

Projected programme variance (weeks) 4

Figure 7.10 Project time control (estimated time adjustments in italics)

Time control

This depends on accurate project programming with appropriate breakdown into recognisable subsections to allow progressive monitoring as the project progresses. The programming equivalent of the cost contingency is called float time and is established as follows. The events to be individually programmed to form the overall project programme are classified as critical and non-critical. Critical events are those whose completion on time is fundamental to the overall programme and these events link together to form the critical path. Non-critical events occur concurrently with critical ones but have some degree of latitude, and this becomes the float time. It follows, however, that if a non-critical event is delayed beyond its float time it becomes critical to the overall programme.

The principle of time control is similar to the variance reporting on cost control but, as can be seen in Figure 7.10, the intention is to monitor delays in critical sections, and flag up project overrun while there is still time to accelerate the remaining works to meet the intended completion date.

There is an interface between cost control and time control, in that a decision to accelerate the work to overcome a delay, that is not the result of a contractor default, will incur a performance bonus payment to cover uneconomic or overtime working. On the other hand, in a properly formulated contract, where time is of the essence, any delay by the contractor will be at his cost risk, either by the contractor covering the acceleration costs or by paying late delivery damages to the client.

Quality Control

This is a matter of exercising enough supervision over the building works as they progress to discover and correct errors of construction technique, poor workmanship or deficient materials. The relative performance of the various procurement routes has already been discussed and the diagram in Figure 7.4 shows that the greatest design and supervision control rests with those contracts where the client retains the services of a design team. Whenever this control is passed to the contractor the quality/profit conflict can easily arise. Figure 7.7 shows that traditional contracts have the best safeguards on quality, and that design and build contracts have the greatest inherent risk.

The time to establish the control functions on a project is at the outset before the contract is signed, because it is easier and more effective to make cost, time and quality limits a prerequisite to engaging a contractor, than it is to negotiate them into an existing contract. Once the contract is let, the client's bargaining strengths are severely limited, and variations instigated by the client, if onerous on the contractor, will be costly to introduce at that late date.

Long-term accountability is a feature of quality control in that problems caused by inadequate construction often do not arise for some time, often years, after completion of the construction. The problem to be assessed by the client is how best to allocate the risk to ensure that adequate protection is available 5, 10 or more years later. The choice depends on the procurement method adopted, because in design and build the contractor carries the responsibility, whereas in traditional contracts it rests with the design team and the client. It is a matter of choice, taking an objective view for each project on the commercial security of contractors, or the long-term protection of design consultants' professional indemnity insurance. Professional indemnity insurance is compulsory for consultants operating within the rules of the major recognised building professional bodies, but one must always seek proof that the cover is in place, and is adequate in its amount. One must also stipulate, in the consultants' appointment contract, the period after project completion for which cover must be kept in force.

It must be remembered that building is an imprecise art and the multitude of components cannot be assembled on site with factory manufacturing precision. Also, design is an evolving art, taking account of new regulations, techniques and materials, which can only be the best available taking into consideration the current state of knowledge. Even the best designed and constructed buildings can develop failures in use so procurement methods should be chosen in the light of professional advice to minimise risk.

On completion

Let us suppose that a new facility has been progressed from feasibility through to physical completion and possession is about to be taken from the contractor. The building will become the responsibility of the facilities manager to run and it will be unfamiliar, so any operating problems will need to be understood. Placing a contractual requirement on the design team and contractor to provide a master set of 'as built' drawings, showing construction details, services routes and equipment locations, is invaluable. Also, the provision of service and operating manuals for installed equipment like boilers, air-handling plant, lifts, and so on, is essential to the continuing smooth operation of the facilities.

The provision of such information is standard procedure in the construction industry and the data should be centralised into a single master reference document held under strict control by the facilities manager. Photocopying should be discouraged, and whenever unavoidable, needs to be controlled. After all, once a master is copied, and then amended to show alterations in the building, there then exists two master copies with conflicting data. One means of control is to adopt a computer-aided facilities management (CAFM) system, which is easily created as part of the building design process. The main benefits of CAFM systems are security of the master records held in protected files on the management computer, easy access to specific information relating to particular components or occupational areas, together with visual indexing of the often extensive data bases of management information.

The use and occupation of buildings is a continuing process and the control of servicing of equipment together with the collection of data on performance is invaluable in guiding future management decisions. Logbooks held within the CAFM system which record all events relating to the building, from routine servicing, to breakdown and wear-out rates, provide data showing durability and, with analysis, may help to predict failures. Failures of insignificant items like light bulbs in ancillary areas can be dealt with on the 'as and when' basis, but items strategic to the operation of the facility must be addressed through planned preventive maintenance processes. The longer logbooks are maintained accurately, the more refined the predictions should become, and the facilities management costs will be more than justified by the increase in productivity. More information on this topic can be found in the book recommended at the end of this chapter.

Conclusion

A consideration when selecting design consultants, contractors, component suppliers or term contractors is that of quality assurance (QA). Those companies which can demonstrate registration under BS 5750, its European equivalent EN 29000 or the international ISO 9000 series, add a further dimension to risk avoidance in any procurement route. When selecting companies it is important to inspect their QA certificate, but one must also insist on checking the assessment schedule. This schedule defines the scope of the quality registration and can be limited to one particular service or product and the offer of the certificate alone can give a false impression that the company is covered for all the services being provided.

Bibliography

Franks J 1992 *Building procurement systems* CIOB
NEDO 1988 *Faster building for commerce*
Park A 1994 *Facilities management – an explanation* The Macmillan Press Ltd

Chapter 8

Built asset management practice

Roy Holmes

Introduction

Built asset management practice is assumed in this chapter to be concerned with the management of maintenance, renewal and improvement work to buildings and their surrounds, and to the services relating to those buildings. The two major areas of work in this field are commonly referred to as **response maintenance** and **programmed maintenance**. Within these two areas a range of work is carried out, which gives rise to special task names, such as cyclical maintenance. The various types of maintenance are described below.

This chapter is developed in a progressive manner which mirrors the actual procedures in many large organisations. The first aspect to be covered is the management of response maintenance, which includes the work process and the IT necessary to ensure that the system is efficient. This is followed by an outline of programmed maintenance, and the various stages that lead to cost-effective management of the processes. It will be seen that response maintenance and programmed maintenance are complementary. Data from response maintenance are valuable for indicating repair trends and for predicting inspection schedules necessary for assessing the potential programme of work.

The application of IT to various maintenance processes is considered, and the methods of data collection and analysis are discussed. Performance standards for maintenance and renewal are examined and methods of work assessment, which are essential for prioritising the programme of work, are considered. Finally, the implications for finance are examined; factors affecting the resourcing of work and methods of forecasting the likely cost burden for renewal are discussed.

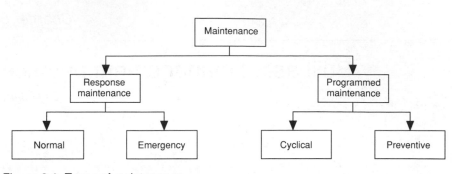

Figure 8.1 Types of maintenance

Types of maintenance

The types of maintenance are shown in Figure 8.1, although this figure has been simplified to prevent confusion. It shows aspects of maintenance which are common to buildings and building services. Figure 8.1 shows two major activities, namely, response maintenance and programmed maintenance. In this chapter planned maintenance and programmed maintenance are synonymous and are taken to mean the organisation of work which has been initiated by management, rather than by the tenant or client.

Response maintenance can be divided into 'normal' maintenance and 'emergency' maintenance; these are categories which reflect the nature of the response rather than the actual work done. For example, emergency work for housing is normally carried out the same day the fault is reported. A list of items, categorised as emergency work, has to be agreed within each organisation.

Programmed maintenance can be categorised by two subgroups. First, preventive maintenance, which consists of work carried out at predetermined intervals to minimise the possibility of elements and components falling below the required standards. Secondly, cyclical work, which would include painting and repairs prior to painting. Periodic maintenance work, which consists of work done for health and safety reasons, such as lift and boiler maintenance, can also be grouped under cyclical work. However, there is another way of expressing these types of maintenance, namely, condition-independent and condition-dependent work. Cyclical maintenance can be categorised as 'condition-independent' work, which is work that is carried out at specific times irrespective of the condition of the elements or components involved. Preventive maintenance can be categorised as 'condition-dependent'; the work should only be carried out when an element has reached its optimum life span and where action is necessary to prevent further deterioration of elements or components. This is discussed more fully below.

These subgroups cover most maintenance activities in the built environment. The major types are now explained further.

Response maintenance

Response maintenance is the name given to work carried out in response to a request from the user of the property, normally the tenant. The tenant is usually responsible for some of the minor repairs and this will be stated in the tenancy agreement. All other repairs are normally reported to the landlord, or to the landlord's agent. When a request is received the response to the request will depend on a number of factors; these include the nature of the request, e.g. whether the problem can be identified without a visit, the maintenance policy, the potential seriousness of the failure and the amount of funds available. In many cases the work will simply be ordered without inspection and prioritised on a simple time basis, ranging from one day to one month, this will be subject to prior agreement with the tenant or client. The tenant or client should be informed of the action taken so that they can make the necessary arrangements for access. The work ordering process is shown in Figure 8.2.

After the work has been ordered the maintenance manager should have some method of checking that the work has been carried out on time, and is of the right quality. This can be achieved though two mechanisms, first, by post-inspection, which normally accounts for 10 per cent of the tasks carried out. Second, by a tenant or client response, where the level of tenant satisfaction is

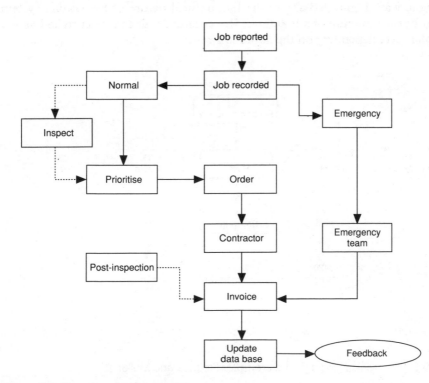

Figure 8.2 Response maintenance

recorded on a card designed for that purpose. On completion of the work the cost of the job is recorded; this may involve the job record being changed. Often the work done is not exactly the same as the work ordered, it is important that the correct job is entered at the invoice stage; this ensures sound data for feedback purposes. In most cases these processes form part of a maintenance package on computer.

Coding response maintenance

Data from response maintenance, in terms of cost and incidence, are extremely valuable for plotting trends and informing decisions on planned maintenance. However, the usefulness of the data depends to a great extent on the coding system used. In 1985 the author published a paper on coding maintenance in buildings.[1] The paper was based on research into maintenance cost trends for housing and school buildings. A number of authorities have used the principles involved in the coding system to develop their own 'in-house' systems and in 1993 the coding framework was accepted, by the National Federation of Housing Associations, as the basis for coding maintenance in housing associations. The coding system recommended is hierarchical in nature and allows the complexity, and the amount, of recording to be controlled in a systematic way. Figure 8.3 shows the hierarchical nature of the coding system for part of the structure of a building. The coding detail can be curtailed at any particular level depending on the data required.

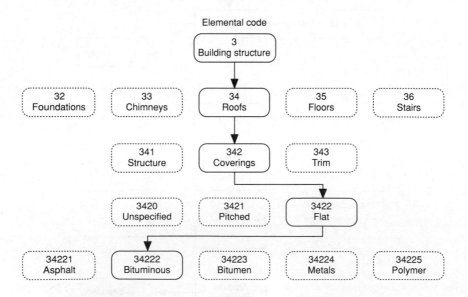

Figure 8.3 Hierarchical coding structure (*after* Holmes and Mellor[1])

A coding frame

Having established a coding structure for the elements of a building there are other details that may be required in the feedback process, or for informing the maintenance operator. These details can be expressed in well-known management terms, i.e. what, where, why and when. What needs to be done to the elements? Where is the element located? Why is the repair to be undertaken? When should it be done? These stages have also been given codes, i.e. **process code**, **location code**, **reason code** and **priority code**. Figure 8.4 shows the coding frame. The extent to which these codes are used depends on the organisation and the use of the feedback.

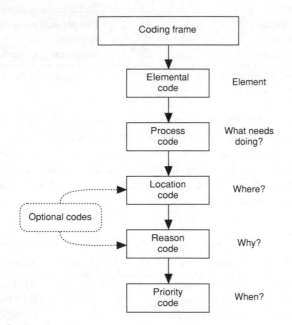

Figure 8.4 Coding frame

This particular coding frame has been developed to various levels of complexity for organisations in the UK and overseas. A vast amount of data can be collected from which cost trends and incidence of failure can be plotted. It is suggested that most elements should be coded to a level of three digits; however, there are cases, particularly when monitoring services and other detailed components, where further levels of coding are justified. The hierarchical nature of the code allows flexibility to suit the detail required.

The process or 'what' code. The second code, following the elemental code, indicates the nature of the work to be carried out. When an order is issued the work required can be referred to as the 'process' to be carried out. Table 8.1

141

shows the original process code. Essentially the size of stock and the use of the feedback data will determine this aspect of data acquisition.

Table 8.1 Process code

Level 1		Level 2 (Renew or replace)	
1	Repair or refix	21	Renew
2	Renew or replace	22	Replace
3	Construct or install	23	Rewire
4	Strengthen or upgrade	24	Rewind
5	Remove	25	Redecorate
6	Ease or adjust	26	Derust and repaint
7	Clean or treat	27	Derust and re-spray
8	Survey or test	28	Repoint
9	Support services	29	Re-grout (pressure)

(*Source*: Spedding and Holmes[2])

The location or 'where' code. The third part of the code deals with 'where', i.e. the location of the problem. Data on location can be helpful to the contractor as well as the maintenance manager. The location code may identify the development, the building, the floor level, an actual room or space and a specific service or duct; the combinations are numerous. Table 8.2 shows a typical coding frame for location.

Table 8.2 Location code

Development	Block	Level	Space	Element
0001	001	00 Basement	01	01 Tank
0002	005	01 Ground floor	03	02 Floor
0003	010	02 1st floor	05	03 Wall
0003	011	03 2nd floor	02	04 Ceiling
0004	002	01 Ground floor	04	05 Duct No. 1
0004	002	01 Ground floor	04	06 Duct No. 2

(*Source*: Spedding and Holmes[2])

Reason code. The fourth part of the code deals with the reason for the work being carried out; this provides the 'why' data. This is particularly valuable for tracking various aspects of maintenance with a view to changing design or specification. For example, the use of this code would be very useful for logging storm damage, or blocked drains, but may prove less valuable for recording reasons such as 'vandalism' (due to the fact that there is a sensitivity about the term and in many cases it is difficult for surveyors to allocate the reason).

After testing the reason code over a period of 3 months, with six surveyors, the research team at Bristol decided that the data acquired did not justify the amount of time spent in recording it – most of the work was being logged as 'fair wear and tear'. Feedback on the 'reason for maintenance' has to be justified by the quality of the data and the likely significance of the analysis. Table 8.3 shows a typical framework for a reason code.

Table 8.3 Reason code

Level 1 (budget)		Level 2 (reason)		Level 3 (result)	
1	Response maintenance	1	Fair wear and tear	1	Malfunction
2	Planned maintenance	2	Vandalism	2	Blockage
3	Cyclical maintenance	3	Storm damage	3	Breakage
4	Annual maintenance	4	Breakdown	4	Insecure
5	Minor works	5	Design fault	5	Dangerous

(*Source*: Spedding and Holmes[3])

In Table 8.3 the code is taken to three levels of detail, the first level dealing with the type of maintenance, the second with the broad reason for the repair and the third indicating the result. The code is valuable for tracking the nature of the failures; it also underpins the decision-making process when seeking new specifications.

The final code for response maintenance is the priority code or 'when' code. With the exception of emergency work, which should be carried out the same day as the reported fault, the priority code will consist of four or five categories, ranging from 3 days to one month. If recorded on computer the data can be used to monitor customer satisfaction and management procedures; the data also serve as a performance indicator for customer satisfaction, where the actual percentage of jobs completed on time can be analysed.

In all the above cases the quality of data depends on orders being checked after the work has been completed to ensure that *actual* work is recorded, together with costs, reasons and date completed.

IT in response maintenance
Most response maintenance is processed through a computer, which allows orders to be checked at any stage of the process. The first stage in the process is the work-ordering stage, the final stage is the invoicing or confirmation stage. When ordering work the maintenance clerk selects the various codes from a menu-driven program and a total code is generated for each order. Data from the first stage, the work-ordering stage, are useful for management control purposes, and for customer liaison, but not for analysis of defects; this is because much of the work actually carried out often varies from the work ordered. When the invoice arrives the actual work done can be checked and the correct coding allocated to the work actually carried out.

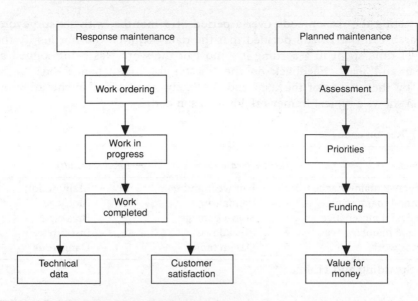

Figure 8.5 Maintenance processes

So far this chapter has dealt with the codes and activities relating to a specific element or component. However, in practice, the order would also have other codes, e.g. district or area, building type or funding account. Many of these codes can be default codes, generated automatically from the address, or from some other aspect of the coding frame. When the invoice is received, and this should be in a format which allows easy data entry, the clerk will check the work done and, if necessary, run through the code menu to change the work code. The cost is then entered, which completes the record. Part of Figure 8.5 shows the response maintenance process.

Programmed maintenance

Programmed maintenance consists of 'condition dependent' and 'condition-independent' work. Condition-dependent work involves inspections of buildings and services to assess the need and the priority of the work, whereas condition-independent work consists of cyclical and other work which is carried out irrespective of the condition of the element or components; this would include health and safety work. Figure 8.5 shows the planned maintenance process; this is expanded in Figure 8.6.

In the case of condition-dependent work an inspection is normally undertaken, depending on the nature of the stock involved. For large, or unique buildings, a survey has to be carried out on each building. With houses, which may have large numbers of similar construction, a sample of the stock can be taken. Cost-effective programmed maintenance work has to be assessed and prioritised, and this is now discussed.

144

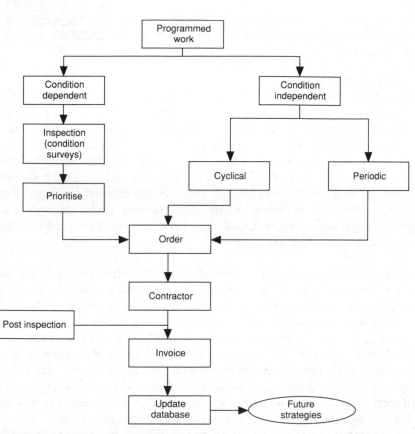

Figure 8.6 Programmed maintenance

Assessing the work required

Condition-independent maintenance is programmed work that is ordered irrespective of the condition of the elements or component. A typical example would be the servicing of gas boilers, which would receive attention annually irrespective of the amount of use. Such maintenance is driven by health and safety factors; the work may be contracted out to a specialist on a term contract. A further example of condition-independent maintenance would be cyclical painting – this is normally driven by policy and may be executed every 4, 5, or more years. The painting cycle is flexible and experience has shown that such work is sometimes used as a budget modifier; towards the end of a financial year the maintenance budget may be overspent and the remaining painting contracts can be held over until the following financial year.

Condition-independent items of maintenance are normally prioritised by policy, health and safety requirements, or some other driving force. A condition appraisal is not usually appropriate. Conversely, condition-dependent maintenance is based on some kind of inspection or survey. The process usually includes a mechanism for indicating the priority of the work; with the use of computers this can be achieved by adopting a point system or weighting factor. The most common method of assessing work is the condition survey; this is now discussed.

Condition surveys

To establish the stock condition a systematic survey must be carried out. Ideally, this should be repeated on a cyclical basis, on a 4- or 5-year cycle. Infrequent inspection leads to the dilapidation of buildings and the attendant problems that often ensue with neglected stock. Frequent inspection can be both costly and unnecessary. The correct inspection interval depends on the nature and use of the stock. It might be said, therefore, that the cost-effective interval for condition surveys is the same as the interval for 'repairs prior to painting' (RPTP), in other words the painting cycle interval. However, experience has indicated that condition surveys should be kept separate from the inspection of RPTP work.

Standardised condition surveys. Depending on the building type, e.g. housing, schools, a sample method may be all that is necessary to obtain a clear picture of the general state of the stock; this is explained in detail later. Having determined the sample size the next objective is to asses the condition of each element. This can be done in various ways. Damen[4] expressed the options as 'direct' and 'indirect' measures; he described the direct method as one of measuring the 'remaining' performance of an element, or component. However, he concludes that such a measure was difficult to assess. The 'indirect' measure is a measure of the manifest or latent defect in a component – this too, as an assessment technique, is not without problems.

An alternative method of assessment, offered by Damen, is called the 'defectscore'. In this method of assessment a kind of value analysis is undertaken which embraces various factors of the maintenance problem, such as gravity, intensity, extent, cause, place or location, etc. The 'defectscore' is then linked with a condition score and from that a proportional cost is produced. The conclusion reached from the development of such techniques is that objective inspection procedures are necessary and possible. The question which remains unanswered is whether such techniques are cost-effective in comparison with other simple methods.

On the other end of the assessment scale is the 'single' survey. These surveys may not be cost-effective for two reasons. First, the data collected are only of value if funds are available to carry out all the disrepair work. If funds are not available, and this is often the case, then the data lose value in terms of accuracy after the first year. Second, data for medium or long-term planning, and for cost predictions, have to be updated on a regular basis. Without this updating facility the data are not representative of the real condition of the stock.

Condition assessment

With assessment that requires surveyors to indicate the level of disrepair, or the remaining life of an element, there is a problem, namely, 'subjectivity in assessment'. If the condition of an element is ranked from 1 to 5 (poor to excellent) how is 'poor' or 'excellent' defined? It is necessary to produce some measurable criteria that will make the assessment objective. This can be done by preparing a schedule that defines the level of deterioration for each major element. For example, for an element to be in condition 1, or condition 5, it must fall into a specific state of repair. In the case of roof covering in condition 1 it may be stated that over half the roof covering is in need of refixing, or that one-third of the roof covering is showing signs of exfoliation. Clearly, there is a need to provide objective assessment guidelines for the surveyors involved.

A cost-effective methodology – grading the stock. Because of the cyclical nature of cost-effective assessment the first task is to divide the stock into groups, which allows a proportion of the stock to be surveyed each year. As stated above, this is often done to match the painting cycle – a 5- or 6-year cycle. In most cases such initial grouping can be done from the experience of the property manager.

However, if the overall state of condition is not known a preliminary survey can be carried out by merely driving around the properties and grading them on a simple scale as follows: ① 2 3 4 5 6 – this would indicate a property being selected for a survey in the first year. Alternatively, the initial sample can be

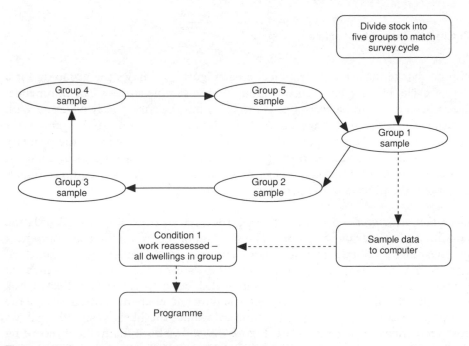

Figure 8.7 Grouping of stock for condition survey

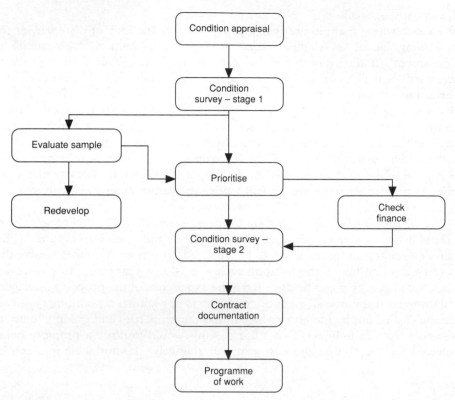

Figure 8.8 Assessment of need

chosen by age, or even geographical area. Figure 8.7 shows the grouping for a 5-year cycle. Having achieved this grouping the sample surveys can commence. It has been found to be cost-effective to carry out the survey in two stages. With housing stock the first stage covers only a sample in each of the groups, or sectors; usually a 10 per cent sample is sufficient. Each element in the property is assessed in terms of need during the next cycle, i.e. the next 5 or 6 years – at this stage no detail information is gathered since it may not be required. Figure 8.8 shows the process of the two-stage assessment.

Condition assessment – first stage. During the first visit the surveyor records the condition of the various elements. The method of recording the condition must be meaningful, simple to understand and quick to implement. A practical approach is to estimate the year, from the date of the survey, in which an element is likely to need repair or renewal. The surveyor simply ticks a box indicating the likely year against each significant element. Alternatively, the estimated cost of the work can be entered against the likely year – this allows cost predictions to be carried out. Figure 8.9 shows both methods of recording the condition of an element. This type of survey gives appraisal information

148

2.0 External work Description	Material	Condition							
		R	S	1	2	3	4	5	10
2.1 Roof (gable/hipped/flat)	Slate			✓					
2.2 Ridge tiles				✓					
2.3 Hip tiles				✓					
2.4 Chimney structure					✓				
2.5 Chimney render	—								
2.6 Chimney pointing					✓				
2.7 Chimney flashings						✓			
2.8 Other flashings						✓			
2.9 Fascias and bargeboards							✓		
2.10 Gutters (OG, HR, BOX)	HR			✓					
2.11 RW pipes				✓					
2.12 Walls – structure							✓		
2.13 Walls – pointing							✓		
2.14 Walls – ext finish/cladding	—								
2.15 Windows					✓				
2.16 Window sill (ext)					✓				
2.17 Doors					✓				
2.18 Porches	—								
2.19 Canopy structure	—								
2.20 Canopy covering	—								

All properties Actual years ➤	92	93	94	95	96	97	98	99	00	01+
External work	0	1	2	3	4	5	6	7	8	9–12
101 Roof structure										
102 Coverings										3000
103 Verges/~~parapets~~										
~~104 Chimney~~										
105 Flashings										
106 Fascias, bargeboards										
107 Gutters/RW pipes					300					
108 Walls structure										
109 Walls pointing										
110 Wall finish										
111 Windows							1200			
112 Sills										
113 Entrance doors			400							
~~114 Porches/canopies~~										
~~115 External stairs~~										
~~116 Balconies~~										
~~117 Soil vent pipes~~										
118 Outbuildings			2500	Replace 'Big six' asbestos sheeting to garages						
119 Boundary walls										
~~120 Fencing/Gates~~										
121 Paths/pavings										
122 Service road										

Figure 8.9 Methods of recording condition data

		Years	5	10	15	20	25	30	35	40	45	50	55	60	
	Sinking fund provision based on elemental life-span							DJM/TE/RH, UWE Bristol							
External elements	Roof structure														
	Coverings									3300					
	Fascias etc							350						350	
	RW goods				200			200			200			200	
	Chimney					50				50				50	
	Point/ren									2000					
	Windows					3000				3000				3000	
	Doors frame					250				250				250	
	Doors ext			200		200		200		200		200		200	
	Frames				300			300			300			300	
Internal elements	Stairs													500	
	Plaster														
	K/Units				1000			1000			1000			1000	
	Doors int						500					500			
	Ironmongery						100					100			
	Floor covers			400		400		400		400		400		400	
Services	Rads						800					800			
	Boiler					900				900				900	
	Thermostats			50		50		50		50		50		50	
	Pumps and valves				300			300			300			300	
	Bath					800				800				800	
	Immersion				60			60			60			60	
	Pipes								250						
	Valves and taps				150			150			150			150	
	Wastes				100			100			100			100	
	Sockets				200			200			200			200	
	Wiring							1000						1000	
	Insulation							150						150	
	Extract			250		250		250		250		250		250	
Ex works	Paving									400					
	Gates				500			500			500			500	
	Years		5	10	15	20	25	30	35	40	45	50	55	60	Total
	Total		0	900	2810	5900	1400	5210	250	11600	2810	2300	0	1010	£43,890
Annuity growth p.a.	2%														
			610	610	610	610	610	610	610	610	610	610	610	610	
			3174	5779	6745	4772	6988	5680	9195	1727	2271	3382	6908	91	

Figure 8.10 Typical life-span and associated costs spreadsheet

from which long-term strategies can be developed, and it also safeguards against unnecessary details being collected. From this sampling process sufficient detail can be obtained to indicate the financial implications of the next programme. This simple method of recording speeds the whole operation up and in a short time the state of the whole stock is established. Having completed the first stage those properties which have elements or components requiring attention in the first year are then revisited, to assess the detail of the elements or components which require attention in the next programme of work – this is known as the second stage of the survey.

Condition assessment – second stage. A second survey is carried out on those elements assessed as being 'category 1' elements, i.e. those elements which require attention in the first year of the programme. The second assessment will provide the quantity and other details necessary for preparing contract documentation. It might be said that a two-stage assessment is a time-consuming strategy but in the case of housing only a sample will have been visited during the first stage and only category 1 work will be assessed in detail. This simplistic method of assessment has been tested on social housing and has been found to be easy to use and cost-effective in terms of staff time. From the first-stage data a 5-year strategy can be developed and the second-stage assessment gives the necessary detail to complete the contract documentation. The simple computer program, which handles the first-stage data, updates all the assessments according to the date the survey was carried out.

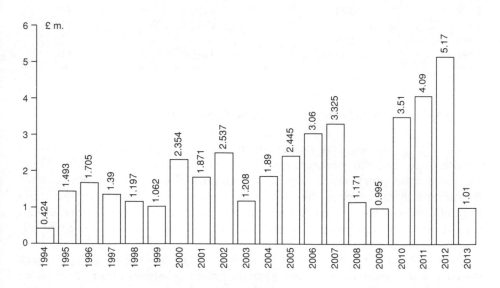

Figure 8.11 Renewal predictions over a 20-year period (*after* Holmes and Marshall[5])

Planning and budgeting

From the two-stage model of data collection a simple spreadsheet can be used to assist decision-making for forward planning and budgeting. Figure 8.10 shows a typical spreadsheet with the life-spans and the associated cost data. The actual life spans can be refined from the condition surveys and the average cost of jobs can be updated to suit the particular organisation.

Table 8.4 indicates the stock age profile for a housing association. These data, together with the data from Figure 8.10, allow cost predictions to be made for budgeting purposes. The cost prediction for the stock over 20 years is shown in Figure 8.11. It will be appreciated that in seeking to plan the financial implications of the predictions in Figure 8.11 some 'smoothing' of activities may be necessary. This may cause some jobs to be brought forward or to be postponed and 'patched' until the finances are available.

Table 8.4 Stock profile for a typical housing association

Year	Units	Year	Units
1969	10	1982	252
1970	69	1983	152
1971	32	1984	273
1972	2	1985	145
1973	0	1986	69
1974	14	1987	125
1975	117	1988	42
1976	208	1989	58
1977	96	1990	238
1978	124	1991	489
1979	29	1992	616
1980	205	1993	22
1981	132	Total	3519

Information technology in built asset management

Information technology has greatly enhanced the planning and organisation of maintenance. Software packages have been developed for most activities. There are three main areas which require IT support; the first for handling work recording and monitoring, the second for condition assessment analysis, and the third for cost predictions. Within these areas a range of linked programmes can be used to supplement the process; for example, an asset register will greatly help with work ordering.

Most building professionals are in favour of the concept of data feedback systems from maintenance management, where designers can learn from performance trends and failure rates. However, for the most part the concept has remained a theory and little has been done in the past 20 years to encourage the systematic gathering of data necessary for enhancing the design process. The same is true in the realm of housing management; many maintenance and renewal decisions are made without the support of cost trends or failure profiles. Little has been done to monitor maintenance activities with a view to producing cost-effective data acquisition.

The nature of the data captured depends on the model used for maintenance management. Basic data are required to improve maintenance strategies, and to support the financing of maintenance; these include data for life-span calculations[6] and cost-in-use exercises.

Performance indicators

Performance indicators are an essential feature of client satisfaction and have been referred to in Chapter 2. In terms of housing maintenance, indicators may include the following: time taken to complete the work, quality of the work, attitude and tidiness of the workforce and the cost of the work; such data can be collected by means of reply cards from the tenants. However, much of the data can be retrieved from the computer, from the response maintenance files and data on quality of work can also be retrieved from the post-inspection cards. In built asset management these indicators include a number of issues, such as the performance of elements and components, performance of contractors and DLOs, the effectiveness of management and client satisfaction.

Performance indicators can be expressed in various ways, e.g. in terms of time, cost, value for money, output, satisfaction and function. For the most part many of these indicators are related to short-term appraisal. For longer-term appraisal data are required on quality, standards, life-span and other criteria which affect life-cycle costing (LCC) and renewal policy. It follows, therefore, that data acquisition should be preceded by a review of data requirements. The first question to be asked might be: 'What management functions are we seeking to appraise?' The second question might be: 'What data are required to help in the appraisal of these management functions?' Having answered these two primary questions the data acquisition process can be addressed.

Data acquisition process

The process of data acquisition depends on a range of factors such as the urgency of the appraisal, the nature of the indicator (whether global or specific), the purpose of the analysis, the flexibility of the coding system, the reporting facility and the validity of imported data. In many cases synthetic data, drawn from parallel studies, and manufacturers' data, can be used and this is often the case with LCC exercises. In some cases schedules can be used, and in other cases sampling techniques can be applied. However, in the medium to long term there is a need to set up a data capturing mechanism for the specific stock in question.

Finance and taxation

The decision to repair or replace will be influenced by available finance. Major repairs can be predicted over a 30 or 60-year period using data similar to those shown in Figure 8.10. The decision to capitalise the major repairs at certain periods depends on the funding arrangement in the organisation. Taxation may also play an important part. Replacement costs may be offset by tax allowances and this should be taken into account when preparing the financial support for the programme.

References

1. Holmes R, Mellor P 1985 *Coding for building maintenance* CIOB, Technical Paper No 47
2. Spedding A, Holmes R 1992 *Review of existing coding and related structure and processes in the maintenance division of the Hong Kong Housing Authority*
3. Spedding A, Holmes R 1988 *Cost-effectiveness of building maintenance in county authorities* SERC Report GR/C/78483
4. Damen AAJ 1988 Meaningless and meaningful maintenance planning *Proc. CIB W70 Seminar*, Department of Building, Heriot-Watt University, Edinburgh, September
5. Holmes R, Marshall D 1993 Condition surveys and predictive modelling. Internal report, Facilities Management Research Unit, University of the West of England, Bristol
6. Published data on the life span of materials and components, such as the HAPM *Component life manual* and the NBA publication on maintenance cycles

Chapter 9

Documentation and cost-effective management of property

Alan Spedding

Introduction

This chapter links with the previous chapter in that it is intended to draw the attention of the reader to the documentation which the facilities manager should prepare in order to monitor the costs of operating the property. The nature of such documentation varies widely between different organisations, but this chapter deals with the main characteristics of costs which need to be reported. Further details on legal aspects of acquisitions and disposal of property and leases are contained in Chapter 4, and consideration of space standards and the like is contained in Chapter 5.

Many organisations operate large buildings or large stocks of property for the purposes of their core business. Studies in the USA and in the UK have shown that a large proportion of such enterprises do not have relatively fundamental data on their property readily available. This problem was not confined to the private sector, and the UK Audit Commission expressed surprise that only about half of public sector authorities studied allocated property operating costs under a limited number of headings to individual properties.[1]

There would be little need for cost-effective management of property if the costs incurred were very small related to the organisation's other operating costs, and if the property had little effect on the core business and the people who use the property. However, this is not usually the case, particularly where provision of accommodation for people is a significant factor in the business activity. The principles of cost-effective management of property are not complex, but the practice varies in complexity according to the need to control cost and performance.

One can suggest that for each building cost centre, such as an element or major component, there is an optimum between cost and performance in use, both of which have practical limits. Figure 9.1 illustrates this concept and

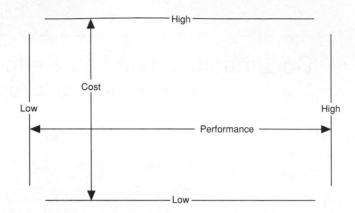

Figure 9.1 Cost performance relationships

indicates that the optimum will lie within the limits represented by the highest and lowest values of each. Naturally, measures of performance will vary between elements, and also the optimum for the whole property may not be simply the sum of the optima for the cost centres. Thus the task of the facilities manager is to try to establish a reasonable balance of cost and performance, while recognising that many elements will interact with others in the property.

If an optimum is selected say for cleaning expenditure, and we call this 0 in Figure 9.2, then it can be seen that increased spending on cleaning may produce an increase in performance at first, say to point 1, but further increases in spending will not produce proportionate increases in performance, and may actually cause other costs to rise in some cases. Similarly a decrease in spending say to point 2, will begin to lower performance, and, in many cases, the graph might show that an attempt to make cost savings causes an unacceptable level of performance to be reached very quickly. This suggests that in many cost centres there may be an area of tolerance which may vary according to money available, and standards envisaged, and that the facilities manager should not always try to achieve lowest cost, particularly in these cost centres which affect others.

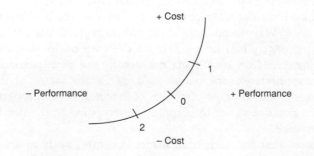

Figure 9.2 Optimum cost and performance

156

Of course, many cost centres will not respond as suggested in Figure 9.2, because some items of expenditure will rise in steps rather than as a curve, and also because our ability to measure performance in some areas may be underdeveloped, particularly in relation to subjective assessment. Nevertheless, we suggest that reports on significant cost centres are needed in order to put the monitoring of performance into a useful framework for management purposes.

However, the studies noted above suggest that many organisations do not have enough information to facilitate effective control of their property. Precisely which data are required in what form will depend upon the needs of the organisation, and the return which the organisation hopes to achieve from the facilities management system. Thus, while some aspects of data and documentation are discussed below, it must always be remembered that the acquisition, storage, retrieval and interpretation of data consume staff time and involve use of equipment and space. It is important, therefore, to match the level of data gathering and documentation to the essentials required for cost-effective management.

Running costs

If we look at annual running costs of buildings we need to be sure of the broad characteristics of the stock. For instance, the pie chart in Figure 9.3 shows percentages of average annual costs of local authority property which will be predominantly non-air-conditioned schools. Such broad-brush charts may, over a period of years, help to draw attention to trends, but facilities managers will wish to compare individual buildings at a finer level of detail. This will require information on the nature of the asset and data which can highlight its cost efficiency.

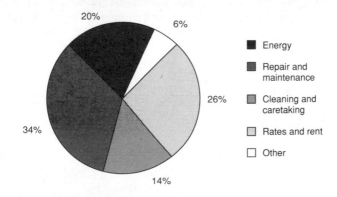

Figure 9.3 Building related costs (*source*: Audit commission/SCALA)

157

For the purposes of this chapter, which deals with the property, it is suggested that data are required on the following:

- asset registers
- condition registers
- maintenance and repair, improvements and alterations
- operating costs, including rent and rates

Such data will normally be stored on computer and should be coded at an appropriate level using a system which allows for data coordination[2] and for linked assessment of performance. A brief synopsis of ancillary services is included later in this section in order to complete the picture and is further discussed in chapter 11.

Asset register

The asset register forms the backbone of a property data system in that it should list all of the physical attributes of the stock at a level which not only serves its own purpose, but also interlocks with other data on cost and use factors. All of these data relate to the expectations of performance built into the property initially, and also as maintained and operated, and a simplified view of the property cost relationship via the asset register is shown in Figure 9.4. Asset registers might only record salient facts such as address of the property, its type, leasing or purchase details, total floor area, department funding or occupying the property and a reference number, such as in an estate management 'terrier'.

While this may appear to be elementary it is common to find that even a coordinated and comprehensive list of this type is not available to all of the departments or sections of an organisation which deal with their property. In some cases different departments may have different reference numbers for a property or group of properties and it is not unusual for such reference

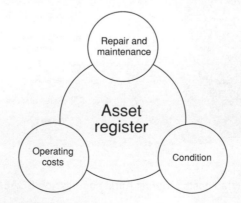

Figure 9.4 Concept of data relationships

numbers to be allocated on a different basis. As an example, three buildings, A, B and C on one estate might be grouped for estate management purposes under one reference for A and B because they are self-occupied blocks and C has a separate reference because it is a building which is leased to a client. However, the facilities manager might wish each to have an individual reference so that cost and performance for each building may be compared. Similarly, a finer level of referencing will be necessary if parts of buildings are leased to different clients. This suggests that the asset register and its parts need to be designed and referenced to allow for provision of different levels of detail should this become necessary.

It is usually the case that relatively static data are the first requirement, and these data may be collected at different levels of detail. In outline, one would expect to see:

1. Site information, location, tenure, area, major legal and physical factors pertaining to its use.
2. Building information, location on site and relationship to other buildings on site, gross/net floor areas, physical morphology, specification of major constructional elements, year and type of original construction, special conditions pertaining to use.
3. Referencing systems and maps or plans, including 'as built' drawings and location of external service installations.

Although the principles of an asset register are universal, the detail to be provided will vary according to the function and intensity of management control. As an example, the Department of Education and Science published a paper on the topic for school buildings.[3]

The extent to which further detail is incorporated will vary according to need, but the building information might give overall areas, numbers and characteristics of major building elements, such as external walls, roof and service installations. This information might be further subdivided so that, for example, service outlets or types of electric light fittings are identified within each area of the building together with the age of component and manufacturer's names. If the referencing or coding system is hierarchical in nature it is likely to be the most suitable for recording such data. An example of such a system was given in Figure 8.3 and, together with location data can provide a potentially powerful management tool. For example, if a particular component is found to be failing at a particular age, the data may be interrogated to identify how many similar components are installed in which location, and remedial action may be planned. Additionally, different areas of the building might be identified with different users or lessees and other user capacity data such as workstations, seating places and the like may be incorporated.

Data may be held in a manual card-indexed or microfiched form, and site and building drawings may also be held in plan chests or microfiched.

However, while it is not essential for asset registers to be computerised it is a convenient way of holding data. Data may be held at different levels and only accessed by staff of predetermined seniority levels if so desired, and similarly only people with particular job functions may be allowed to alter or update information. If the system is linked to a computer-aided draughting package with associated data base, or to a geographical information system package, then drawn information can be easily linked to descriptive and numerical data. Naturally a good computer-aided facilities management (CAFM) package may provide all of the required functions, plus other useful facets. Ideally information about the building should be held in such a way that the system can be interrogated from site level down through individual blocks or sections of the building to particular features. Thus the users might ask the system to display data on the number and location of fire doors, or home in on a particular referenced feature and list its constructional characteristics.

Obviously the length and complexity of the asset register will depend upon management's view of the uses of such records. If the data are arranged in pages, then a typical page may be as illustrated in Figure 9.5. In this example a three-digit elemental coding system based on that illustrated in Figure 8.3 has been assumed and the latest update is the first quarter of 1994. The tenant reference will allow for different tenants in different blocks or levels to be located. The sub-element windows is coded 420 and is part of the main element SFIF (structural fixings and internal finishes). Location may be subdivided into levels and also into position, which could be coded by face of building. There are two construction references, which are type of material and/or manufacturer plus form which refers to the shape or constructional type, such as horizontally hinged. The quantity may be expressed in area, length, number or other appropriate units. The last three columns are shown as containing life cycle data, such as date of renewal if different from age of

Property Name			Head Office		A/R Pag		0037		Update		194
Property Ref			003		Record begins		0031		Ends		0045
Tenant	002		Building/block No		005		Date Const		175		
Element			Locn		Const		Quant		Life		
Main	Sub	Code	Level	Posn	Type	Form	Area	Nr	Ren	PLS	RL
SFIF	WDW	420	01	–	36	3	–	26	–	30	11
			02	–	34	3	–	22	92	30	28

Figure 9.5 Typical coded property asset register

building, planned life span and remaining life based on time elapsed which is automatically updated.

As always, the level of detail to be provided must be planned with its eventual use in mind, and management must remember that accurate data cost money, to provide, input into the system and keep up to date. An assessment of which data might be needed for management purposes and their frequency of use might be undertaken although there will always be deficiencies in an economical system. Thus, while there are some excellent computer-based packages related to, for instance, cable management, it is up to management to visualise how often spaces will be changed and whether simple drawn information, plus colour-coding and labelling of the cables *in situ* is sufficient for future purposes.

Whether or not the asset register is relatively simple or complex, the objective is to quickly obtain details of the property and to associate other data with that property in a coordinated manner.

Condition register

There are different uses for a condition register, and the intended use will affect the type of condition survey employed and the format in which the data are presented. Typical examples of the purpose of condition registers are:

1. To record condition at a particular time:
    (a) as a basis of an agreement when handing over property
    (b) in order to satisfy health and safety, or other requirements
    (c) in order to provide a basis for establishing a value of the stock, possibly in comparison with a notional new-build cost
    (d) to estimate remaining life of elements and components
2. To provide the basis for planned repairs and maintenance, and related budgetary calculations.
3. To provide a record of condition which can be updated so as to assess periodically the effectiveness of the property maintenance policy.
4. A mixture of the above.

The condition register is likely to be more dynamic than the asset register, because any repairs and maintenance, or any programmes of refurbishment or improvement will change the condition of the asset, even if the nature of the asset is unchanged. An example might be that of replacing old timber windows with new timber windows of a similar type from the same manufacturer. In such a case the only requirement might be to update the remaining life of the components, and to change the condition assessment to 'as new'.

The author, however, has examined condition registers which were extensive and carefully undertaken, but which were only used for a single, limited purpose, such as (1c) above. In a typical case the new build cost of each property was estimated and broken down into constructional elements in a similar manner to Figure 9.5. An extensive condition survey was undertaken and the condition of each element was assessed as a percentage of brand new. Thus a 50 per cent condition, for instance, was assumed to be worth 50 per cent of its new cost and so a total 'value' for all of the stock related to 'new' value was summated. This exercise produced a snapshot of the condition of a large stock of buildings expressed in comparative monetary terms. However, the method of evaluation did not provide a management tool to help with future upkeep of the stock. Although it is not suggested that this exercise was cost-effective, it was also designed to highlight the lower 'value' properties, which were then considered for refurbishment or disposal.

In many cases, and particularly as in (1) above, the condition register may simply be an extra set of records on the asset register. As an example, the state of the asset may be recorded to provide a linked condition register. The condition information might be recorded in the previous example of an asset register by adding (or substituting) columns which record date of inspection, actual condition and reassessed remaining life as Figure 9.6.

Obviously if the condition survey is to be repeated periodically then the system employed for recording data should allow for easy updating as repair and maintenance work is undertaken, or as condition deteriorates. In the case of condition surveys, or tests which are required as a result of legislation, then these must be planned and recorded in accordance with predetermined schedules. In cases such as in (2) and (3) above, the condition register may be produced in different ways, as discussed in Chapter 8, and a computerised facilities management system might be used which carries data in a different format. Much will depend upon the extent of the stock, the financial and professional staff resources which are available and the organisation's view of what the condition should be. If an alphabetical or numerical scale is used to record condition, say 1 to 5 (poor to excellent) then is the organisation aiming to have all properties and constructional elements and components at least average, say condition 3? Alternatively are they aiming for condition 5? If there is a target level, then the condition survey process should lead to management action to ensure that repairs are done so that the building condition is brought to that target level.

Where money is not available to undertake all of the desirable work, the computerised condition register can be called upon to highlight all substandard

Condition		
Date	Cond	R.L.
293	4	15

Figure 9.6 Addition to asset register to code condition data

items and the asset register will note those which are approaching a critical age, so that management may monitor deterioration.

It is possible to envisage that a link between records of work done, processed through a computerised work ordering and accounting program, might automatically update the condition register. One might question whether such a system could be effective if automatic, but a procedure for updating condition records as work is completed is needed even if the system is not completely automatic. Such condition records, when examined in conjunction with records of money actually spent on the upkeep of the property, will provide a picture of the cost-effectiveness of policy, and can also enable comparisons to be made between buildings possibly of different age or constructional type.

Costs of maintenance and repair, improvements and alterations

It is difficult to separate maintenance and repair costs from those related to improvements and alterations, because many repairs include an element of improvement, such as when a computerised automatic control is used to replace a defective and obsolete manual control in engineering services. However, the British Standards[4,5] remind us that maintenance is concerned with maintaining performance and that repair is to restore an item to an acceptable condition. Thus it is sensible to try to keep to these definitions in order to separate the virtually unavoidable costs of operating the building from other policy-led costs. In this way cost comparisons may be made and related broadly to other running costs.

Such costs need to be summarised into categories in order that management may anticipate the need for future spending and can check actual against forecast cash flows. The facilities manager has to undertake such forecasts, but can expect little help from purely historical cost records. Some historical records will be useful where work has to be done at regular intervals and where directly employed staff, such as services engineers, are to be costed to the maintenance headings. In the case of service installations in particular, programmes of preventive maintenance will be planned and it is likely that other elements will need some regular servicing. However, it is not necessarily the case that preventive maintenance for all elements saves money and a balance needs to be struck. Such preventive maintenance, particularly that required by legislation, will be the subject of regular report to management. What is needed is a good condition inspection regime linked to an assessment of probability of failure based on past cost records which identify weaknesses in the stock. Obviously, where a number of similar properties are being managed it is more likely that some potential weaknesses may be identified, than where complex individual, or idiosyncratic, buildings are being managed. It must also be remembered that not only building, but external works, maintenance costs need to be monitored, and allocated to headings such as car parking, landscaping, recreation and the like.

In a similar manner to human pathology we can postulate probable maximum and minimum life-spans of elements and components together with reasonable averages and can build in expectations of necessary maintenance. However, the almost unique nature of each building means that cost forecasts and records of actual expenditure usually do not coincide.

Coding systems for maintenance work may be detailed, as indicated in Chapter 8 and such detail will be conveniently recorded and classified on the basis of a computerised ordering system. In terms of numbers of orders, much maintenance work consists of relatively small items which can be coded to elements or subelements, such as doors, lighting, plumbing and the like. The associated costs can be summarised and monitored on an average annual cost basis, while planned and preventive maintenance can clearly be more reliably forecast, coded and allocated to elemental headings.

However, there remain the large planned replacement jobs, or the large unplanned jobs due to unexpected failures which need coding for record purposes. Where these cut across elemental boundaries they might be coded under the dominant element of failure and given a policy or 'special project' designatory additional code. In this way the larger failures and the larger policy-related work can be monitored, perhaps over a period of years, and budgets adjusted accordingly.

Improvements and alterations are not really part of the maintenance budget because they will have been ordered as a result of separate management policy decisions which the facilities manager will have translated into operational terms. They will be undertaken in order to provide for new and different space uses, to comply with new legislation, or in response to changing workplace standards and the like. Consequently such work will require changes to the asset registers which will probably also cut across a number of elemental and space utilisation records. Costs of such work could be allocated between a number of elemental groupings, but this is not likely to be of any value to management processes. It is likely to be more sensible if costs are allocated to the dominant elemental group where identifiable, or a special project code, and explained by coding to a suitable category from a reason code such as indicated in Table 8.3. A typical example might be repartitioning or other costs caused by moves of staff or 'churn' and recorded under a policy heading of 'change of use' which would allow management to request reports on total costs of all changes of use in the stock.

The extent of implementation of elemental, reason and related codes will depend upon the uses which management foresee for such data. For instance, it will be important in a stock of multi-storey high-rise properties to record the detail of component breakdown in lift mechanisms, together with reason codes, and response times of lift engineers to emergency call-out. However, it is unlikely that a fine level of detail will be needed in most other elemental repairs. Reports may therefore be requested in detail for some elements but not for others, so codes may not necessarily be employed at the same detailed level across all of the elements.

The costs of repairs and maintenance represent an area of budgets where management may choose to make savings by deferring work or reducing standards. In the case of many other costs involved in operating buildings, management may not realise how these can interact with the condition of the building. Lack of maintenance to windows, for example, might result in heat loss and higher fuel bills, or poor upkeep of internal finishes may create problems of cleaning, possibly resulting in lack of care or vandalism to the building. Therefore, maintenance levels must be kept in mind when looking at the other costs of operating buildings.

Operating costs

The term 'operating costs' is intended to mean costs of keeping a building operational. It is not intended to include staffing and management costs which are related to the core business function, including computing, fax, communications, catering services and the like. However, building provision for these may be included under the asset register and the relevant elemental maintenance records. Operating costs may include:

- energy costs
- water and waste/rubbish disposal
- insurances
- rent and rates
- cleaning
- facilities management charges
- ancillary services and amenities

Energy costs

Costs of energy, such as used for heating and lighting purposes, can be assessed from details of specifications and manufacturers' data, related to expected performance and use factors under various operating conditions. The actual expenditure on energy can be monitored and any significant divergences can be investigated. It is worth while checking the energy efficiency of the property if there is any doubt and the Department of the Environment's Energy Efficiency Office may give some assistance with consultancy on this topic. It may be possible to zone areas of a property to compare costs incurred by different departments, but this is not usually practicable particularly in older buildings. It is, however, interesting to keep energy costs under review and to compare them with costs from other similar properties, or averages from published information.[6] Energy costs can be subdivided by type of fuel and allocated to elemental headings where possible. Storage facilities for oil and solid fuel, as well as substations for electricity and gas storage or metering accommodation, will be allowed for in the asset register.

It is necessary also to account here for the staff who are employed to manage the service installations on a day-to-day basis, perhaps apportioning their time between this and any other duties, which they undertake. They will be required to sign that they have carried out their scheduled duties on a regular basis so that unnecessary damage, for instance due to unexpected frost, will not occur.

Facilities managers are likely to be unable to change the fabric of the building or the service installations except when significant refurbishment is being undertaken. Therefore control of energy costs needs to be undertaken on an active basis by ensuring that energy-saving responsibilities are allocated to staff, and recent studies indicate that considerable differences may be found between typical offices and those which conform to good practice.[7] In practice, it is not impossible to find that energy costs in buildings are in excess of 50 per cent more than the minimum good practice total energy costs. While some air-conditioned buildings may use double the energy of some non-air-conditioned buildings, attention to economising in use of services generally is likely to be rewarding. For example, the boiler plant is often over-designed and higher levels of control and taking some boilers out of multi-boiler installations can be beneficial. The running hours of equipment and lighting are often poorly controlled and air-conditioning fans can be wasteful. Natural lighting may be adequate in many offices for parts of the year, and replacing older installations with modern lamps and reflectors can show useful savings. Implementation of an energy management policy can be monitored and its success measured by the levels of consumption related to before and after comparisons, as well as by reference to other similar buildings.

Water and waste/rubbish disposal

Water supply may be covered by rates or metered and both water and disposal charges may be subject to negotiation, but should be monitored. Such records may give warning of undetected problems, such as where greatly increased water consumption results in the identification of a serious leak in the structure of a swimming pool.

Insurances

Insurances need to be carefully and economically managed, and the services of a disinterested broker or other professional adviser will usually easily be repaid. The adviser should be covered by professional indemnity insurance, and must be given all relevant information. The extent of the risk will need to be defined, particularly in the difference between owned and leased property. The coverage of the policy may affect other costs, such as maintenance and testing of boilers, sprinkler installations and other specified installations, and it is possible to take out an 'all risks' policy based on rebuilding costs, although the exact nature of the cover needs to be checked carefully. Facilities managers should check the effect of change of use, or occupation, of the property and should note that void property will affect insurance cover. Obviously a programme of regular inspection and upkeep of the property will be a useful factor in negotiating economical insurance conditions, and conversely if the value of the property has dropped below the cost of reinstatement then the insurance money may not cover full rebuilding particularly in a period of building cost escalation. In such cases a low specification replacement may be adequate and should be negotiated on. If the building is rendered a total loss, then the old structure will have to be demolished and cleared away, and the insurance should include such an eventuality. Inspections are also necessary in order to ensure that tenant's business practices do not affect the insurance.

In addition to building insurance the extent of contents insurance must be considered, and the risks clearly defined. It is not unusual for such insurance to be placed with insurers other than the building insurers particularly where terms of a lease place constraints on choice.

In cases where organisations own a large number of properties they may be selective as to whether to insure as the premium payments may be higher than the liabilities they expect to incur on an assessment of probable risk. Where other risks are insured, say in the case of lost revenue due to fire, then this should be counted as part of the core business costs.

Rent and rates

Rates for non-domestic properties are based on the rateable value of the property as assessed by valuation officers appointed by the Valuation Office modified by a nationally determined multiplier. The rateable value is related to the rent at which the property might be let, currently based on the 1988 value, if the tenant undertakes to pay all usual rates and taxes, repairs and insurances, and the like which are necessary to maintain the property at the rental level. A revaluation to be effective in April 1995 is already in preparation. Valuations may be made on a basis of evidence of rental levels for comparable properties, or on another basis depending upon the function of the property, such as an assessment of the effective capital value based on new-build, or related to receipts or profits expected from the operation of the property.

The facilities manager should note that empty properties are still liable for rates, although probably at half the occupied rates. There are specified revaluation years, and the facilities manager might seek the advice of a valuation expert in order to consider whether to appeal against an assessment, although there are conditions as to when and under which circumstances an appeal may be made.

Rents and covenants are referred to in the lease which is an agreement for a period of time often incorporating a review at specified intervals. Leases are commonly for 25 years with provision for rent reviews every 5 years, usually based on current market rents. Traditionally such reviews of rent are in an upward only direction, although there is in the current property market some resistance to this in newly negotiated leases. Covenants attached to the lease will refer to matters such as payment of rates by the occupier, internal or full repairing terms and insurances. Full repairing and insurance (FRI) terms are common and place these obligations on the occupier. Usually there is a specified timetable for rent reviews and the facilities manager must be aware of the procedures specified. Disputes may go to arbitration or to an expert for adjudication. It is worth while to have a clear view of the levels of rentals which may be considered reasonable in an area so that forecasts of future costs may be as accurate as possible. Where it is intended to make alterations to rented property the approval of the landlord will usually be required and the facilities manager should establish whether or not alterations might cause extra rent to be sought by the landlord. Alternatively, if improvements are to be made, will the landlord reimburse the tenant?

Of course, obligations to decorate at regular intervals and to repair are usually placed upon the tenant, who is usually required to relinquish the property in a state of good repair at the end of the tenancy. There is usually not a clear definition of the standard of repair expected, but the age of the property, location and other factors should be borne in mind when assessing what is reasonable. It is therefore prudent to have the property surveyed before leasing so that the condition is agreed. Any initial repairs to bring the property to good condition can then be negotiated. At the end of the tenancy a schedule of dilapidation is prepared if necessary by the landlord's agents and agreed with the tenant who then is obliged to undertake the necessary work.

Cleaning

Cleaning costs will consist of regular scheduled daily or other periodic tasks, both internal and external, plus other work related to particular needs. The schedules of cleaning must be specific to the surfaces involved and must be adhered to. While it is likely that cleaning costs will be allocated pro rata to space occupied, or charged as an overhead, there may be specific cleaning operations attributable to particular departments, which may be billed for the work. The facilities manager will need to set up a system for checking the quality of cleaning, whether done by in-house staff or contracted out, and the specialist cleaning of carpets and soft furnishings for instance is recognised to be of considerable importance in reducing 'sick building syndrome'. Also regular or periodic outside cleaning jobs to keep gutters, gullies, drains and the like operational must be scheduled. It is now common to see schedules in public areas, which may have to be signed by the cleaning staff every 2 hours, for instance. Such schedules may also give a telephone number for complaints to be logged.

Facilities management charges

These charges may be levied on each property as an overhead, or may be subsumed into general overheads. Facilities management staff and their space and equipment, the cost of the data system, CAFM and space planning will be charged here. Also the costs of acquisition and disposal of property may be included as well as relocations. Ancillary services and the contracts arrangements will be managed and costed by the facilities management department. It is possible to make a charge based upon the total costs allocated by area managed, but the principle should be that of ensuring that the cost of the facilities management department, or consultant, is subject to monitoring as is the case with other services.

Ancillary services and amenities

These may cover a spectrum of provision, such as:

- internal and external security
- lift attendants/commissionaire services
- telephone exchange and operators, and fax services
- porterage and mail collection and distribution
- sampling environmental quality and other health and safety aspects
- keeping toilet accommodation and staffrooms appropriately stocked
- refreshment service and servicing vending machines
- attending to plants and exhibited materials, signage and decorative features, both internal and external
- first aid service
- office equipment and furniture

Service charges

The comments noted above will apply to service charges and these will be payable under a leasing or tenancy arrangement for a building. There may be a problem where buildings are leased in that clear agreement is needed on standards for the rented space and the 'landlord's common parts' of the building so that there is compatibility with the organisation's required standards in their own property. Where a company occupies part of an office building, for example, the costs for common areas and for the occupier's space will be apportioned between the tenants according to the method agreed in the lease or tenancy document. This document will also record the cost heads under which charges will be made. Service charges are based on actual costs incurred and will be supported by invoices and receipts. Typical service charge headings are:

- energy costs
- insurances
- cleaning
- security

- repairs and maintenance of the building
- lift maintenance
- mechanical and electrical services
- management charges

Obviously rent, rates and taxes are payable and the facilities manager may have to keep track of costs of buildings owned by his organisation and others which are leased in whole or in part. Also, the ability to claim tax relief on items of expenditure out of revenue must be maximised.

Care must be taken when comparing one set of service charges with another, as the basis of calculation may be different. Usually, energy costs include electricity to the common parts of the building, such as foyers, staircases and general circulation space, as well as to building services plant as a whole. Gas or oil will also be that consumed by services plant and equipment. Insurances will usually cover the fabric of the building, property owner's liability and possibly loss of rent. Repairs and maintenance to the fabric of the building and services will be included, although maintenance and repairs to lifts, and mechanical and electrical services installations, may be charged separately from general repairs and maintenance, as indeed may maintenance to fire-fighting systems. In some cases a reserve fund contribution may be charged which is designed to provide for major replacements, such as heating plant, but the setting of such a charge in an equitable manner is a difficult process.

An interesting survey was undertaken into London city office service charges in 40 buildings in 1987.[8] The report indicated that a range of newer buildings were significantly more expensive to maintain per square foot than pre-1970 buildings, that service charges for buildings of over 20 storeys were more than double those for buildings of less than 10 storeys when expressed as cost per square foot and that maintenance charges per square foot for buildings over 150 000 square feet were over double those for smaller buildings. A summary of Savill's findings over the whole data base which included air-conditioned and non-air-conditioned properties is illustrated in Figure 9.7.

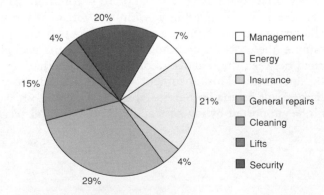

Figure 9.7 Office service charges (1987)

This figure cannot be compared directly with Figure 9.3 as a different cost base is employed, and because the service charges include the common parts of the building but not all running costs. When one examines the main conclusions, it is probable that the increased cost of maintaining the newer buildings, many of which are large, tall buildings, related substantially to the provision of air conditioning and its upkeep. With foresight, the report noted that maintenance costs were not an essential part of rental negotiations at that time, but that the situation of supply and demand in the City of London may well be different by the early 1990s. A later survey[9] used a larger sample of buildings in London and part of the findings are summarised in rounded-off percentage terms in Figure 9.8 for non-air-conditioned buildings.

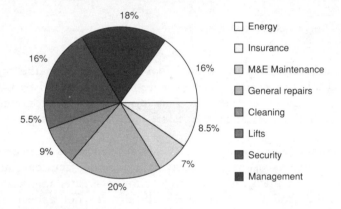

Figure 9.8 City office service charges (1992)

The report noted that cost reduction has now become a main priority with companies, and constraints were being placed on energy consumption of buildings, and non-essential maintenance. This clearly mirrors the situation in which most public sector property has been for many years, and raises the question of the longer-term cost consequences of not undertaking maintenance. The 1992 survey revealed some striking differences from the 1987 survey in respect of London city buildings. For instance, total services charges in the sample of newer buildings were lower than in 1987 when adjusted for inflation, while pre-1970 buildings were higher. In terms of height the costs in buildings of up to ten storeys were proportionately higher than in the previous survey, and in terms of size the smaller buildings have significantly increased in service charges when compared with the 1987 sample.

Another report involving a wider geographical spread of buildings[10] averaged service charge costs from a sample of 172 small to large buildings in the 1992 calendar year. Costs, inclusive of VAT, are expressed in terms of net lettable space, and, of course, exclude extraordinary expenditure such as major items of capital replacement and periodic repair and redecoration. The 1992 average

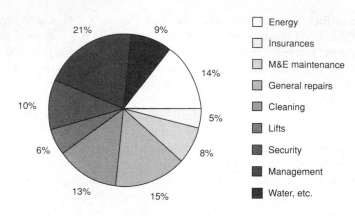

Figure 9.9 Service charges (1992)

service charge of £4.05 per square foot was lower than the previous year's average, and higher costs of security were counterbalanced by tight control of staffing and management charges. This input identified economies of scale in the larger buildings. Average charges are shown in percentage terms in Figure 9.9.

These comparative findings are of interest to facilities managers in so far as they may indicate cost trends. Leaving aside the fact that the samples of buildings are not identical, the surveys show a greater importance of energy costs in 1992, and the larger-sized buildings do not appear now to be as significantly more expensive to run per square foot. The difference between air-conditioned and non-air-conditioned buildings is however significant, particularly in older buildings, and energy costs are becoming more important overall. Security costs are also proportionately significant, and there is some evidence that relative repairs and maintenance costs have fallen overall, possibly due to a combination of factors, such as tight building prices, reduced programmes of maintenance, power of facilities managers to negotiate better terms when they operate larger stocks of buildings and technical improvements in design. The cost of cleaning varies between categories and may reveal policy differences between occupiers.

The facilities manager with a relatively static stock of property is in a good position to monitor such costs and to record broad changes in management policy, taxation and tariffs, and to identify trends, and will probably express costs in terms of median or average costs per unit of floor area. Alternatively costs per unit of occupation might be used as long as consistency is applied.

The importance of units can be illustrated by a simple example from the author's research into maintenance expressed at 1980 average prices.[11] (See Table 9.1)

Properties were selected to be as representative as possible and it will be seen that secondary schools each cost nearly seven times as much as primary schools

Table 9.1 Importance of cost unit parameters

Type of school	*Number of schools*	*Average cost (£ p.a.)*		
		Per property	*Per m²*	*Per pupil*
Primary	10	22 377	2.63	21.25
Secondary	50	3 329	3.14	17.83

to maintain over the period studied. However, prices per pupil showed that secondary schools cost about 20 per cent more than primaries, and cost per square metre was 16 per cent less. These conclusions illustrate a typical example of potential confusion unless cost units are consistently used for comparison. Cost per property is subject to fluctuation according to the size of building, but there are cases where it can be used as long as buildings are similar in size. Cost per pupil is subject to variability according to how many occupants the building contains when cost data are collected. Costs per square metre will differ according to size and height of the building, and the surveys referred to above illustrate this. Nevertheless, rent is usually paid according to floor area occupied and this unit is most commonly used for monitoring comparative costs. It will, of course, be appreciated that where a standard allowance of floor area per person is company policy, then cost per unit of floor area and cost per person will follow similar trends. It is also important to be clear as to whether costs are related to gross floor area or net lettable or usable area in commercial buildings.

An implication of the comments above is that owned freehold property has to bear costs which can be more actively managed by the facilities manager than can leasehold property, that age, size and number of storeys affect costs as well as whether air conditioned or not, and of course quality and location can be expected to affect costs. In some cases of course, the facilities manager will be in charge of property, some or all of which is let to other organisations. In this case records of expenditure on the property will need to be carefully kept and apportioned as agreed with the occupiers. The question of quality is a difficult one to comment upon in general terms, as running costs are not necessarily lower in a 'high quality' property, and often the reverse holds true. However, the facilities manager will require to forecast running costs in order to be able to compare alternative building solutions at procurement or leasing stage. It must be borne in mind, however, that good building management practices can result in substantial energy savings so that some potentially expensive buildings can be operated at a more economical level without any significant loss of comfort and the fitting of a building energy management system may be investigated in appropriate cases.

Benchmarking

The collection of data on cost and performance is of doubtful value unless clearly defined uses are planned. However, at an appropriate level it is worth while keeping a cost data base to assist in monitoring performance and comparing with other properties. The concept of benchmarking is concerned with defining which key data are needed for effective economical premises management, collecting such data, analysing trends in cost and performance according to yardsticks such as unit of area or per person and making comparisons year on year and with other organisations where possible.

This chapter has dealt with costs of operating the property and these costs, at least, should be summarised for report to management together with brief comments. A commentary is needed to explain why differences between targets and actual achievement have occurred. As an example, maintenance costs may be unusually high in one year due to a flat roof recovering contract, or rewiring, and reference to the asset register should indicate if such work had to be done before the expiry of the planned life span. Costs of energy might have risen due to changes in VAT, or due to a severe winter in the case of heating or very hot summer in the case of air conditioning. Other costs relating to operating the premises, or providing amenities, furniture and the like may be recorded against a yardstick, such as area or per capita and updated by a published or in-house cost index, so that trends may be examined.

It is difficult to compare costs of operating facilities management departments, particularly where there are some functions which are contracted out and where others are not. However, it is a starting point to relate management costs to the total operating costs. Unfortunately many published tables and diagrams are not as specific as is desirable when one wishes to attribute and compare costs to functions, and typical percentages quoted for management range from just over 10 to nearly 30 per cent of total operating costs (excluding rent or capital repayments). Differences occur between functions of buildings and some of these are evidently due to the inclusion of some staff associated with managing services which might be attributed to the core business rather than operating the building. Other differences can occur according to the complexity of the building and the extent of managerial control felt to be necessary, and Figures 9.7-9.9 above may reflect some of these factors.

As implied above, shape and size of buildings will affect costs, and the quoting of costs related to floor area therefore can give rise to misleading conclusions. Thus, the facilities manager needs to know much more about the physical characteristics of the property and its operating regimes in order to make balanced comparisons. In the case of management costs, it has been suggested[12] that the staffing, accommodation and equipment costs of the whole maintenance organisation in a large county authority might amount to a little over 10 per cent of the annual cost of the work done. If one takes into account the total running costs of a private sector stock of buildings, then the added complexity of managing the work to a commercial standard, together with a level of monitoring which gives better control over performance, one might suggest that the 10 per cent noted above is rather low for non-air-conditioned premises. However, the facilities manager should monitor performance against management costs on an annual basis. Of course, it might be pointed out that savings achieved by management in running costs would have the effect of making the facilities management service look more expensive as a percentage, which emphasises the point which is often made that performance of the property must be looked at as a whole.

There are other indicators of performance which are not necessarily expressed as costs but which do nevertheless closely relate to the operating costs. For instance, sampling of efficiency of heating and cooling service installations, adequacy of natural and artificial lighting levels, either general or task oriented, sampling of air quality or pollutants in the building and provision of space per person in different departments, and these can be objectively measured. Other factors, which are dealt with in chapters 10 and 11, are those which are less easy to measure or to attribute to cause and effect, but which are very important to the organisation. Much thought has been given to these factors[13] and these include staff satisfaction with the working environment including its perceived quality, use of space and need for privacy, avoidance of distraction, but easy communication with other staff, satisfaction with the facilities department reactions to requests for remedial action in cases of malfunction or failure of elements, or lack of control over environmental conditions. In many cases such issues are interrelated and the facilities manager's prompt attention to perceived problems might affect employees' performance, absenteeism and the like. It is therefore often worth while to prepare records of time taken to respond to problems from date, or time, of first notification to the facilities management department, or contractor, through to the commencement and completion of remedial work.

Objective measures for all of the relevant factors are not easily available, so some measures based on regularly repeated satisfaction profiles may be employed. Clearly, as with any subjective factors, staff perceptions will change over time, as indeed will the actual people employed, so that level of detail involved in questionnaires, for instance, must be only just sufficient to elicit the information needed. For the organisation's management purposes the data obtained should be put together as part of a targeted, coordinated and economical reporting system on the effectiveness of the management of the facilities.

Budgeting for effective management

An important precondition to good budgeting is a sound system of recording costs against major headings as discussed above, plus adequate measures to forecast or at least provide for future costs as adequately as possible. Clearly the organisation will need to account for all income and expenditure and to allow for taxation, but this chapter is only dealing with the property-related budget. Allied to this must be arrangements to monitor cash flows and to make adjustments when new factors occur. Naturally most budgeting starts with records of previous years' cash flows both in revenue and capital terms.

In some cases a figure based on the assessed capital value of the stock in new condition is used, and about 1.8 per cent is a common figure. This figure broadly equates to 100 percent replacement of the cost over a 60-year loan period but clearly has no basis in need, and it is more logical to budget for major repairs on anticipated life of elements adjusted by inspections, plus allowances for day-to-day and preventive maintenance work. The use of a guideline percentage figure, or some other fixed starting point for budgeting, can mean that historic maintenance costs may turn out to confirm the percentage to the satisfaction of management although the condition of the property may be gradually deteriorating. This is why condition and quality of work done must be monitored regularly.

Many organisations use the previous year's budget and adjust it for the coming year allowing for cost escalation, changes in stock and changes in policy in relation to the upkeep of property, but it is not appropriate to use this approach for larger items of expenditure, or for those which can be more accurately forecast. Probably, updated historic costs will be used for the smaller and more numerous items, such as day-to-day response maintenance, as these cannot be foreseen. However, as indicated in Chapter 8, expensive maintenance and other large items can be planned for some years ahead based on condition and life span data. Budgeting for such problems does not guarantee that they will need attention when forecast but smoothing out of peaks and troughs of work by bringing some items forward, or delaying others if possible can help to ensure that funds may be available. A coordinated view of budgetary headings helps the process as long as virement between budget headings is allowed, so that an unexpected need for spending under one heading may be funded from another.

The aim, however, must be to budget as accurately as is possible based on the facilities management records plus bids and forecasts from departments and sections of the organisation. These bids should be built up on a standard pro forma so that all appropriate budget headings are included, and will frequently be based on expected expenditure per quarter of the year. The budget will itemise proposed expenditure under the headings previously discussed, under maintenance and repair, improvements and alterations, operating costs, and any service charges. Decisions may also have to be taken as to whether to refurbish or seek to dispose of one property and acquire another by leasing or new-build and this option appraisal must be undertaken and the conclusions budgeted for with an appropriate lead-in time for design, construction and resettlement of staff. Taxation must be taken into account, although such liabilities will be the province of the accountant, once the building-related costings have been done. The situation regarding tax is not simple because of a range of factors. For instance, taxation, which may change from year to year, may be affected by the definition of the property as trading or investment property. The country of location of a company can affect liability for tax on disposal of property and rents, of course, will be liable to tax, while some benefit from capital allowances on building services plant may be available on acquisition, stamp duty will be payable. Therefore there may be occasions when adjustment of categories of expenditure, or moving of receipts or liabilities from one year to another may legitimately be undertaken to the advantage of the organisation.

These considerations mean that smoothing of proposed workload, as well as expenditure, during the coming year needs to be considered. Quite apart from disruptions to the organisation due to maintenance or other work there is the question of peaking of cash flow demand and the potential load on the facilities management department.

Unfortunately, it is often the case that proposed budgets exceed guideline target figures issued by top management and prioritisation of larger jobs must be undertaken in order to try to bring proposed expenditure closer to what is known to be a practical limit. Where a number of properties have to be managed there may be sensitive issues involved in deleting work from initial budgets, and the facilities manager may be exposed to criticism and attempts to go to higher authority to ensure work is done for one department or building rather than another. It helps in such cases if there is a set of guidelines which state the major priorities of the organisation and the author and colleagues are at present undertaking research work funded by the Science and Engineering Research Council on this topic. It is interesting to note, even when policy guidelines are prepared, how often these are modified in practice as circumstances change or as guidelines produce unanticipated results. Therefore such prioritisation needs sensitive implementation even though the rules in some instances are quite unambiguous. On the other hand policy guidelines may provide the facilities manager with a useful tool when negotiating an initial budget figure with management.

Subsequent to the preparation of the initial budget, negotiations usually take place on the total amount and the timing of proposed expenditure. This may mean some adjustments to planned jobs, and departmental heads should be kept informed of changes in case they wish to reorder their requests. Once approved by top management the proposals need to be translated into documentation for action. Small jobs may need little planning but larger ones may need a lead-in period for obtaining quotations and arranging for space to be vacated while the work is done. Also the scheduling and consolidating of work or purchases into cost and management-effective packages need thought. As jobs are ordered they can be coded for data retrieval, but invoices will need to be checked to ensure that the outcome and final cost of the work are recorded instead of commitment figures. A proposed cash flow profile might be made so that actual expenditure can be checked on a weekly or monthly basis,

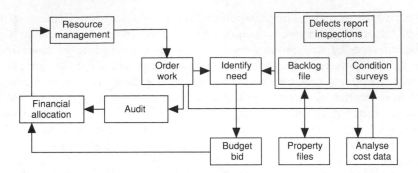

Figure 9.10   Maintenance data model

together with committed sums so that deviation from projected cash flow can be identified early. The end of financial year spending then needs to be reconciled, bearing in mind that larger jobs will run over the end of the financial year.

A diagram of the overall process is given in Figure 9.10, which was produced elsewhere in respect of building maintenance[14] but is typical of the processes involved. At the centre of the diagram is the identification of need based upon information contained in the right-hand processes, which relate to the collection of information on need and its analysis related to the current state of the property. Needs leads to the preparation and submission of a budget bid, as a result of which an allocation is made. The management of resources then involves planning of work and contracts and their ordering which is then subject to monitoring and audit. The process of ordering, suitably corrected for any changes, then provides data for analysis of trends and performance which helps to identify need for future budgets.

Risk

All management tasks are subject to the element of risk, and financial risk is a factor in property costs and budgeting which must be allowed for to some extent. It is often the case that a percentage on cost estimates, or a lump sum, is added to budgets at the planning stage. Management of risk cannot be an exact science, but some thought should be given to problems which might arise during the coming budget period, and what their cost consequences might be. A task of the facilities manager is to minimise risk of interruption of the core business and consequential loss of profit, or clients. However, some risks will be in respect of the building, its occupants, people and property adjacent to it, and the environment. Therefore the facilities manager should try to identify potential risks, to assess their possible consequences and to seek to reduce them, or at least be prepared for them. In financial terms, some of the costs referred to above are foreseeable, such as rent, rates, insurances, preventive maintenance and the like, and insurance itself is a means of passing on an element of risk, Other costs are controllable to some extent, but involve some uncertainty perhaps due to weather conditions, vandalism and unexpected failure. In matters related to energy consumption, sick building syndrome or other health and safety matters, staff training may be utilised to reduce the chances of things going wrong. Back-up procedures need to be in place to try to ensure that if problems occur, such as a fire in the offices, then swift action is taken not only to mitigate the problem, but also to bring duplicate records and other measures into action to ensure that the organisation is disrupted for the minimum time. Such measures will cost money and their implementation will relate to management's perception of the risk of the situation occurring and the cost of preparing for, and or insuring, against it. However, the message is that measures to reduce the liability to risk can be costed, together with sinking funds or contingency resources, and identified clearly in the budget.

Computing and property data

Facilities management data storage and analysis processes lend themselves to computerisation. As was noted in the comments on asset registers, data may be stored in a manual system quite economically, but extraction of data and analysis for reports is speeded up if a computerised system is used with data which are coded in a compatible manner by each of the departments or groups contributing those data. Some of the uses of the computer in facilities management will be referred to in Chapter 11, particularly in respect of space planning and the recording of associated assets. Also, computer-based building management systems (BMS) are capable of providing information on the current state of use of service installations, security and a wide range of other matters, should a high level of control be required.

While various separate programs are available an integrated CAFM system is potentially more useful in generating useful displays and reports. Much of the inertia which tends to prevent such systems being implemented stems from two factors; firstly the idiosyncratic nature of organisations, and secondly the staffing resources needed to set up the system with current data, measured plans and the like. Once the system is set up then maintenance of the data base should be a much less onerous job, particularly as the data should be collected for management purposes anyway. The manager is then able to generate responses to possible alternative policies on matters such as partitioning, workstations, layout and costs. In order to achieve this ability to respond, the heart of the CAFM system will be a computer-aided design (CAD) program allied to a compatible structured data base. The data base should be capable of providing support to the facilities manager in a range of functions, but particularly in keeping track of the cost centres referred to previously in this chapter.

Obviously the CAD base to a CAFM system will enable spaces to be analysed, but also other attributes to the space to be recorded for asset control and departmental cost reporting purposes. Coordinated data can be kept in the data base for easy updating and speed of retrieval. Such data may include space and personnel allocations, asset registers, furniture layouts and inventories, locations of electrical and communications cabling, outlets and sockets of maintenance and cleaning regimes can also be recorded. If maintenance work orders are issued via the computer system, then virtually automatic coding to job and cost headings may be done. This function is potentially one of the most useful to the facilities manager, providing not only a means of recording progress of work programmes but also keeping running cost totals for budget control and reporting purposes. As with the design of management systems generally, management must choose the scope and level of detail to be computerised in the light of the resources to be deployed.

References

1. Audit Commission 1988 *Local authority property, a management handbook* HMSO
2. Spedding A, Holmes R 1992 *Co-ordinated databases and budgeting for effective property management* Report to SERC GR/F 26102
3. DES 1986 *Property information systems and the educational building stock* Architects and Building Branch Paper No 10
4. BSI 1984 *Glossary of maintenance management terms in terotechnology* BS 3811
5. BSI 1986 *Building maintenance management* BS 8210
6. BMI Ltd *Property occupancy cost analyses* Building Maintenance Information Ltd, Kingston upon Thames
7. DoE 1991 *Energy efficiency in offices* Energy Consumption Guide
8. Savills 1987 *Property management costs* London
9. Savills 1992 *Central London occupational costs survey 1992* London
10. Jones Lang Wootton 1993 *OSCAR: office service charge analysis 1993* London
11. Spedding A, Holmes R et al 1983 *Maintenance in schools* Bristol Polytechnic
12. Spedding A, Smith V 1987 *Control of maintenance in a county authority* Building Maintenance, Economics and Management, Spon
13. Becker F 1990 *The total workplace* Van Nostrand Reinhold
14. Spedding A 1987 *Management of maintenance – the need for and uses of data* Building Maintenance, Economics and Management, Spon

The indoor environment: strategies and tactics for managers

Adrian Leaman and David Tong

Introduction

Previous chapters have looked at property, design processes and costs in the light of the creation and operation of assets. However, we should remind ourselves that buildings are designed to create environments indoors which are substantially less varied than the natural environment outdoors and they also provide spaces for activities. These two functions – climate control and space provision – are basically what buildings are for. Controlling environmental variation increases human potential by allowing more functions and activities to take place over longer periods of time than they could otherwise. The most effective ways of combining materials and spaces to provide comfortable, healthy buildings which were best suited to local climates emerged over many generations. Now, the introduction of new materials and technologies, and the changing expectations of building occupiers for higher comfort and health standards, have fundamentally changed our approach.

As comfort and health conditions have seemingly deteriorated, especially in offices, the relationship between comfort and health is being investigated anew, with old principles rediscovered and new ones formulated to cope with modern conditions.[1] As a result, our perceptions and understanding of what is meant by the 'indoor environment' are changing quickly. Table 10.1, for instance, summarises the most important indoor environment parameters which were measured in a 1988 British study of an office building which was known to have problems relating to 'sick building syndrome' (SBS).[2] It was found that there were significantly high levels of sulphur dioxide and high dust levels, bacteria and fungi were found in the water-spray humidifiers and bacilli spores in the condensate trays of the induction units. Table 10.1 gives some of the ranges found, and shows how these compare with typical office levels and occupational exposure limits.[3] Ten years previously, only comfort would have

Table 10.1 Summary of most important indoor environment parameters from a study of a UK office building known to be 'sick' (*Source:* Thomson Laboratories and Building Use Studies[2])

Factor	Units	Range found	Typical office level	Occupational exposure limit
Temperature	Degrees centigrade	21–26	18–25 (comfort zone)	Not applicable
Humidity	Per cent relative humidity	10–55	20–60 (comfort zone)	Not applicable
Lighting	Lux	300–2200	350–750 (comfort zone)	Not applicable
Carbon dioxide	Parts per million	390–400	400–600	5000
Carbon monoxide	Parts per million	<0.5	<1	50
Sulphur dioxide	Parts per million	0.01–0.08	<0.1	0.005–0.01
Nitrogen oxides	Parts per million	<0.005	0.005–0.01	3(NO_2)
Formaldehyde	Parts per million	0.04–0.08	0–0.06	2
Total volatile organics	mg/m^3	0.46–0.65	0.1–0.5	Not applicable
Airborne particulate matter	mg/m^3	0.17–0.22	0.04–0.1	10

been studied in research programmes in respect of the indoor environment, not ill health. At the time of writing (1994), the agenda has broadened even further to encompass not only comfort and health, but also energy efficiency and human productivity.

Like the 1988 study, most other research into SBS, and earlier work on comfort and indoor air quality, has had a technical focus. Quite justifiably, the search has been for causes of discomfort and ill health which can be investigated by standard scientific means. This work continues, as exemplified by the 1993 Proceedings of the Indoor Air Conference, the vast majority of the 650 papers from which were of a technical or scientific character.[4] However, as a more rounded view of the sick building problem develops,[5] it is appropriate to consider how facilities managers deal with indoor environment problems so that remedial efforts can be encouraged and guidance can be improved while technical research continues.

Management and the indoor environment

Facilities management grew as a profession in the UK in the 1980s because technological and organisational developments made building-related decisions more complex and also more profound in their consequences for occupants. At the same time, it was becoming more obvious that some buildings, notably offices, were performing much less well than their designers intended: they were hotter, and noisier, especially in deep-space, open-plan environments, for instance. SBS emerged as a recognised workplace problem, and Legionnaires' disease also came to prominence. It became clear that traditional building management practice was failing to prevent an apparent deterioration in the quality and performance of the indoor environment.

Not only that, failures of building management practice helped to create the conditions where environmental problems such as SBS develop. SBS was not, as first thought, primarily a 'designed-in' problem created by mistakes in architectural and building services design which could be easily rectified by better design alone, but more a management problem resulting from failures to deal with adverse user responses which resulted from new design scenarios. Also, in certain circumstances, poor line management helped to create organisational cultures which increased the sensitivity of building occupants to environmental conditions, thereby creating vicious circles of deterioration.

The main types of management failures, drawn from the authors' experience of research and consultancy in these areas, are set out below with examples. They are broadly split into strategic and tactical, reflecting different levels of management involvement, and environmental and cultural, emphasising physical environment problems on the one hand, and organisational on the other. Where possible, published references are given to support the examples. Otherwise, information is derived from internal Building Use Studies client data and reports.

Tactical environmental failings

Inadequate performance standards

A common example is the failure to set ventilation rates at the recommended levels.[6] Lack of adequately distributed fresh air can result in poor indoor air quality and is often associated with SBS. This association has led many to think that poor ventilation is a cause of SBS, which can be eradicated by improving the ventilation. Like many other conditions in buildings, this is not necessarily true. Complex chains of causality can sometimes mean that a symptom is being mistaken for a cause. Also ill-conceived interventions can unwittingly make the problem worse.

While improving ventilation rates may help, lack of ability to cool offices is often perceived by occupants as being more fundamental for their personal well-being. Failure to appreciate the importance of cooling (as well as heating), and light levels which are often set too high (especially for VDU-related tasks), are commonplace in respect of basic performance standards. Additionally, standards are not reviewed and updated because, as noted below, managers usually lack feedback data on the achieved indoor environment and on the occupants' perceived responses to it. Data on performance are a vital ingredient in the evaluation of standards in use.

Low maintenance and cleaning standards

Achieved maintenance and cleaning standards are often poor or very poor. These problems are suspected to be extensive[7] but have not yet been studied fully. Poor maintenance and cleaning are management issues because they usually represent ineffective monitoring of delegated or subcontracted tasks. Sometimes they are made worse by the more general housekeeping problem of untidiness, where cleaners and engineers have difficulty gaining access to areas requiring attention (which may suffer from poor design in the first place!). Proper cleaning, diligently and regularly carried out, is probably the most cost-effective measure that can be applied in any office building because it reduces dust and airborne contaminants, thereby making the building feel fresher for the occupants.[8] It also introduces a regular discipline of monitoring and tidiness which is related to quality control and which helps to identify defects much faster. Sadly, cleaning tends to be the first, not the last, cost centre to be cut when savings have to be made.

Strategic environmental failings

Lack of building performance data

Studies of energy use in British buildings[9] have illustrated that facilities managers usually lack even the simplest performance data, such as for energy costs and consumption. It is almost certain, therefore, that managers will also lack information which is more difficult to obtain, such as for temperature, ventilation, lighting and air quality. Another example is data on absenteeism, due to sickness, which is rarely if ever related to building occupancy. This means that it is seldom possible for facilities managers to determine how different buildings compare in terms of the level of sickness absence. In the studies reported earlier[2, 3] 42 per cent of the staff in the building (which was known to be 'sick') reported that they had left work early at least once in the past month as a result of their chronic symptoms. Twenty-six per cent said that they did this on up to 5 days a month. These data are a rare exception. There are, in general, few building performance data and hence it is not usually possible to relate organisational performance to building performance.

Failure to anticipate the consequences of change

Office environments have been altered increasingly frequently because of a growth in team-based working and marketing-led business operations. Problems arise when these replanning exercises are not accompanied by consideration of their effects on the indoor environment. An obvious example is the failure, following alterations between cellular and open plan formats, to make changes to the air distribution system. For example, it is commonplace to find that workstations have been placed immediately next to perimeter window walls. In naturally ventilated buildings this can deny occupants access for control of windows, blinds and radiator valves. In some air-conditioned buildings with perimeter induction units, workstations can block access to the units for maintenance and tempt staff to use them for extra storage space, thereby blocking the vents. Replanning often ignores the existing switch locations, so that the light switch for the newly partitioned meeting room is located in the adjacent workspace! There are many such instances of lack of care and forethought when areas are being replanned, which often lead to a deterioration in conditions.

Failure to understand the non-linear nature of building complexity

Managers are often caught out by changes in the magnitude of problems they face. This is because the relationship between complexity and management input is not linear. There are thresholds of complexity in building design and if a threshold is crossed (and what constitutes a threshold will vary between buildings) the management effort needs to be increased disproportionately. This means that buildings of high complexity may need considerably more management input than might be intuitively predicted, as illustrated in Figure 10.1. In general, it may be best to provide space and services which are self-managing or manageable by individual occupants, so that they do not become an extra burden for management.[10]

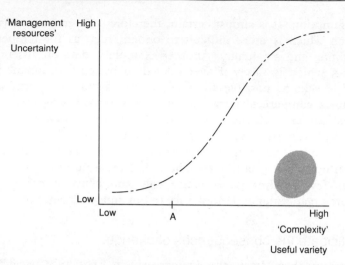

Figure 10.1 Thresholds of building complexity
The graph shows how building complexity (bottom axis) is related to the management resources required to run buildings so that they function well. If a building is located on or close to the curve, then it will probably be efficient, healthy and comfortable. The shaded area represents problem buildings, like sick buildings, where the management input is far too low to cope with the complexity of the building systems and services.

Generally speaking, buildings become physically much more complex once the limits of natural ventilation have been exceeded beyond about 15 m depth of space (represented by A). This is the point at which the S-curve begins to rise steeply. Often, management underestimate how much more time and effort have to be put into running buildings of this type, especially those which are open plan and air conditioned.

This diagram, and others accompanying it, are explained in more detail in reference 10. In general, the more complex a building is, the more uncertainty is built in to the way it operates. Management resources must be devoted to dealing with the consequences of this uncertainty which, if left to proliferate, quickly makes the building unnecessarily expensive to run, difficult to use, uncomfortable and, in some circumstances, sick.

Slow response of systems

As buildings get larger and more complex, they tend to lose the ability to be responsive to occupants' attempts to change the conditions in them. Naturally ventilated, shallow-plan buildings often have this capability because many of the control systems, such as blinds, openable windows, radiator valves and so on, are often domestic in character and simple to use. They also provide occupants with rapid feedback on whether they have operated correctly and whether they are effective. Speed of response to desire for change is very important for occupants' perceptions of comfort. People will tend to tolerate objectively worse indoor conditions if buildings have reasonable controllability and good responsiveness, as Figure 10.2 shows. In air-conditioned buildings, where there is often much slower perceived response of the physical control systems, and people tend to have less control anyway, they tend to be less tolerant of objectively better conditions!

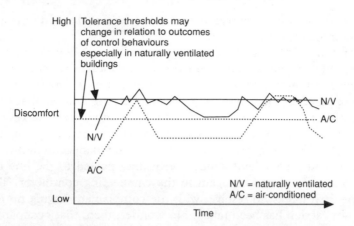

Figure 10.2 Tolerance thresholds in naturally ventilated and air-conditioned offices
This represents likely differences in performance between naturally ventilated and air-conditioned offices with respect to users' tolerance of the conditions and the ability of the building to respond when people become uncomfortable.

Naturally ventilated (sometimes called 'free-running') offices often have higher user tolerance (because they usually offer more user control) and more rapid response, but the control systems only tend to alter conditions marginally, especially in the height of summer when conditions are most uncomfortable.

Air-conditioned ('close control') buildings have lower user tolerance because of their slower responses, and often run for longer periods of time either inside or outside the comfort zone.

Beyond the failings which directly result in poor physical indoor environmental quality, management can create a culture within organisations which increases the sensitivity of staff to environmental deficiencies so that SBS develops in physical conditions which are tolerable in a more supportive culture. Again there are strategic and tactical factors.

Tactical cultural failings

Responding slowly to complaints

Slowness of physical response in buildings can be compensated for by excellence in the management system's speed of response to complaints. A remarkable instance of this was found in a study of the relationship between occupants' environmental control and energy efficiency carried out in 1992.[11] One of the air-conditioned buildings was found to use only as much energy as the naturally ventilated offices in the study. It would be expected to consume at least twice or perhaps even three times as much. This building was also perceived as much the most comfortable by the occupants. On inspection, there seemed to be nothing special about its physical systems, other than that they were well-chosen and appropriate. The real difference was the quality of the

187

management and maintenance regime and the exceptional speed of response to occupants' complaints.

It has been found[12-14] that where management fail to take prompt, corrective action to remedy environmental complaints, staff morale is reduced and the likelihood of reporting of symptoms increased. Experience shows that response times are hampered by poor reporting, record keeping and feedback systems, but perhaps more importantly by a cynicism about the validity of the complaint. In some instances, complaints procedures are exceptionally slow and bureaucratic, involving three or four levels in the management hierarchy. It is common to find a complaint about overheating passed to the line manager responsible and then passed on again to the engineering contractor. This may take days, or even weeks, to resolve, with the complainant having no feedback on what, if any, action has been taken. No wonder, then, that occupants prefer systems which give instantaneous responses, even if conditions are not substantially improved by the control action/s.

A different approach to the management of complaints was outlined in a recent research seminar.[15] In one facilities management department, complaints were seen as part of an open dialogue between users and managers in a 'customer-led service culture'.[16] Users were allowed to assign a priority status of their choosing to a request for action, which, after an initial settling-in period, they did in a responsible manner. The result was a shared appreciation of priorities between managers and users.

It has been estimated that a dissatisfied person will tell an average of nineteen others about their experience, while they will tell only a few about a satisfactory experience.[17] There is increasing evidence to show that dealing with customer complaints quickly and courteously can turn a hostile customer into a customer for life. This also applies in buildings, where dissatisfaction is often contagious. Once a building acquires a reputation for being poor, it is often extraordinarily difficult for management to reverse the situation. The last thing they should do is to try short-term, cheap and gratuitous approaches like dummy (placebo) controls to placate staff. The deception is only short-lived and like many knee-jerk 'solutions' it will almost always make the problem worse.

Ignoring job stress

It is generally accepted[18] that staff working under stress are more sensitised to environmental conditions and therefore may tend to report more symptoms of SBS. Reduction of work-related stress is a management responsibility. Job stress is not 'building-related', that is caused by building factors alone, but it can be significantly exacerbated by poor conditions, bad management or ill-working building services equipment.

Failure to consult staff in design and planning decisions

Just as there is a lack of performance data on the achieved indoor environment in buildings, there is a general lack of data relating to user evaluations of environmental quality. It may not be myopic to hope that this may improve in the European Union with the implementation of Directive EC 90/270 which requires users to be consulted in the evaluation of workstations where visual display screen equipment is used. Although staff may spend on average about 25 per cent of their time at a VDU (with a range from zero to 100 per cent), workstations and VDUs are still a relatively insignificant part of the total indoor environment. By concentrating too much attention on the single issue of VDUs, many other equally important topics may be ignored or treated peremptorily.[19]

Staff surveys and consultations are of most use in either diagnosing existing problems or providing factual data for management to make decisions on new projects. It is usually best to concentrate on surveying facts and attitudes based on experience, rather than asking staff what they would like to have. By asking people about their preferences (especially for nice-to-have facilities like swimming pools), expectations can be raised to unrealistic levels which are then not fulfilled (the pool is taken out of the scheme because it is too expensive). It is much better to survey what people actually do and how they really behave, so that need can be judged on a realistic understanding of problems and opportunities.

Strategic cultural failings

Facilities management issues not prioritised

Steele and Wilson[20-22] have found that some senior operational managers tend to ascribe a low value to workplace environmental issues and treat them in a discontinuous fashion. This must inevitably hinder the efforts of facilities managers to optimise quality, but it is a viewpoint which is difficult to change because lack of building performance data means it is impossible to link building and organisational performance. The way in which research data can help overcome this inertia among senior operational managers is explored at the end of this chapter.

Over-reliance on technocentric philosophies of environmental control

There is widespread belief that centralised, automated control mechanisms can deliver a predictable environment of acceptable quality. Recent research[23] has begun to question the validity of this belief. The focus on users who feel that they lack environmental control arose because work on SBS found that occupants with low perceptions of control were more likely to have chronic SBS symptoms.[22] The ill-conceived response to these findings was to provide occupants with as many controls as possible. Where this happens, control functions are likely to conflict with each other (for example, blinds for glare control conflicting with open windows) thereby making the environment worse, not better and making people more frustrated. Ideally, buildings should operate so that they have (a) baseload comfort conditions which keep as many people as possible comfortable for as long as possible and (b) the ability for occupants to change the conditions quickly, should they wish to do so. It is the second of these which is often absent or ignored, especially in buildings with centralised control systems running under the automatic supervision of a building management system (BMS). Managers often mistakenly assume that the BMS will provide for all their needs, but this is rarely so, and the buildings fail in just those areas where their occupants are most sensitive, i.e. lack of control when conditions are bad or uncomfortable.

Managers investing in complex electrical control systems are often making a conscious effort to improve environmental management, yet this can be counter-productive in terms of the well-being of staff. The results are beginning to suggest a number of challenges and opportunities which could promote better management practices.

Control systems and environmental management

Modern control and energy management systems offer great potential for improving comfort and health and providing a measurable return on investment by reducing energy consumption. However, many systems achieve none of this. This is because it is often assumed that if they work properly, in the engineering sense, they will do the job required. In practice, automatic provision of pre-set, 'ideal' conditions can prove disappointing because perceived comfort and control come not so much from particular control devices but from systems which react rapidly when people find conditions unsatisfactory. Rapid response can be achieved either by simple 'domestic' controls (say an openable window or light switch), well-configured electronics, or an effective manager, or by combinations of all of them. The most important thing, as suggested previously, is that these systems combine together to produce a rapid response when environmental conditions become uncomfortable.

In the study previously mentioned,[11] the building which had one of the lowest energy consumption figures and the highest occupant satisfaction also had a centralised electronic control system. The crucial factor in the success of this building appeared to be that users' perception of control was high and that the facilities manager had a clear 'bias to action'.[24] He intervened quickly, often before occupants complained, on the basis of information provided for him by feedback from the BMS. This helped to create a culture of responsiveness even though the electronic control systems themselves could be slow to react or were outside the immediate control of occupants. In another similar building, where energy consumption was three to four times higher, comfort ratings were lower and the perceived degree of control was also much lower. In this case, the constraints imposed on the tenant by the landlord's management and maintenance requirements made it impossible for the tenant building managers to respond quickly to problems. These results show that systems need to be treated in a context-sensitive manner; they cannot be installed on a 'fit and forget' basis as the designers in the latter case assumed.

Conclusion: a virtuous cluster?

If, in considering the control environment within a building, we accept that fast and effective management response is a key component of the users' perceived control system, then it is instructive to remind ourselves of the link between environmental control and human productivity. A relationship has been found between users' perceived ability to control their environment and their perceptions about the effect of the workplace on their productivity (Figure 10.3].[25] People perceive that, as control increases, so does their productivity, the more so for control over heating and ventilation (cooling was not assessed in this particular study). Determined management action and rapid response increase users' perceptions of control, which in turn affect their perceptions of productivity, leading to greater tolerance of discomfort when it does occur. As perceived control is also associated with lack of building-related ill-health symptoms and there is an additional ingredient in that improved control procedures also help to achieve energy savings, there is increasing evidence for the presence of a virtuous cluster of beneficial attributes.

But most buildings do not work like this. Many of them have the attributes of vicious, not virtuous circles: sick buildings themselves are an example of a vicious circle, so is vandalism damage. We estimate that less than 10 per cent of the British office stock have most or all of the attributes of the virtuous cluster (energy efficiency, high levels of cleanliness, responsiveness, comfortable and healthy staff and positive productivity). We believe that, although many buildings are management obstacle courses with many poorly thought-out design features, design by itself is not the main problem. Managers tend to blame designers for failures and designers, of course, blame the managers. No matter how well a building is designed, if the basic management disciplines are not in place – like basic housekeeping – then, eventually, the indoor environment will deteriorate and the occupants will suffer.

We have said in this chapter that there are three basic management disciplines which lead to a comfortable and healthy indoor environment. These are (a) cleanliness, (b) responsiveness of control systems and (c) energy efficiency. Being good at any one of the three will eventually lead to all the others because they are all part of the same quality control system applied not to a single product or service but to the building as a whole, including its occupants. Cleaning, for instance, does not just purge the environment of dust

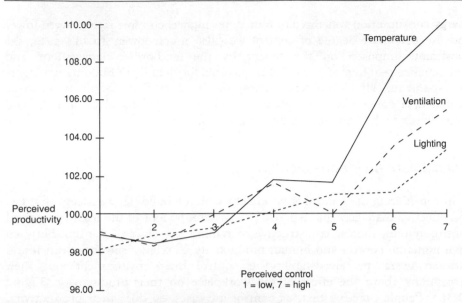

Figure 10.3 Perceptions of productivity and control

These data are from a sample of 4500 respondents in 50 buildings. Respondents were asked to rate their personal productivity (vertical axis) and their perceived control over temperature, ventilation and lighting. The majority of the sample rated control as low (1, 2 or 3 on the scale) and also reported loss of productivity (shown as less than 100 per cent on the scale). The sample of people reporting higher control gets smaller further up the scale (with about 200 respondents reporting high control (7 on the scale)).

People report higher productivity when they also perceive that they have higher control, and this is most marked for temperature, and rather less so for ventilation and lighting.

and bacteria, it introduces a discipline of inspection and monitoring. This is the reason why so many great businesses have founders who were obsessed with cleanliness. Cleaning not only is good for consumers' perceptions of the quality of products (especially foodstuffs) it is also a wonderfully simple way of achieving defect and waste control in the production process. The following example, although stagy, illustrates the point well:

As a fish-frier and restaurateur, Harry Ramsden was the ultimate perfectionist, believing first and foremost in absolute cleanliness, making sure that every corner of his premises was spotless before the day's business began and in a similar state before they closed for the night. To make sure that he was completely au fait with everything in his shops and restaurants, Harry prepared a list of daily tasks which he, as the proprietor (or one of his staff duly delegated) had to carry out. The list had 100 items! It was pinned to the back of a cupboard door and Harry never left until every single job had been carried out and ticked off from the list. It covered everything for ensuring that there was an adequate supply of flour for batter-making to his all-consuming preoccupation with cleanliness. This was a fetish with him. He searched high and low for a cleaner he could trust to regard proper hygiene with the same religious zeal as he himself observed. At last he found this paragon, a Mrs Ireson, and as he triumphantly announced at the end of his exhaustive search to young Harry he carried out a small demonstration. 'Watch this,' he instructed, dropping a match on to the floor. 'She won't miss it' and it was a small victory for him as Mrs Ireson came into view, duly spotted the match and whisked it into her dustpan. Harry oozed with satisfaction. 'I told thee,' he beamed delightedly.[26]

Rapid response is a topic which has been given far less emphasis in buildings than it warrants. An early study by Haigh of controls behaviour in British schools set out some of the central points:

A number of good reasons for designing a partnership of user-operated and automatic controls have been illustrated: the user's desire for instant results once a crisis of discomfort has been reached, the absence of any option to reduce temperature other than energy-expensive measures such as ventilation, the lack of incentive to take time to re-adjust the situation unless there is an appreciable drop in temperature [and] the lack of any acknowledgement of the considerable occupied times during the day. These observations would begin to suggest a control system with an internal logic to complement that of the users, and with additional energy goals.[27]

We have said that it is essential that buildings not only provide baseload comfort conditions but are able to respond instantly when occupants become uncomfortable or want to make changes for other reasons. To achieve this, there is often no need for extravagant electronic systems, only for extremely robust, stable and predictable responses from the controls. Haigh gives an example – 'The "old-fashioned" winding handle controls on high-level ventilators allowed very precise adjustment of the amount of opening, far more useful than the minimal stays provided with the more recent [school] window.'[27]

The third essential, in our view, is energy efficiency. Evidence shows that buildings which are energy-efficient are also likely to be more comfortable for their occupants. It is also possible to link discomfort to lower productivity, as Figure 10.4 shows.[28] So there are staff productivity gains to be made from energy efficiency as well as cost savings and environmental benefits. Of course, better energy efficiency does not cause better productivity: it is only one element in a complex physical and management system whose outcome is both better energy efficiency and higher productivity. To link them as causal is spurious (as with many other factors in buildings as well).

We are now closer to understanding what kind of management system produces both an objectively better indoor environment and one which is better suited to the needs of the occupants. We have given some clues as to how this may be achieved. We have also shown that the two are not necessarily linked. Seemingly 'good' objective conditions (as measured by thermometers and hygrometers) do not necessarily produce favourable responses from the occupants. It is the behavioural context that matters most, not solely the physical conditions, as many mistakenly think.

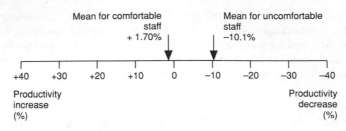

Figure 10.4 Productivity comparisons for comfortable and uncomfortable staff

These data come from analysis of 1640 respondents in 58 office buildings in the UK surveyed by Building Use Studies in 1993. They show the importance of designing to avoid discomfort. The sample has been divided into two groups: staff who report that their office environment is relatively uncomfortable overall (points 1, 2 and 3 on a 7-point comfort scale) and those who say that they are comfortable (points 4, 5, 6 and 7). The scale runs from 1 (uncomfortable) to 7 (comfortable) with 4 being the neutral point.

Staff were also asked to assess their personal productivity on the scale shown in the graph. The difference in reported productivity between the two groups is striking. Staff reporting that they are uncomfortable show producitivity losses of greater than 10 per cent; those who are comfortable report gains of just over 1 per cent, a difference of 11 per cent. Uncomfortable staff make up 33.73 per cent of the sample; comfortable 66.27 per cent. For all staff together, mean productivity shows a loss of 2.3 per cent.

Conclusion? Do not solely design for providing comfortable conditions: make sure that staff can avoid discomfort, because this is much more important.

References

1. Kirwell S, March C, Venables R (eds) 1990 *Buildings and health: the Rosehaugh guide* RIBA Publications, London
2. Thomson Laboratories in association with Building Use Studies and the Ove Arup Partnership 1988 Unpublished report for the Building Research Establishment, Ref F3/3/879
3. Leinster P, Raw G, Thomson N, Leaman A, Whithead C 1990 A modular longitudinal approach to the investigation of sick building syndrome. *Indoor Air '90*, vol 1. Canada Mortgage and Housing Corporation, Ottawa, pp 287–92
4. Seppanen O et al (eds) 1993 *Proceedings of the Sixth Conference on Indoor Air Quality and Climate, Indoor Air '93*, Helsinki, six vols
5. Raw G 1992 *Sick building syndrome: a review of the evidence on causes and solutions* Health and Safety Executive, Contract Research Report No 42/1992, HMSO, London
6. Wilson S, O'Sullivan P, Jones P, Hedge A 1987 *Sick building syndrome and environmental conditions* Building Use Studies, London
7. House of Commons Environment Committee 1991 *Sixth report: indoor pollution* HMSO, London. See especially the evidence presented by the Heating and Ventilation Contractors Association
8. Roys M, Raw G, Whitehead C 1993 Sick building syndrome: cleanliness is next to healthiness. *Indoor Air '93*, Helsinki, July
9. Energy Efficiency Office 1991 *Energy consumption guide for senior managers* Energy Consumption Guide 10 produced as part of the Best Practice Programme

10. Leaman A, Bordass W 1993 Building design, complexity and manageability. *Facilities* September
11. Bromley A K R, Bordass W T, Leaman A 1993 Are you in control? *Building Services* April
12. Rask D R, Lane C A 1989 Correcting maintenance deficiencies to solve sick building syndrome. *ASHRAE Journal* 5: 54–6
13. Leaman A 1993 Fast is never fast enough. *Facilities* March
14. Leaman A 1993 The importance of response time. *Building Services* March
15. Unpublished report of a seminar held at the Building Research Establishment as part of a research project entitled 'User and automated controls and management in buildings', carried out by Building Use Studies, in conjunction with William Bordass Associates
16. Referred to in Fortuna R M 1990 The quality imperative, chapter 1 of Huge E C *Total quality: a manager's guide for the 1990s* Kogan Page. Original source not quoted in reference
17. Tong D 1992 Beware the single issue. *Facilities* December
18. Macpherson R K 1980 What makes people accept a thermal environment? In Cowan H J (ed) *Solar applications in the design of buildings* Applied Science Publishers, London and Hedge A *et al.* 1987 Environmental, psychological and organizational correlates of employee health in offices: a proposed model. *Proceedings of the Human Factors Society 31st Annual Meeting* vol 2
19. Thomson-MTS and Building Use Studies (in press) *Attitudes to noise as an occupational hazard* Forthcoming contract research report from the Health and Safety Executive
20. Steele F 1986 *Making and managing high-quality workplaces* Teachers College Press, New York
21. Wilson S 1985 *Premises of excellence* Building Use Studies, London
22. Wilson S, Hedge A 1987 *The office environment survey* Building Use Studies, London
23. Bromley K, Bordass W T, Leaman A 1993 Improved utilisation of building management and control systems. *CIB/IEA Symposium on Energy Efficient Buildings* Stuttgart, March
24. 'A bias to action' is one of the components of management excellence noted in Peters T, Waterman R H 1984 *In search of excellence* Harper and Row
25. Raw G J, Roys M S, Leaman, A 1990 Further findings from the office environment survey: Productivity. *Proceedings of the 5th International Conference on Indoor Air Quality and Climate* Toronto, Canada, vol 1, Canada Mortgage and Housing Corporation, Ottawa, pp 231–6
26. Mosey D, Ramsden H Jnr 1989 *Harry Ramsden: the Uncrowned king of fish and chips* Dalesman Books, p 22
27. Haigh D 1981 User response in environmental control. In Hawkes D, Owers J *The architecture of energy* Construction Press, pp 45–63
28. Leaman A 1993 Productivity comparisons for comfortable and uncomfortable staff. *Facilities* August/September

Chapter 11

Facilities management and the organisation

Alan Jordan

Introduction

This chapter brings together many of the factors raised in previous chapters and views facilities management as the coordination of buildings, work and people into a single interactive system. It deals with energy and environmental issues, company culture and contract maintenance, security and space allocation, costs and catering. In other words, a diverse range of vital activities which can be simply summed up as 'getting the best from buildings for the benefit of the organisation'.

In that view, the term 'facilities management' includes support services outside of the core business such as:

- lease terms and negotiations
- rent reviews
- building services
- engineering maintenance
- project management
- space management
- cleaning and security
- graphic services and reprographics
- catering
- office services
- budgets and cost control
- IT, voice and data
- purchasing and contract negotiation
- car fleet management

Facilities management therefore embraces a series of vital functions to support all types of organisations using any and every type of building. This rationale holds firm regardless of geographical location; whether an organisation operates worldwide or is confined to a small town; and whether a business uses an elaborate network of nationwide branches or operates from a 'back office' central headquarters complex.

It will be appreciated that the field of business management with its related areas of applied psychology, behaviour of people in organisations and studies of structures is well served by extensive literature. However, the effects of IT and computerisation on organisations, and also on buildings, are everywhere to be seen, and who can doubt that we are only in an early stage of profound change. Therefore this chapter is written with the assumption that the importance of business management knowledge, *per se*, will be appreciated by the reader, who will also recognise the need to delve further into that field as necessary.

Consequently this chapter will commence by briefly making a link between the core business and the facilities management function.

The business organisation

Businesses have tended to define themselves in product terms, so that what they are and what they do has been assumed to be understood by simply stating what they produce, or the service they provide. The fashion for vertical integration as well as horizontal development in many fields led to the growth of very large organisations with widely dispersed properties and a wide range of activities. Some reversal of this trend has been pointed out, as companies realised that their reputation and strength had been built on what they do best, and that diversification had, in many cases, led them into fields where they were not able to operate profitably. Other pressures related to shifts in competition not only regionally but in some cases worldwide have been accompanied by social and technical change and by the growth of internationalism in business.

These pressures have required corporate cultures to acknowledge the pace of change and to plan for it. They have caused many organisations to re-evaluate their property in the light of possible new business goals. Of course, the core business will dictate property needs, and, for example, the needs of a large insurance company will not be the same as an electronics production facility. Business will, however, need to define current and future property strategy in the light of core business needs.

Planning of facilities therefore must be closely linked to policy making at company board level, and company strategy, which is designed to lead to organisational change and improvements in efficiency, may be directly translated into a property strategy which supports change and improvement. Against this background, some of the more significant factors which may affect the business organisation and its choice of property are:

- nature of business
- corporate image
- culture and expectations
- location of customers and suppliers
- budget and affordability
- new products and other initiatives
- growth projections
- ratio of staff grades and functions
- working practices and attendance patterns
- use of IT
- frequency of change

Change and facilities management

Naturally all business organisations are usually in a state of change to some extent or other, because of increasing, or decreasing, markets for their products or services in some fields. It is rare for any business organisation in the private sector not to have competitors, and the public sector is not exempt from change. Therefore most organisations find it useful to set out their business strategy in the form of mission and goals statements which can be related to business objectives.

Such statements can then be used to examine operational needs of the organisation, and the current management structures of the company and its departments. In a large company, individual departments will set mission and goals statements in the company context, against which the company can identify gaps in planning, and also measure success in achieving aims through periodic reviews. The setting of goals also enables the company and its departments to look at strategic planning to ask themselves if they are carrying out functions which do not fit with their core business, or its essential support. Facilities management, of course, is part of such statements and the organisation must decide if it wishes to operate an in-house facilities management service, if it wishes to outsource, or out-task some support services, or indeed if it wishes to employ a facilities management consultant to provide the whole service. A danger of the last course of action is that the facilities management service might not identify clearly with the mission and goals of the organisation and may not, therefore, take an active role in board-level policy making. The following sections examine the practice of facilities management and some of the alternatives open to the company.

The organisation and facilities management

In addition to organisational factors within the company, the organisational structure of a facilities management department relates to the diversity of the types of property to be serviced. A major factor is the size of the operation and the geographical spread of the portfolio. Thus, in a relatively small company perhaps the personnel manager or finance director will carry responsibility for all property management issues.

An organisation which occupies nationwide offices will probably include a large facilities department to manage a significant budget. In some cases this function may be located in a central headquarters, or may extend to a regionally based network of facilities managers with specific knowledge of local regional conditions and contracts. Similarly, a large department may include various professionally qualified experts in such fields as general estates management, building surveying, quantity surveying, building services engineering, architecture and interior design. Some may even count lawyers and accountants among their numbers.

Property strategy

As has been noted earlier, in most organisations facilities management is often closely linked to strategic decision making. In non-manufacturing companies, property frequently represents the second biggest outlay after payroll and so the costly burden of too much space needs to be avoided. Perhaps worse still is having too little space, which could severely inhibit operations and thus prove to be financially disastrous. This principle holds equally true for a large multinational or for a small professional office. Plans for defining the size and design of the portfolio, building location and available budget can be referred to as a property strategy. A complete property strategy has three distinct items:

1. A procedure which helps to ensure the organisation's requirement for space is met as closely as possible. Acquiring and, depending on the market, disposing of space can be a lengthy process – designing and building an office block can take 3 years for example. However, most businesses need to react quickly to their changing markets and it requires careful planning and a sound approach to be able to react to changing requirements with minimum disruption.
2. A specification of facilities and standards the organisation needs from its property. Even within office blocks, design standards for floor width, cabling systems and air conditioning can vary considerably and, indeed, air conditioning may be considered unnecessary. The specification should define the ideal accommodation for the particular organisation, and it should be kept up to date.
3. Finally a property strategy should define the criteria to be used for decision making. Most of these will be financial, for example: which costs to include to assess the complete picture and how to compare alternatives. The criteria cover both acquisition and disposal decisions, and actions required to maintain the value of the property.

Office services

At the other end of the spectrum of activities, an increasing number of organisations consider office services to be part of the facilities management responsibility. The scope includes many of the diverse services which support principal business roles such as:

- post distribution
- telephones
- records management
- print
- fax/telex
- stationery provision
- courier services
- furniture
- storage and distribution
- reprographics
- travel arrangements

The effective management of these 'cinderella' services is essential to the well-being of the organisation, and since there is never a second chance to make a first impression, their performance can be critical. While the services are largely hidden from view, the results are not and the effects of poor performance have an immediacy rarely felt in other business activity. For instance, post, telephones, fax, telex, records, print, reprographics, courier services, distribution and so on are directly or indirectly supporting the ability of an organisation to communicate with customers and staff. If they are badly organised, the effects on business can be catastrophic.

Although many of the common core services operate within very short time-scales, they must be developed within the long-term strategic framework of the business. It is essential that facilities managers responsible for these areas are well briefed on the primary objectives of the company and understand how their functions support the strategy to achieve these goals.

In practical terms, the work in this area is often seen as a series of mundane tasks. It is important to motivate staff and retain their goodwill. Sharing goals and a vision for the future will enhance their ability to achieve them and will:

- Help staff to raise their sights above day-to-day activity.
- Give them the information to understand where they fit in the grand scheme of things and secure their commitment, loyalty and enthusiasm.
- Bring suppliers and contractors into the organisation, to show them how their equipment and service affect overall performance, and to make them feel part of the team and share the vision.
- Orient the group to be customer led, developing objectives with customers

in mind, checking regularly that where you aim to be is where they want you to be. It will help to let customers know how you are doing and how they can help you to achieve your objectives more efficiently in line with their requirements. Encourage them to visit unseen 'cinderella' sections and share the experience, thereby increasing their understanding of what you do and how you do it and enhancing your partnership with customers.

Service reviews

Each service should be assessed on a regular basis against three criteria:

1. Is the service level provided in line with user requirements?
2. Can technology be used to improve service levels or reduce costs?
3. Which employment method is most appropriate?

Too often the service levels of today are relevant to the needs of yesterday. For example, a large company employed over 20 internal post room staff to receive, sort and distribute incoming mail. The facilities manager conducted a survey among user departments and found that all received the same number of pick-ups and drop-offs each day. On investigation it was found that different departments had different requirements and instead of a uniform six drops per day some areas were content with one or two. However, some who were directly driven by incoming mail did need the six-a-day service. Following the survey, service levels were adjusted to suit the actual requirements in each department and resulted in a significant reduction in cost.

Technology

Most of the traditional office service areas have benefited from developments in technology over the past few years. Traditional switchboard operations have been revolutionised by the advent of direct dialling facilities to internal extensions and the development of on-line directory systems. Other features such as teleconferencing, user directory on-line amendments, tie-line facilities and so on have all made an impact in this area. Internal electronic mail systems allow staff to correspond instantly via on-line terminals. This can drastically reduce the amount of internal paperwork and resultant physical distribution requirements. Other developments include optical character-reading equipment and intelligent mail room equipment (envelope stuffers, franking machines, etc.). A gradual movement towards computer storage of records using micro systems and optical discs has made enormous inroads for records storage and management. Even simple systems such as mobile racking and traditional microfiche are worth considering in certain situations.

Smarter systems and procedures mean that the facilities manager frequently needs to review employment policy. Sound employment policy and labour flexibility are not mutually exclusive. Flexibility can fit particularly well in areas where workload fluctuations are common, using a combination of the following:

- full-time staff
- part-time staff
- job sharing
- temporary staff
- short-term seasonal contracts
- flexible working hours
- shift working

Achieving the correct balance will give the optimum service at minimum cost and enable you to react to changing demands.

Types of facilities management services

There are a number of issues associated with placing contracts for services not directly connected with the main core business. Outsourcing, as this practice has become known, is often used as a synonym for the global term 'facilities management', but this should not be the case. Outsourcing of contracts is merely one tool or method available to the person responsible for the overall facilities management. A company may choose not to outsource at all, but to directly employ and control staff for support services such as cleaning, building maintenance and security. This could be for a number of reasons such as company culture, location or commercial security.

Depending on the range of responsibilities under the control of the facilities manager, the more commonly contracted services are likely to be:

- cleaning
- security
- landscape maintenance
- mechanical and electrical services maintenance
- building maintenance
- projects
- catering
- rent and rates reviews
- acquisitions and disposals
- pest control
- waste clearance
- office move labour
- lift maintenance

Other services could include:

- reception staff
- switchboard staff
- health and safety consultancy
- photocopier maintenance
- vehicle management
- property consultancy
- disaster planning back-up
- print design and production

The range is extremely varied and these lists are by no means exhaustive. For example, the management of IT could also be included although this is often considered to be a specialist area and constitutes a sector in its own right. However, these lists demonstrate the significance of contract management within the facilities management function, and hence the need to have a good understanding of how to maintain tight control over the expenditure incurred and the quality of service provided.

Contract management principles

Each organisation will have its own definition of what constitutes core and non-core business and this will dictate which elements of the operation should remain under direct staff control and those which can be put out to contract. The issue of control, or rather the lack of it, when placing contracts outside the organisation can create feelings of risk or uncertainty. This need not be the case and the reader should reflect on some of the contractual matters discussed in Chapter 7. A well-managed contract will be just as reliable as an in-house managed function as long as good selection, specification setting and performance monitoring are carried out.

Four basic categories of contract management have evolved in recent years:

1. Dispersed.
2. Centralised.
3. Partial grouped or bundled.
4. Totally outsourced.

Dispersed contract management is generally the organisationally immature end of the spectrum, although for some organisations the arrangement may be very appropriate. The contracts are controlled by various managers within the organisation who historically may have an interest in particular areas. For instance, the personnel manager may look after the catering contract as it is seen as part of the employee benefits package. An office manager would look after the photocopier or reprographics services contract, internal plant maintenance contract, furniture contract and office cleaning contract. This would leave the engineering manager to control contracts for mechanical and electrical services, building maintenance, lift maintenance and so on.

Centralising the control of service contracts has become fairly commonplace for many organisations in all industry sectors. This allows a uniform approach to administration, supplier selection and monitoring of performance. Responsibility and accountability are focused and problems are more easily resolved. The facilities manager will often use directly employed subordinates to control a number of contracts. Deputy managers may often have other non-contracted duties such as messenger services, or project management responsibilities.

Bundling normally occurs when the number of contracts under management become unwieldy for one person to control. Grouping contracts or 'bundling' puts a number of contracts under the management of one supplier. A common grouping can be cleaning, security and catering – three of the more labour-intensive services. This development has come about in two ways: clients wanting fewer points of contact and reduced administration, and the desire of some contracting companies to expand their range of services and make use of more effective site management.

Total outsourcing takes bundling one stage further, putting all service contracts under the direct management of a facilities management company. The internal facilities manager creates a partnership with the management company to enjoy one point of contact, one invoicing system and can often reduce the in-house costs of administering the range of contracts. There is a risk of having all your eggs in one basket, but if the selection process has been carried out properly, and appropriate controls are adopted, any risk should be reduced to an operationally acceptable level.

Total outsourcing does not mean that all contracts have to be carried out by one company. In fact, given the range of services often required by large organisations, it is highly unlikely that one company can supply the complete range required. However, it does mean that one company can manage the range of services specified as a series of individual contracts for each service, bundling where appropriate.

Contracting out

The amount of effort given to working with contractors should be relative to the value and sensitivity of the business to be placed. One-off contracts may also be considered in a different light from those which require a long-term relationship. Some of the most critical and visible facilities management services will obviously benefit if you employ contractors that you can work with for a long time. Bear in mind that the effort and cost of changing contractor (say every year) can be considerable.

Consider the workload created by going to the market every 12 or even 24 months, for say an average portfolio of 12 contracts. In such a case contractors may not see your company as long-term viable business and will only invest a commensurate amount of effort and goodwill. Try to phase contract review periods to achieve a steady workload throughout the year. Having all contracts running for 12 months from January to December could be a recipe for disaster.

Selection

The selection of contractors should not be restricted by the facilities manager's own knowledge. One should try to cast the net beyond those companies which may be familiar, and there are a number of points to consider in the selection process:

- Trawl the market in a professional manner, sending contractors a detailed questionnaire about themselves and the services they provide.
- Remove the 'three quotes' barrier by giving a cross-section of contractors in the field an opportunity to respond.
- Concentrate on the quality aspects of performance which are measurable (product, paperwork, service/delivery standards) and clearly set out how you want them to respond.
- Provide contractors with appropriate information on your own company.
- Give contractors a set amount of time in which to respond and be firm on this: it is their first test of delivered service.
- Investigate individual contractor trading viability through a recognised agency, or perhaps via a bought-in on-line system.
- Analyse the information they provide and the way they provide it; categorise the contractors; and negotiate on the component parts to optimise the contract.
- Let contractors know if they have been unsuccessful or have failed to impress, with reasons.
- Try to remove assumptions about abilities by testing them, perhaps visiting other sites under management for example. This approach will make new and existing contractors aware that they cannot afford to be complacent about your business.

Specification

It is important to approach potential contractors with a clear specification. This may seem fairly straightforward but in practice a number of pitfalls can occur. Perhaps this is best illustrated by considering some problems which could arise from a cleaning contract:

- Ground-floor windows of a five-storey building naturally get dirtier than those for the upper floors due to soil splashback and proximity to the road. What about a more frequent cleaning service for the lower levels?

- The external cladding used on a building is susceptible to marking from certain agents. No one has told the cleaners and unfortunately the wrong chemicals are used to remove some long-standing accumulations. The cladding is damaged and requires remedial work. Who pays?
- The glass revolving door and side panels at reception do not get cleaned. The window cleaners assumed this was the general office cleaner's responsibility. Who should deal with this?
- A commercially sensitive R&D department does not want windows cleaned internally during out of office hours when nobody is around. Was this made clear to the contractors?
- Window cleaners are not keen to use harness arrangements from the roof cradle systems. What are the legal and health and safety implications?
- Contractors complain they have not been paid within 21 days. Your company's payment cycle is 28 days. What should be done?

These simple examples demonstrate the need for a detailed specification if the two parties are to work together and achieve a good relationship which provides a quality service at the appropriate price.

It is probably not possible to pin down every eventuality within the contract specification and, if it were, it would probably become a procedural millstone for both parties. But it is essential to cover all the critical factors in delivering a service or product. Some of the more common issues are:

1. Time:
   - When is the service to be delivered?
   - Frequency?
   - Any restrictions?
   - How will *ad hocs* or emergency call-outs be specified?

2. Staff:
   - Who is to provide the service?
   - Qualifications needed?
   - Dress/overalls?
   - Is security vetting appropriate?
   - Restrictions?
   - Variations?
   - Relating staff to various sites?
   - Procedural detail.
   - Agreed procedures to be adopted.
   - Areas to be covered.
   - Equipment to be inspected or used.
   - Checklists.
   - Appropriate technology.
   - Training.
   - Quality and standards.

- Performance measurement.
- Safety.
- Specialised requirements.
- Legal obligation.
- Training and local procedures.
- Equipment and materials to be used or not used.
- Reporting of defects, hazards and accidents.

3. Security:
   - Observing local regulations.
   - Security vetting.
   - Restrictions on working areas.

4. Management information:
   - Cost indices.
   - Checks on services provided.
   - Regular reports.
   - Key data reporting.
   - Exception reporting.

5. Cost:
   - Overall contract cost.
   - Payment periods.
   - Authorisation procedures.
   - Identified rates.
   - Cost initiatives.

Establishing a tight, yet not overwhelming specification is the basis for an almost self-monitoring system of contract management. Facilities managers will often be controlling a large number of contracts, either directly or through an outsourcing organisation, so the need for these to be self-monitoring or largely trouble-free is essential. To achieve this three ingredients are required:

1. A clear specification (with supporting contract).
2. An effective management reporting system.
3. A streamlined administration system.

Vetting

The time involved in vetting contractors with the objective of selecting the right one can vary considerably. The facilities manager may decide that the initial response to the specification is enough to form a basis for making a decision. Alternatively, the duration, value and sensitivity of the contract, together with the requirements of the work, may warrant a higher level of vetting. Some of the questions which may be asked are:

- What is the financial position of the contractor?
- What other contracts does he have?
- Could he be bought or sold and what would the effect be on your contract?
- Does the contractor rely on substantial support from a third party and what would be the impact if this support is withdrawn?
- What contingency or disaster planning back-up can the supplier provide?

It is also worth establishing the effect the specific contract will have on the contractor, by asking:

- If your contract value is a high percentage of the contractor's turnover, will he be able to handle it?
- If the contractor employs additional staff or invests in additional equipment to obtain your contract, how will he be affected if you terminate or do not renew the contract?
- Conversely, if your potential contract value is a small percentage of the turnover, will larger customers take priority?

If you intend to reduce the initial list to a shortlist, you will need to consider how competitive each contractor can be, and to what degree they are prepared to meet the contract terms and conditions. Does the contractor contractually agree service levels, how long will prices remain fixed, and are there hidden costs?

For high-value facilities management contracts it may be necessary to consider such a lengthy list of criteria, and it is always advisable to create a checklist for testing the sensitivity and value of a contract.

Measurement

It is important to agree how contractor performance will be measured. The service delivered by contractors will also provide tangible evidence of the facility manager's own performance within the organisation. The effective management of contractors is therefore essential to the success of most facilities managers, and it is not safe to assume that once a contract is in place, the original requirements will always be met. It is therefore essential that the original contract clearly defines the service level required and the way in which that service will be measured. Feedback should be encouraged and poor performance acted upon immediately. The feedback mechanism and an agreed frequency of review will provide the facilities manager with the chance to build up a dialogue with contractors. It is important to do this soon after contract start-up so that a pattern of meetings and reviews is quickly established.

In providing a service there are a number of elements upon which measurement criteria may be based:

- physical evidence that the service has been carried out

- clear technical specifications
- accuracy and timeliness of delivery
- absence of complaints
- proactive response and good planning
- clear paperwork produced within an agreed time-scale
- ability to resolve problems within specified periods

If specific criteria are identified against which performance may be monitored, beware that they do not involve a lot of unnecessary administration. Make your measurement benchmarks clear, simple and unambiguous. Ideally you should identify a method that is self-measuring, can be checked with minimal effort and is immediately apparent to the client.

Model contracts

Model contracts can offer a method to ensure that all contractual angles are covered and that document preparation time is kept to a minimum. Most facilities management contracts can be covered by a model contract format. The term 'model contract' means a standard framework or significant draft which can be used with minor amendments. Models should be created with legal input either from internal advisers or from a commercial solicitor.

Model contracts have a number of significant advantages: they avoid reinventing the wheel every time a product or service is purchased; they ensure consistency of approach with adherence to agreed quality standards; and they increase the facilities manager's ability to protect the company contractually. There are also some drawbacks: they can encourage tunnel vision and if company requirements or the industrial sector change, then model contracts can soon become outdated.

Successful model contracts should be written in plain English so that everyone can understand the obligations and implications; they should be fair and reasonable to both parties; and they should lay great emphasis upon the product specification. But no contract, however tight, will protect a loose specification. A basic model contract should contain:

- definitions
- scope
- duration
- risk/property
- purchase price
- contractor's obligation
- confidentiality of service – jurisdiction
- your company's obligations – full specification
- appendices to the contract – warranties
- service arrangements
- termination – force majeure

- liquidated damages – waiver and assignment
- operational procedures

Single source contracts

Any decision to move towards single source supply in the facilities management field must be made after weighing a number of benefits and disadvantages for your particular circumstances. The advantages include:

- One point of contact for all services.
- Less time in day-to-day management.
- Less time in reviewing and negotiating contracts.
- Less administration and paperwork.
- More influence over a single contractor.
- The ability to tap into a wide range of skills from one source.
- The potential for a good long-term working relationship.
- Savings from economies of scale and fewer senior management positions.
- Flexibility of labour within the contract.

On the other hand, some of the disadvantages can be:

- Reliance on one organisation for a range of very visible services.
- Alternative contractors may be limited if your grouping of services is large or unusual.
- Parts of the overall service may be expensive compared to alternatives: this could be masked in the overall contract.
- Your contract site manager may not receive all the support he needs from his own organisation which could dilute his effectiveness.
- You may suffer from one bad constituent service and find it difficult to eliminate this aspect if it is bound up within the total range of services.
- Legalities may be very complex.
- You have to achieve empathy with the single contact person but this may not always be easy.

Monitoring facilities performance

In the same way that you will have developed a contract specification for your suppliers and contractors, you may also find it useful to establish an internal 'contract' between your facilities management department and 'client' departments. This type of internal contract is often known as a service level agreement or SLA. It will identify which services are to be provided, the timing and standard of delivery and the value of the service.

You may find that the expectations of your internal 'customers' exceed affordable budgets. This can be resolved by defining service requirements with 'clients' – directors, partners or senior managers responsible for profit centres. Your 'customers' are the internal staff who receive the service within the levels of affordability agreed by your 'clients'. You can redefine SLAs with particular clients and customers as frequently as is necessary until a true agreement is achieved, based on a common understanding of the requirements and associated costs.

The next step is to decide on the best way of monitoring facilities performance by selecting some key performance indicators, deciding on how best to measure them, and defining an appropriate reporting frequency to monitor performance trends. These data will enable the facilities manager to tackle any issues arising from the monitoring exercise.

Help desks

A useful tool in establishing performance monitoring is an on-line help desk. Help desks offer a number of benefits to the facilities manager and his customers:

1. One telephone number.
2. Call logging to give:
   (a) ownership
   (b) tracking
   (c) reporting
   (d) trends
3. Common approach to customers.
4. Focused customer interface.

Sophisticated systems can accept work requests in two formats: electronically passed messages and/or conversational requests by telephone or written requisition.

The information typically recorded by the help desk may include:

- originator
- date and time of the request
- nature of the problem or work required
- urgency

Work orders can be created by the system and status information is automatically registered for future reference. Help desk operators can monitor the status and progress from their own screen, and details of each request are stored to provide data for performance reporting and trend monitoring.

211

Feedback

Another useful technique is the use of performance expectation graphs or PEGs. This relies on customer feedback to score facilities management performance over a set period or following a specific project. Facilities management staff score their own performance and the results are compared with customer perceptions. The resulting perception reports enable the facilities manager to concentrate on differences of opinion or poor scores. A typical feedback questionnaire might address the following aspects:

- willingness, helpfulness, overall attitude
- ability to help resolve specific problems
- effectiveness in delivering to agreed terms
- quality of written communication
- efficiency in delivering a day-to-day routine service
- general comments

Another important indicator of facilities performance can be the efficiency of space management since the use – and abuse – of space is a key driver for expenditure. Facilities managers may find it useful to plot the space allocation for each department as demonstrated in Figures 11.1 and 11.2. These plots reflect divisional structure for quick comparison against the organisation's average allocation. Figure 11.1 shows the average amount of workstation space allocated to all the staff from different departments and Figure 11.2 shows the average total space occupied, including support space such as meeting rooms, storage areas and circulation space. Armed with this powerful information, facilities managers can evaluate their performance in managing space, exploring the reasons for different space allocation. By showing internal customers the cost of providing facilities based on space allocation, you can start to pose some searching questions in departments where norms are significantly exceeded.

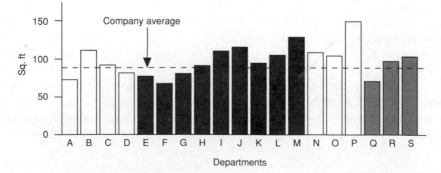

Figure 11.1 Average space per workstation

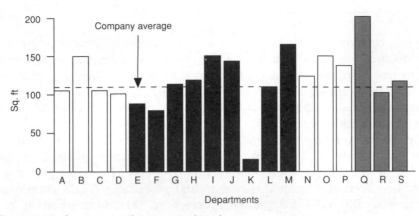

Figure 11.2 Average total space per head

Quality and the environment

This information will also help the facilities manager achieve the goal of providing a total quality environment. Productivity and quality in the workplace are inextricably linked by a single objective: getting it right first time. Quality is about continually meeting customer expectations – providing the service needed to an agreed standard. In this respect staff and not management will usually have the biggest impact on success, and total commitment is a prerequisite.

Clearly, therefore, a motivated workforce needs to feel involved in all aspects of work, including the design of the work environment, to achieve high productivity. Few will deny that a happy, well-motivated workforce aligned to a single business aim, and sharing in business success, will be productive.

However, there are two sides to the coin. Productivity and quality are also about efficiency: providing the right service at the right time but also at the right cost. One of the dangers of active participation in workstation design is that staff expectations may be raised beyond the levels of affordability. The key is often to put the higher-level considerations to staff by placing operating costs in perspective against productivity – in other words, greater involvement. As we have seen, premises costs may be the second largest expense after staff costs for many organisations, and the single biggest cost driver here is space allocation. Simple graphic presentations showing the relationships of space guidelines and department space allocations to the bottom line will help staff to understand the underlying need for effective design. In this way their involvement will be constructive and help to achieve a truly productive workplace.

Finally, it is worth emphasising that the common theme throughout space management should be to provide a total quality environment by constructing facilities which take account of people factors and productivity as well as straightforward economics. Indeed these aspects are probably synonymous, because as costs and expectations rise, the aim must be to deliver not only an efficient solution but also a well-thought-out one.

TQM and BS 5750

Quality has become a major management theme across all economic sectors. Initially focused on manufacturing, quality concepts and systems have now spread to service industries and the facilities management sector in particular. There are two distinct approaches to managing quality: total quality management (TQM) and quality assurance such as to BS 5750 (or ISO 9000 to quote the international standard).

At the risk of over-simplification, TQM is concerned with culture while BS 5750 is about systems. TQM emphasises the importance of attitudes; the generation of enthusiasm and commitment to quality. BS 5750 places the emphasis on effective, documented systems and procedures. TQM enthusiasts might criticise BS 5750 for the bureaucracy of this documentation and certification criteria, while BS proponents dismiss TQM as little more than missionary zeal. A more balanced view is that enthusiasm without a framework of procedures is as likely to be ineffective as systems operated without commitment.

Whichever quality approach or combination is selected, it is important to involve suppliers and contractors. A good start is to ensure that they have their own well-documented quality service procedure, perhaps involving them in training programmes for in-house facilities staff. The aim should be to take every opportunity of raising their awareness of your own quality approach by making appropriate reference to your requirements at the contractual stage. As far as internal customers are concerned, the services provided by in-house or contracted facilities resource should be seen as a seamless operation. This can only be achieved if contractors and suppliers are fully aligned with your own approach to quality.

The use of IT to support facilities management

Given the diverse range of functions within the facilities remit, there is probably no one single IT system capable of meeting all the requirements for strategic and tactical applications. However, a number of systems are available which can be tailored to meet specific objectives in different organisations. The business objective for a facilities management IT strategy might be to provide for: 'the coordination of property information to assist the facilities manager to meet statutory obligations and service level agreements within budgetary constraints'.

The critical requirements for this business objective could be:

- Gathering relevant data, and storing historic data for trend analysis.
- Updating and identifying sources of data, noting the frequency of updates.
- Regular reports on key management information, including analysis of stored current and historic data.

- Provision of key modelling functions, including forecasting and projections based on current data.
- Tools for *ad hoc* modelling, to answer specific 'what if' queries.
- Controls to validate processes for the previous requirements.

Applications

In broad terms there are potential applications for IT in many areas of facilities management:

- Property management, including lease details, floor areas, rent and rate review.
- Cost control by on-line commitment account systems with full cost analysis by component and premises, relating to individual invoices.
- Space management using computer-aided design and numerical data.
- Utility management, linked to BEMS.
- Planned preventive maintenance, with routine maintenance based on hours.
- Geographic information systems indicating preferred locations linked to customer distribution or other geographic criteria.

CAD

Regardless of detailed requirements, most facilities managers today would consider a computer-aided design (CAD) installation to be highly desirable. CAD provides many opportunities to work more efficiently, both strategically and in day-to-day terms. At the higher level an automated system will help the analysis and understanding of key data at each stage of the strategic planning cycle. By presenting information in a systematic format directors will be helped in corporate decision making. It will enable options to be evaluated and cost-effective solutions to be reached on the issues affecting office space, running costs and property strategy. At the tactical level, the most obvious application for CAD is as an electronic drawing board, but it is also a powerful tool when used as a menu-driven data base for asset management and budget tracking.

An automated system is quick, and it should be accurate and should help to coordinate different disciplines such as data-cabling and furniture layouts, bringing benefits such as increased ability to explore alternative layouts, greater flexibility, higher job satisfaction and improved presentations.

There are many systems on the market and the specification required will be influenced by some of the factors which affect your general approach to space management. In making a selection there are two key requirements: a data base for decision making, and a design tool. Perhaps the best way to develop an effective system is to install well-proven but relatively inexpensive equipment to meet defined needs, and a PC is probably adequate for most applications if it is allied to a comprehensive software package.

'As built' drawings
These drawings are an accurate record of the premises, following initial construction or subsequent alteration, and are intended to show construction, location of services and design loadings. They are the starting point for future alterations, and to be effective over the life-span of the premises need to be preserved and kept up-to-date. They are particularly important when the expected life of the premises will exceed living memory.

Benchmarking
Indicating a point or points of reference for comparison.

Breakdown maintenance
The operation of restoring an item to a state in which it can fulfil its original function after a failure in its performance. (BS 8210:1986)

Built assets
Physical assets that have been designed, constructed or engineered and which form part of the support system for an organisation or its clients. Typically these would include all buildings and building services, as well as those external works and ancillary services that support users' needs.

Condition-based maintenance
Preventive maintenance initiated as a result of knowledge of an item's condition gained from routine or continuous monitoring. (BS 3811:1984)

Condition survey
The technical examination of the components or elements of a building.

Corrective maintenance
The maintenance carried out after a failure has occurred and intended to restore an item to a state in which it can perform its required function. (BS 3811:1984)

Cyclical maintenance *see* preventive maintenance

Emergency maintenance (*see* response maintenance)
The maintenance which it is necessary to put in hand immediately to avoid serious consequences. (BS 3811:1984)

Estimate
An assessment, based on a detailed breakdown of the resources, etc. involved, of the cost expected to arise in respect of a given thing or service. This is usually calculated before the expenditure occurs and before the true costs are known. (BS 3811:1984)

Facilities management
The practice of co-ordinating the physical work place with people and work of the organisation integrates the principles of business administration, architecture and the behavioral and engineering sciences. (Library of Congress)

Feedback
A written or oral report of the success or failure of an action in achieving its desired result, which can be used to influence design, performance and costs. Feedback may be computerised. (BS 3811:1984)

Life cycle costs
The total cost of ownership of an item, taking into account all the costs of acquisition, personnel training, operation, maintenance, modification and disposal, for the purpose of making decisions on new or changed requirements and as a control mechanism in service for existing and future items. (BS 3811:1984)

Maintenance
The combination of all technical and associated administrative actions intended to retain an item in, or restore it to, a state in which it can perform its required function. (BS 3811:1984)

Maintenance programme
A time-based plan allocating specific maintenance tasks to specific periods. (BS 3811:1984)

Outsourcing (*see* out-tasking)
The procedure adopted to discover and introduce suppliers and service providers from outside the organisation, often on a competitive basis of price, quality and performance. The supplies and services secured by outsourcing may previously have been satisfied from within the organisation.

Out-tasking
A term sometimes used instead of outsourcing; applied usually to the provision of distinct individual services as opposed to bundles of services.

Performance indicatiors
Indicators set by management for assessing the performance of a particular service. These indicators may focus on issues such as service delivery, management efficiency, standards and costs.

Physical asset register
A record of items including information such as constructional and technical details. This may be combined with an inventory. (BS 3811:1984)

Planned maintenance
Maintenance, organised and carried out with forethought, control and the use of records, to a predetermined plan based on the results of previous condition surveys. (BS 8210:1986)

Preventive maintenance
Maintenance carried out at predetermined intervals, or corresponding to prescribed criteria, and intended to reduce the probability of failure or performance degradation of an item. (BS 3811:1984)

Professional indemnity insurance
Insurance maintained by a consultant as a safeguard against losses or expense caused directly by that consultant's professional failings. It is particularly important on occasions when design services or project management consultancy is involved.

Programmed maintenance *see* planned maintenance

Quality assurance
Planned and systematic actions that provide confidence that an item will satisfy given quality requirements. (*Glossary of Building and C.E. Terms*, BSI)

Real estate
Concerned with, or dealing in , property or land.

Remedial work
Redesign and work necessary to restore the integrity of a construction to a standard that will allow the performance of its original function. (BS 8210:1986)

Repair
Restoration of an item to an acceptable condition by the renewal, replacement or mending of worn, damaged or decayed parts. (BS 8210:1986)

Residual life
Period of time during which a building or component may reasonably be expected to continue to fulfil its present function provided it is given normal routine maintenance. (BS 8210:1986)

Response maintenance
Maintenance work carried out as a result of a request from the building user. The term is often used in place of the terms day-to-day maintenance, emergency maintenance, and tenant-requested repairs.

Sinking fund
A fund formed by setting aside income to accumulate with interest to pay off debt.

Smoothing of activities
The delaying or acceleration of programmed work to achieve a smooth financial curve that matches the revenue profile.

Term contracts
Contracts for the supply of services that can be defined in terms of the type of activities that may be required over a predetermined period but are indeterminate in quantity. Such contracts traditionally run for between one and three years.

Terrier
A register of a landed estate; an inventory.

Variance reports on projects
Management reports usually concerning time and cost allocations where a model or budget is set in advance over a period of time, often on a six- or twelve-month rolling basis, and the actual time used or cost incurred is monitored against the model. The differences between the actual and the model values becomes the variance for reporting purposes.

Index

absenteeism 175, 185
air distribution system 185
alterations 58, 64–5, 158, 163–5
ancillary services 158, 169, 200–201
annual equivalent technique 26, 29–30, 31
appeals 46
appraisal
    development 26, 27–8, 29
    information 17–18
    investment 26, 35, 36, 39, 96
    option 20
    see also life cycle appraisal
'as built' drawings 6, 135
asbestos 67–8
asset registers 158–61, 165, 174
assets 7, 26, 40

benchmarking 7, 88, 95, 174–5
benefits see cost-benefit analysis; costs and benefits
bills of quantities 124
breach of condition notice 48
briefs and briefing 76
BS 5750 214
budgets 90, 95, 131, 132, 152, 175–8
buildability 124, 125, 130
building
    elements 159

form 83–4
management systems (BMS) 179, 190
requirements 79–80
services 75–6
shell 74–5, 84
team 77
Building Regulations 47, 64, 103
Building Use Studies 183
buildings, shape and size of 174
built asset management 2, 6, 6–7, 137
    see also information technology; maintenance
built estate 9, 12
bundling 204
business environment 2, 89–90, 185
business organisation 197

capital operating budget 90, 95
cash flow 27, 28, 41, 99, 163, 177–8
    see also discounted cash flow technique
cellurisation 87, 88
change see estate change; forecasting; managing change
Chartered Institute of Building (CIOB) 3, 6
    educational framework of 2
    handbook on maintenance management 1, 3

Steering Group   1–2
Chartered Institute of Building
    Services Engineers   2
chemicals   67
'churn'   164
civil liabilities   63
cleaning   64–5, 165, 168, 169, 172,
    184, 191–3, 205
coding
    frame   141
    maintenance   140
    structure   141
    system   21, 140, 143–4, 159, 164
comfort   181, 183, 191, 193, 194
company strategy   197
compensation   60–61
competitive outsourcing   130
complaints, response to   187–8
completion   135–6
complexity   185–6
computer-aided
    design (CAD)   179, 215
    draughting   160
    facilities management (CAFM)
        system   135–6, 160, 169, 179
computing   4, 179–80
condition
    assessment   147–51, 163
    registers   158, 161–3
    survey   97, 146, 147, 161, 162
condition-dependent work   138, 144,
    145
condition-independent work   138,
    144, 144–5
conservation areas   47
construction
    economics   5
    existing, work to   126–30
    new   120–26
    management   124–5
    manager   124–5
Construction Regulations   64–5
contract management   203–10
Contract Procedures   6–7
contracting out   4, 202–3, 204–10

contractor performance   208
contractors, selection of   129, 130,
    205, 207–8
contracts
    acquisition procedures   51–3
    forms of   118–19
    management   124–5, 127
    model   209–130
    negotiated   125–6
    performance specification   130–31
    single source   210
    traditional   123–4, 127, 134, 135
Control of Substances Hazardous to
    Health Regulations 1988
    (COSHH)   67
control systems   131–5, 189–90,
    190–91, 192
    see also estate control plans
controllability   186
conveyances and transfers   53–4
cooling   184
core business   4, 7, 10, 155, 165,
    178, 196–7
corporate style   88–90
cost
    and performance   155–7
    centres   157
    control   131–3
    identification   105–7
    records, historical   163
cost–benefit analysis   26, 27, 32
cost-effective management   155
cost-in-use   7, 26, 29–32, 94
costs and benefits   102–4
    intangible   103, 108
    tangible   102–3
costs, average   172
covenants   56, 167–8
critical path   134
customer-led service culture   188
cyclical maintenance   137, 138

data   7, 38, 152, 155, 158, 159–60,
    161, 162, 169, 174, 179–80,
    184–5, 215
    acquisition   153–4

decision-making
  levels of 77, 78, 91
  strategic 12–13, 16, 21
defects maintenance period 123
demand and supply 77, 78
demolition 44, 45
departmental arguments 122
depreciation 39, 40–41
design
  and build 121–3, 127, 131, 134, 135
  and planning process 74, 93
  briefing 76, 117
  decisions 74, 75, 88, 95, 109
  failures 123
  flexibility 122
  options: assessment 83–7
deterioration 98
develop and construct 122–3
developer 25, 27
development
  appraisal 25, 27–8, 29
  constraints on 43–9
  decision to 25–6, 27
Development Plan 46
direct labour 129, 130
disclaimers 63
discount rates 99–100, 107–8
discounted cash flow technique (DCF) 28, 32, 39, 99, 108, 110
discounting 27, 28, 99–101
display screen equipment 68, 184, 189
documentation 7, 155
domestic controls 190, 193
durability 95
duties, legal 61–3

economic life 101
efficiency 2, 5, 7, 183, 191, 193
electricity 66–7
employees 61–3, 175, 185
  see also staff morale
employment policy 202

energy 14, 17, 98, 184–5, 190
  costs 95, 165–6, 169, 170, 172, 173, 174
  efficiency 183, 191, 193
enforcement notices 47, 71
environment *see* workplace environment
environmental assessment 46
environmental conditions 15, 181, 213–14
equipment 68–9, 169
estate change 20
estate control plans 12, 13, 20–21
estate information 13–14
estate management 12–13, 25
  'terrier' 12, 158
estatecode 20

facilities management 1, 2, 3, 4, 5–6, 7, 8, 26, 168–9, 196–7, 198–9, 202–3, 212, 214
  see also computer-aided facilities management
facilities manager 25–6, 32, 33, 35, 39, 74, 76–7, 96–7, 101, 109, 115, 122, 155, 163, 166, 167, 172, 173, 178
feedback 186, 188, 212
finance 8, 9, 154, 213
fire precautions 66
first aid service 169
float time 134
flow chart 116
forecasting 19–20, 110
forward planning 151–2
freehold estate 49, 50–54, 173
fuel costs 106–7, 107, 165–6
full rental value (FRV) 37
functional life 101
functional suitability 14, 14–15, 17

general development order 43
geographical information system 160
glazing 95, 104–5, 106, 108

growth potential   38
guarantee   123

hazards *see* risk; workplace hazards
health   181, 183
health and safety statutory compliance
   14, 16, 169
Health and Safety at Work, etc. Act
   1974   61–3
help desks   211
human potential   181

identifying needs/requirements
   79–82
improvements   158, 163–5
income capitalisation method   36–8,
   39
incomes: varying, terminable, variable
   39
indoor environment   65–6, 181, 193
information   10, 13–14, 17, 25,
   117–18, 207
information technology   2, 4, 91–2,
   93, 197, 203, 214–15
   in built asset maintenance   143–4,
   152–4
injunction   48
inquiry, planning   46
insurances   58–9, 135, 166–7, 169,
   170
intelligent buildings   4, 93
interior layouts   76, 79–82, 84–6, 88,
   89
internal rate of return (IRR)   28
International Facility Management
   Association (IFMA)   5
investment appraisal   26, 35, 36, 39,
   96
investment in real property   6, 32, 40
   see also return on investment

Joint Contracts Tribunal   118

land registration   49, 53
landlord *see* leases

layouts *see* interior layouts
leasehold estate   49, 54–61, 173
leases   37, 167–8, 169–70
   compensation   60–1
   content of   54–9
   tenure, security of   59–60
legal obligations   61–3
Legionnaires' disease   68, 183
legislation   70–3
life cycle appraisal
   case study   104–9
   whole life   94–101, 109–10
life cycle costing   4, 6, 94, 96–7,
   99–104, 153
life of a building   101, 103, 151–2
life-spans   150, 151, 153, 164
lifts   169, 170
lighting   66
listed buildings   46–7
Local Plan   46
location (of property)   35
location code   141, 142
lump sum tender   121

mail   169
maintenance   2, 64–5, 70, 94, 121,
   137, 158, 163–5, 178, 184
   costs   94
   type of   138–52
   see also cyclical maintenance;
      programmed maintenance;
      response maintenance; repairs
      and maintenance
management
   charges   170, 174
   contractor   125
   control   155, 143
   failures   183
   information   207
   response   187–8
managing change   77–9, 185, 186,
   198
manpower   9
market forces   122
mechanical and electrical services
   170

menu-driven program   143, 215
milestones   131
modernisation   97

National Joint Consultative
    Committee for Building   129
negligence   63
net present value (NPV)   28, 100,
    101, 108–9
noise   66
notification requirements   69–70
novation   123
nuisance   63

obsolescence   17, 39, 40–1, 97, 101,
    102
occupancy   106
    profile   98
occupant satisfaction   190
office equipment and furniture
    68–9, 169
office services *see* ancillary services
open-plan   183
operating costs   155, 158, 165–9,
    174–5, 213
operational requirements   121
optimum between cost and
    performance   155–7
ordering   177–8
organisations
    characteristics of   79, 197–8
    corporate goals of   9, 11
    efficiency of workplace   2, 5, 7
    strategic plan of   19
outsourcing   130, 198, 202
owners   97–8

pay-back   98
performance
    cost and   155–7
    of building   96, 158, 184–5, 212
performance
    indicators (PIs)   18, 153, 175
    monitoring   157, 210–12
    specifications   130–131

physical condition   14, 17
planning
    concept   86–8
    contravention notice   48
    enforcement   47–9
    permission   43–9
    policies   46
post-occupancy evaluation (POEs)
    14, 19
practice environment   7–8
premises, building and facility   115
present value (PV)   99, 100
pressure systems   69
price competition   122
pricing   131
priority code   141, 143
process code   141, 141–2
procurement
    fast start-up   119–20
    fast track   122, 125
    flow chart   116
    of building work   6–7
    'one stop shopping'   117
    operational flow   115–7
    see also completion; construction;
        contracts; control systems
productivity   191, 192, 194, 213
professional bodies   3
professional indemnity insurance
    135
profitability   33, 34, 41
programmed maintenance   137,
    138–52
property *see* freehold estate; leasehold
    estate
    development   6, 26
    investment portfolios   32–3
    management   10–11, 25–6
    manager   25
    operating costs *see* operating costs
    policy objective   11–12
    strategy   199
    see also strategic property
        management

property management, operational 39–40
prosecutions   71

quality   35, 134, 187–8, 213–4
   assurance (QA)   136, 214
   control   134–5, 213–14

rates   165, 167–8
rationalisation   12, 20
reappointment   123
reason code   141, 142–3
refreshment service   169
refurbishment   96, 162
renewal   137, 151, 153
rent-review clauses   37, 56
rents   37, 55, 165, 167–8
   full rental value (FRV)   37
repairs and maintenance   4, 57, 64–5, 121, 154, 158, 163–5, 168, 170, 172
   see also maintenance
residual method   28
resource   9, 11, 12, 13
response maintenance   7, 137, 138, 139–44
responsiveness
   of management   187–8, 191
   of systems   186–7, 190, 193
retrofit   97
return on investment   33–5, 41
right of entry   49
risk   62, 119, 121, 122, 123, 124, 126, 134, 135, 136, 178–9
   analysis   28, 96
rolling account   28
room dimensions   65
running costs   95, 97, 105, 157–8, 171, 173, 175

safety   14, 16, 61–3
scenery   76
searches and enquiries   50
security   169, 172
   of tenure   59–60

sensivity analysis   28, 29, 108–9, 110
service
   charges   57, 169–73
   level agreement (SLA)   210–11
   levels   201
   life   103
services   7, 75–6, 170, 196
servicing   163
settings   76
shallow-plan   186
sick building syndrome (SBS)   168, 179, 181–3, 188, 189
'single' survey   146
sinking funds   179
space   4–5, 6, 65, 81–2, 169, 213
   budget   82
   utilisation   7, 14, 15–16, 17
specification   205–7, 210
staff morale   188–9
'standing time'   129
statutory nuisance   63
statutory obligations   14, 16, 61–70
stop notice   48
strategic decision making, framework for   12–13, 16, 20–21
strategic property management   2, 5, 6, 9, 11–12, 21–4
stress   188–9
Structure Plan   46
support services   7, 196
surety   56
surplus buildings   19
surplus land   19
surveys and reports   51

taxation   37, 41–2, 97, 154, 174, 177
technocentric philosophies   189–90
technological life   101–2
technology   201–2
telephones   169
temperatures   65–6, 106
tenancy agreement   139
   see also leases
tendering   121, 122, 123–4, 129
term contractors   129, 130

terminal value (TV)   28, 41
time control   133, 134
time horizon   101–2, 107
'time value of money'   99
   see also valuation
timing   51
tolerance thresholds   187
total quality management (TQM)
   214
tree preservation orders (TPOs)   47

U-value   105
uncertainty   96
   see also risk
use classes order   44
user interests   77

valuation   26, 27, 35, 39
value of property   35, 36, 162
vandalism   191

variance report   131, 132
VAT   41–2, 174
VDUs *see* display screen equipment
ventilation   65, 184
'virtuous cluster'   191

water and waste disposal   165, 166
whole life cycle (LCC) appraisal *see*
   life cycle appraisal
'wish list'   121
work assessment   145, 148
work ordering process   139, 143
workplace
   environment   5, 7, 65–6, 175,
      181, 189, 193, 213
   hazards   66–9, 69–70
   organisation   2, 5, 7
   requirements   81–2

yields   38–9